Privatization

Privatization

Toward More Effective Government

Report of the President's Commission
on Privatization

David F. Linowes, Chairman
Annelise Graebner Anderson
Michael D. Antonovich
Walter F. Bish
Sandra Mitchell Brock
Garrey E. Carruthers

Richard H. Fink
Melvin R. Laird
James T. McIntyre, Jr.
George L. Priest
Ralph L. Stanley
Walter B. Wriston

University of Illinois Press
Urbana and Chicago

Illini Books edition, 1988
Manufactured in the United States of America
P 5 4 3 2 1

This book is printed on acid-free paper.

ISBN 0-252-06058-X

Contents

Preface

Our democratic government must be responsive to citizens' changing needs, rather than be captive to inflexible ideologies. In the deliberations of the President's Commission on Privatization, we sought better methods of meeting the needs of the American people so that both public and private institutions deserve and receive people's confidence.

This report is about the programs, services, and activities of the federal government, and the most effective delivery systems. We address alternative approaches that can best provide for the social good. In this we believe the report makes a contribution to our enduring national discussion about the proper limits of government in our society.

In all our deliberations, our primary considerations were the American consumer who is in need . . . of education; of loans for school, home, farm, or business; of transportation; of health care; of other social services. We weighed the potential risks of failure of new private efforts against costs alleged in failures of government performance. We were attentive to the concerns of federal employees. We considered the complexities inherent in performing uniquely governmental responsibilities through mechanisms other than those of federal agencies. We clearly acknowledged that the government's role as maker of policy, and creator and enforcer of standards, must never be compromised.

Our recommendations are deliberate attempts to identify and encourage improvements in service where convincing evidence demonstrated that they are needed. For the most part, we opt for incremental approaches. We recognize the need to build upon success, and we recognize that the American people are not likely to embrace initiatives that depart too widely from their traditional experiences.

The American people have often complained of the intrusiveness of federal programs, of inadequate performance, and of excessive expenditures. In light of these public concerns, government should consider turning to the creative talents and ingenuity in the private sector to provide, wherever possible and appropriate, better answers to present and future challenges.

Our task was broad and our time was limited. Throughout the six months of the Commission's existence every effort was made to hear from leaders in the respective issue areas. We heard from those who would be affected by our recommendations, as well as from those who would be

vii

responsible for implementing them. Obviously, both the breadth and depth of our examinations were limited in scope by time constraints.

During our six public hearings, we heard testimony from 140 witnesses. We held ten business meetings, conducted extensive in-house research, and made two site visits related to topics being examined (including a trip to England by several Commissioners at personal expense). We reviewed a lengthy list of government activities and selected our topics for study based on several factors:

- Is there evidence of inadequacies of services currently provided by government? Are there extensive complaints of poor or insufficient service? Are there studies indicating waste of resources?
- Are there indications that private providers are interested in supplying the service, but are impeded or prohibited by current laws and regulations? Does the government sustain its advantage over private providers by relying on subsidies?
- Do current programs reflect basic principles—such as the idea that free people should be responsible for their own development and the principle that government programs must be accountable to public officials?
- Are there frequent complaints that federal policies work against people's best interests, even when they work as intended?
- Is the activity likely to be affected by major changes in needs, technology, or other near-term factors that might affect performance, whether retained by government or transferred to the private sector?
- Is a similar good or service already being provided in the private sector? Is government competing with business?

In carrying out our work, we drew upon experts in each of the areas we addressed. Many of these fields are technically complex, and many of them involve intense differences, even among experts, about the proper roles of government and the private sector. We stressed practical concerns, such as the level of public interest, the degree of public need, the availability of private services, and the likelihood of popular and legislative support for the recommendations.

The final chapter, "Economic Public Policy and Privatization," shows how privatization is much more than a set of specific changes in who performs an activity and how. It is part of a fundamental political and economic rethinking that today is reassessing the roles of government and the private sector in the modern welfare state—a rethinking that is having an influence on all segments of American opinion.

We have only begun. Our study is not exhaustive. It is the hope of this Commission that the recommendations in this report will be adopted and thereby lay the framework for further examinations for involving the talents of all segments of our nation—including the private sector—in helping to solve problems and meet the needs of all the people.

Work of this scope and magnitude is dependent on the cooperation and assistance of a great number of people and institutions. We owe much to many individuals from both the public and private sectors . . . officials of agencies of the federal government, members of Congress, governors of states, union officials, trade association representatives, and scholars at universities and research institutions, all of whom contributed generously to our efforts. I offer special thanks to all.

Many government agencies provided us with a variety of assistance. In particular, I want to thank Comptroller General Charles A. Bowsher for the useful information the General Accounting Office staff was able to provide; and to Interior Secretary Donald P. Hodel, who responded promptly and graciously from the outset by furnishing us five capable staff members as well as financial assistance. My appreciation also goes to the Departments of Commerce, Defense, Energy, Justice, Transportation, and Treasury; and the Agency for International Development, Environmental Protection Agency, and Federal Trade Commission for providing their support; and to Director James C. Miller III of the Office of Management and Budget for responding cooperatively to all our requests for information from his agency's experts.

To the Commissioners, I extend my deep appreciation for their dedication to the demanding schedule of hearings and meetings. Their concern for each of the issues was demonstrated by the countless hours devoted to studying the overwhelming literature and staff documents, culminating in intensive deliberations at our business meetings.

The members of our staff performed tirelessly. Their diligence in uncovering all sides of the many issues, researching and analyzing extensive literature, and preparing in-depth papers for the Commissioners was invaluable. They performed with unusual devotion, applying limitless hours to the task. To each of them, I offer my sincere personal gratitude.

DAVID F. LINOWES
Chairman

Executive Summary

The President's Commission on Privatization was established on September 2, 1987 "to review the appropriate division of responsibilities between the federal government and the private sector," and to identify those government programs that are not properly the responsibility of the federal government or that can be performed more efficiently by the private sector.

The Commission reviewed a broad spectrum of government activities:

- Low-Income Housing
- Housing Finance
- Federal Loan Programs
- Air Traffic Control and other FAA Functions
- Educational Choice
- Postal Service
- Contracting Out: Military Commissaries; Prisons
- Federal Asset Sales: Amtrak; Naval Petroleum Reserves
- Other Programs: Medicare; International Development Programs; Urban Mass Transit

In all these representative areas, the Commission found potential for improved efficiency, quality of service, or both, to be derived from increased private sector participation in the provision of services. In some areas, such as the Naval Petroleum Reserves, the Commission found that the public would be best served by complete government divestiture. In other areas, such as Housing, Education, and Medicare, the Commission found that the continued need for public sector support could be served by means of vouchers, which act as vehicles for private sector participation, and hence, competition. In yet other areas, such as Air Traffic Control, Postal Service, and Urban Mass Transit, the Commission found that a combination of private sector initiatives, from contracting out to asset sales, may best serve the public interest. However, federal workers should be assured that normally any staff reductions resulting from the implementation of Commission recommendations should be handled through attrition. In addition, any recommendation supporting increased contracting out should be implemented only after full consideration has been given to employee interests.

The following are summaries of the Commission's findings and recommendations in each area:

Low-Income Housing

Rather than financing new public housing construction, the government should provide housing subsidies to eligible low-income households in the form of vouchers enabling them to rent acceptable housing in the private marketplace. To the greatest extent possible existing public housing should either be sold to or managed by the residents. By giving residents a larger stake in their own housing by selling it to them, contracting with them to manage it, or by allowing them discretion in choosing it through a voucher program, the long-term quality of their housing will be improved at a lower cost per household.

Housing Finance

The federal government should assume a more neutral position with respect to direct housing finance programs (Farmers Home Administration, Government National Mortgage Association, Federal Home Loan Mortgage Corporation, Federal National Mortgage Association, Federal Housing Administration, and Veterans Administration). In addition, the federal government should refocus the mortgage insurance activity of the Federal Housing Administration so that it does not compete as directly with private mortgage insurers. Rather, it should direct its efforts, as originally intended, toward home buyers who have been turned down by private insurers. Similarly, the Federal National Mortgage Association and, by extension, the Federal Home Loan Mortgage Corporation, should not be allowed to compete on an unfair basis, and thus should be fully privatized, including the elimination of all federal benefits and limitations.

Federal Loan Programs

The federal government should phase in a loan asset sale program in order to avoid large uncertain liabilities in the future. Moreover, federal loans should not be sold with any type of recourse that would create a future liability for the government. When federal loan assets are sold, the legal and contractual rights of the borrowers should be protected and the private sector owners should be required to abide by the stated collection policies that are used by the agency that makes the loan.

The federal government also needs to implement better accounting methods and introduce better incentives to make the budget accurately reflect the impact of the various types of loans it makes. In particular, a market valuation method of identifying the subsidy cost of its credit programs would enable policymakers to more accurately weigh the costs and benefits of direct loan and loan guarantee programs. In order to reveal hidden subsidies, the federal government should phase in a policy of purchasing reinsurance for all loans it guarantees, and the agencies should be required to obtain annual appropriations to pay for the reinsurance.

Air Traffic Control and Other FAA Functions

The FAA should continue to regulate the national airspace system for the foreseeable future for reasons of safety, public service, and efficiency. However, portions of that system can and should be considered for private operation or for contracting, when such options would improve air commerce. In this regard, the federal government should reduce its direct role in the development of airports, by encouraging each airport to develop its own sources of funding from the full range of beneficiaries of aviation services. In particular, the portion of national airport and airway expenditures borne by users should be increased. Airport operators should be allowed to charge peak-hour takeoff and landing fees to alleviate congestion, and to charge passenger facility fees as a means of generating revenues. The FAA should retain authority over the en route centers, but some center activities should be subject to contracting out. In addition, the FAA should move incrementally to a system of private airport traffic control towers, and should privatize its system of flight service stations and system maintenance service.

Educational Choice

The federal government should foster choice options, including the use of vouchers, to achieve the nation's full range of educational goals. Congress should adopt policies to increase parental choice in education at the elementary and secondary levels, just as it now fosters choice in higher education through GI Bill payments and Pell Grants. Private schools should be able to participate in federal programs providing educational choice to parents, but the federal government should remain sensitive to retaining the values represented by the public schools and should ensure that the full range of civil rights guaranteed by the Constitution is protected.

The federal government should encourage choice programs targeted to individuals in the lower percentiles of the current elementary and secondary student population. The schools are failing these children now, and alternatives beyond current programs should be explored. Finally, the Secretary of Education should use discretionary resources to conduct additional research on educational choice initiatives that might expand the range of educational options for children.

Postal Service

The private express statutes, which mandate the postal monopoly, should be repealed to allow competition in the provision of any and all postal services. The benefits conferred by competition, in terms of quality of service, cost efficiency, and the incentives for innovation, clearly outweigh the costs of transition to a free market. However, there must be a gradual phase-in period and compensation of postal employees for possible loss of benefits or earnings. The U.S. Postal Service should seek private sector involvement, with consideration given to selling it as an Employee Stock Ownership plan. As part of the phase-in process, the monopoly restrictions on the carriage of third-class mail and on rural delivery should be lifted immediately. Similarly, the restrictions on private delivery of urgent mail should be loosened and the prohibition on private use of letter boxes should be repealed immediately. At the same time, the Postal Service should more actively pursue contracting out opportunities in all its functions and ensure highest and best use of all its assets.

Contracting Out

The federal government should not compete with the private sector in the provision of commercially available goods and services. Contracting out through the competitive bidding process should be pursued more aggressively through the Executive Branch as a means to procure the same or better level of service at reduced cost. This process should include appropriate in-house competition and adequate safeguards against employee displacement. Employee Stock Ownership Plans (ESOPs) can also be devices for furthering competition and contracting. Although Fed CO-OP is still a demonstration program, it, and other ESOP options, should be pursued by the federal government. Public policy goals and the operational needs of government should not be threatened if proper attention is devoted to developing work specifications and administering contracts.

Military Commissaries. Private sector businesses should participate in managing and operating military commissaries in the United States in order to achieve greater efficiency through competitive stimulus.

Prisons. Contracting the administration of jails and prisons at the federal, state, and local levels could lead to improved, more efficient operation. Problems of liability and accountability should not be seen as posing insurmountable obstacles to contracting for the operation of confinement facilities, although Constitutional and legal requirements apply. Contracted facilities may also be required to meet American Correctional Association standards.

The Bureau of Prisons and the Immigration and Naturalization Service (INS), in cooperation with the appropriate government agencies, should prepare cost studies, following the guidelines of OMB Circular A-76, comparing the cost of contracting with total government costs for administering existing facilities. In addition, the Bureau of Prisons and the INS should be encouraged and authorized to pursue lease-purchase arrangements for the addition of new facilities and the Department of Justice should continue to give high priority to research on private sector involvement in corrections.

Federal Asset Sales

Divestiture of federal assets should be pursued either where federal ownership is unnecessary for achieving public policy goals or where private ownership, in combination with covenants, regulations, or other protections, could better achieve these goals. Statutory prohibitions on studying divestiture of federal assets cannot be justified. Without adequate study, there is insufficient evidence to determine whether public or private ownership would best serve public policy goals.

Amtrak. Private sector initiative in the provision of intercity passenger rail service should be encouraged. The federal government should adopt a multi-year plan to move Amtrak or major portions of its operations to the private sector, in conjunction with repealing Amtrak's exclusive rights to provide intercity rail service. As part of the multi-year plan, federal subsidies should be incrementally reduced, and a deadline should be set for the Department of Transportation to decide whether Amtrak or portions of its operations should be continued. Capital needs should be funded by the federal government only if the purchase can be justified as a means to reduce the federal subsidy and to facilitate the eventual transfer of Amtrak to the private sector with no additional commitment of federal funds, including government loan guarantees. At the same time, Amtrak should contract out operations wherever the level of service can be performed at an equal or improved level and cost savings would result—taking into consideration the interest of employees. It should charge states and other users the full costs associated with providing rail service and trackage rights.

Naval Petroleum Reserves. The federal government should begin immediately to divest itself fully of the Elk Hills, California, and Teapot Dome, Wyoming, reserves. The military purposes for which they were acquired can now be better met through alternative means. In developing the sale, some level of access to light Elk Hills crude oil for smaller refiners and producers, as well as structuring the sale to maximize the number of potential bidders, should be considered.

Other Programs

Medicare. Private sector competition, by means of vouchers, in the provision of health care financing (health insurance or HMOs) for the elderly can impart critically needed cost-containment incentives in this market and offer a broader choice of health plan options. The government should act to increase competition and private sector participation in health care financing under Medicare by encouraging the use of vouchers or capitated payments to purchase private health care financing. Since the private sector is naturally reluctant to assume greater risk without compensating benefits, some risk-sharing plan, such as the use of risk-corridors, should be considered in the implementation of any voucher system.

International Development Programs. Developing countries, for a variety of reasons, often have extensive state ownership of business enterprises. In many cases, these enterprises could be made more efficient and innovative if turned over to the private sector. The Agency for International Development (AID) should increase its support of privatization in developing countries by channeling its funds and expertise as much as possible toward the private sector or by aiding host governments in converting state-owned enterprises to private entities. AID should support employee stock ownership plans and debt-equity swaps as means of facilitating privatization efforts in developing countries, and should encourage multilateral financial institutions and regional banks to act more decisively in private sector lending and divestiture in less developed countries.

Urban Mass Transit. Various means of increasing private sector participation in the provision of urban mass transit, including contracting out, employee stock ownership plans, and stimulating competition, can result in improved service in many areas. The federal government should administer its grant programs so as to foster public-private partnerships and healthy competition among public and private providers of mass transit service. At the same time, the limitations and requirements of Section 13(c) of the Urban Mass Transportation Act should be interpreted and amended so as to grant transit authorities the ability to achieve economies through privatiza-

xvi

tion. UMTA should allow grantees to sell UMTA-funded equipment to private operations where service is being permanently contracted out or reduced, and UMTA should be reimbursed only for the federal share percentage of the proceeds.

The Commission believes that increased private sector participation in activities currently performed by the public sector has great potential for increasing the efficiency, quality, and constructive innovation in providing goods and services for the benefit of all the people.

Chapter 1

Introduction

The United States is experiencing a renewed interest in the systematic examination of the boundary between public and private delivery of goods and services. The interest has been stimulated in part by concern that the federal government has become too large, too expensive, and too intrusive in our lives. The interest also reflects a belief that new arrangements between the government and the private sector might improve efficiency while offering new opportunities and greater satisfaction for the people served. The President's Commission on Privatization was created to assess the range of activities that might properly be transferred to the private sector and to investigate methods by which such a shift could be accomplished.

There are essentially three techniques for the privatization of service delivery. The first method is simply selling the government's assets. The sale of Conrail in 1987 is an example of the sale of an enterprise as a functioning unit, in this case, through a public stock offering. Instead of selling an enterprise, the government could also sell assets piecemeal, examples are the sale of obsolete military bases, loan portfolios, or surplus equipment. In 1982 the federal government privatized the National Consumer Cooperative Bank by relinquishing the asset value of government-purchased stock and the associated right to name directors to the bank's board. The bank was separated from the government and left to function as a private entity without further assistance.

The second technique is contracting out, whereby the government enters into contracts with private firms to provide goods and services used by the government or demanded by the public. Contracting usually results in cost savings because the process is opened to competition among vendors. Contracting has been encouraged since 1955, when President Eisenhower approved a policy that "the Federal government will not start or carry on any commercial activity to provide a service or product for its own use if such product or service can be procured from private enterprise through ordinary business channels."

Contracting out is widespread and increasing in popularity at the state and local levels. Included in contracting is franchising, under which the government awards an exclusive right to deliver a public service to a private contractor, who then is paid by consumers rather than by the government. Franchising is commonly used for services such as water, electricity, gas, telephone, and cable television.

The third main form of privatization is the use of vouchers, under which the government distributes purchasing power to eligible consumers, who then must spend the funds received on designated goods or services. For example, housing vouchers provide low-income families with the means to obtain better housing in the rental market. Food stamps provide purchasing power to lower income families, enabling them to buy more or better food than their income otherwise would allow. The GI Bill following World War II provided education vouchers that could be used at a wide range of schools at the individual veteran's discretion.

User fees have been classified as a method of privatization, although they do not involve the transfer of government functions, but resemble privatization in that they place the burden of paying for the public service on those who benefit from it, rather than on taxpayers in general. The fees charged to barge operators to use government locks and canals are one example. When user fees are insufficient to cover the true cost of the government service (as is often the case), taxpayers must subsidize the shortfall.

Also considered privatization, deregulation of industry has been one of the most important forms of curbing government and relying more heavily on the private sector. Deregulation in some cases results in competition between private suppliers and the government for the consumer's dollar. For example, since 1979, when the Postal Service began to allow private carriage of urgent mail, private express couriers have grown dramatically, to the point where the Postal Service share of the express mail market is only 12 percent. Under the private express statutes, however, private services are still prohibited from delivering first-class mail.

State and Local Privatization

Contracting out in the United States has been employed most widely at the state and local levels. From coast to coast, government bodies, principally in response to pressures from taxpayers for greater efficiency, have been relying increasingly on the private sector to get the job done.

Since 1932 San Francisco has franchised garbage collection to private companies. Today, drivers own their trucks and are responsible for collections. In 1975, a study showed that San Franciscans were paying $40 a year for the private service, whereas New Yorkers in two comparable neighborhoods were paying $297 a year for municipal collection.

In 1977, Little Rock, Arkansas, contracted out its city hall janitorial services and achieved a 50-percent cost savings. Through similar programs, Cypress, California, saved 20 percent and Phoenix, Arizona, 57 percent.

Orange County, California, reduced costs about 33 percent by contracting out its electronic data processing requirements.

Bringing in private management is another privatization measure being used by local governments. The American Water Works Company manages government-owned water and sewer facilities for more than 95 communities with more than 500,000 people in western Pennsylvania. Sonoma County, California, reduced its annual operating subsidy to its county hospital by 50 percent, after turning the operation over to a for-profit hospital management chain. York County, South Carolina, has turned virtually all its municipal hospitals over to for-profit management companies.

Since 1899, Vermont law has allowed school boards of towns with no public or union district high school to pay for the tuition of the town's high school students at any approved (nonparochial) secondary school "within or without the state," up to an amount (for nonpublic schools) equal to the average tuition rate for a union district high school. In 1985, 95 Vermont towns containing 24.2 percent of the state's high-school-age population used this education voucher system, and surveys have shown strong parental acceptance and satisfaction with it.

Innovative privatization efforts such as these are under way in numerous state and local governments throughout the country. Privatization is growing because it delivers major savings or improved service quality, or both, to local taxpayers.

Privatization at the Federal Level

In the fiscal 1988 budget, the Office of Management and Budget proposed a number of privatization initiatives. These included the sale of the five power-marketing administrations, two oilfields owned by the Department of Energy, excess real property owned by the General Services Administration, the Federal Housing Administration's rural housing insurance fund, auction of the unassigned radio frequency spectrum, termination of federal crop insurance, sale of federal helium equipment assets, sale of Export-Import Bank loans, and Amtrak. The budget also included proposals for additional contracting out by the federal government.

One innovative proposal, advanced by the Office of Personnel Management, is called "Fed CO-OP." It proposes to spin off government entities as independent, for-profit companies with the current government employees as shareholders. By offering employees an ownership stake in the privatized activity, the plan seeks to build support within a group normally opposed to proposals to reduce the federal role. To date, however, no entity has been spun off under the Fed CO-OP plans.

The 1987 sale of Conrail marked the first major privatization initiative to come to fruition. This was followed later in the year by the sale of loans by the Department of Education and the Farmers Home Administration. Even during the period when no highly visible privatization initiative surfaced, use was being made of the contracting out procedures, most notably by the Department of Defense.

Although much more might have been attempted in recent years at the federal level, there is growing interest in privatization, both in the divestiture of federal government assets to the private sector and in the more aggressive use of contracting.

Privatization Worldwide

A worldwide trend toward privatization has accelerated dramatically in the past few years. It has encompassed governments of all political persuasions, including some in Communist countries, which are coming to appreciate the large gains in efficiency that involving the private sector can achieve.

The unquestioned champion for sweeping privatization is Britain. Prime Minister Margaret Thatcher's government has made the sale of government commercial entities one of the principal themes of her administration. Among the entities sold to workers, consumers, and the general public are British Rail Hotels, English Channel Ferry Service, Jaguar (automobiles), British Petroleum, British Aerospace, Britoil, National Freight Corporation, Gibraltar Dockyard, the British Telecom system, British Gas, British Airways, British Airports Authority, and Rolls Royce.

The Thatcher government's sale of more than a million government-owned housing units to residents affected the approximately 40 percent of British families who formerly lived in this "council housing." By selling these units, the government divested itself of money-losing facilities, eliminated costly operating subsidies, received income in the form of sales payments, and made independent homeowners out of dependent government residents. The result not only was beneficial to the residents and to the Exchequer, but has now even won considerable political support from the opposition Labor Party.

In Japan, former Prime Minister Yasuhiro Nakasone had initiated the partial privatization of some of Japan's worst money-losing government enterprises, notably Japanese National Railways (JNR). In 1983, JNR was losing $25 million a day and had accumulated $120 billion in debts. Steps to sell part of the giant Nippon Telegraph and Telephone are also proceeding.

Privatization in France has been a top priority since March 1986, when Jacques Chirac became Prime Minister. In fact, the principal economic minister has been retitled the Minister of State in Charge of Finance, the Economy, and Privatization. France has announced plans to transfer 65 companies to private hands by 1991, for a total price of at least $50 billion. A major goal has been to increase share ownership among the French people, and in the first year the number of French owning corporate shares rose from 2 million to more than 5 million. The government views the effort as reviving the prospects for French firms to compete internationally and strengthening the French stock market.

Turkey has sold the Bosporus Bridge and the Keban hydro plant and has 30 more state-owned enterprises on the list for eventual sale. The sale of the national airline began with sales to airline employees, then to the general public, then to domestic and foreign investment firms.

The Italian state holding company, IRI, has begun selling many of its commercial assets. In Spain, part of the state-owned auto manufacturer was sold off to Volkswagen, and a state-owned ball-bearing factory will follow. The government bus and truck company has been sold to General Motors.

In the People's Republic of China, workers are being allowed to buy shares in their enterprises, which are slowly being freed from state and party control. Free markets are springing up in cities such as Guangzhou, Shanghai, and Chengdu. A stock market has been allowed to open in Shenyang, and extensive agricultural privatization has dramatically improved China's capacity to feed its people.

Even the Soviet Union is moving cautiously in the same direction. In November 1986 the Supreme Soviet issued a decree allowing a range of private sector activities. In Estonia, worker-owned radio and television repair shops have achieved important efficiencies and new levels of consumer satisfaction. Independent production cooperatives also will be encouraged under reforms advocated by General Secretary Mikhail Gorbachev. Among many further such examples in Communist nations, Cuba has embarked on a public housing sale akin to that in Britain, and Hungary allows groups of workers to lease state-owned factories and keep the profits they earn.

In Latin America, where inefficient state-owned corporations have been major recipients of foreign bank loans, numerous governments are moving to transfer their holdings to the private sector. Costa Rica has been one of the most enthusiastic. With help from the U.S. Agency for International Development, a trust fund has been established to buy companies now owned by the state holding company and to sell them to private investors. Costa Rica has converted a key agricultural complex into a 200,000-member agricultural cooperative.

Even in Africa, where socialized economies are almost taken for granted, the movement is gaining a foothold. All the government enterprises in Togo are for sale. The government of Kenya is firmly committed to a similar course. In late 1985 Guinea closed all its state-owned banks and created new banks in which private shareholders have a stake. Ivory Coast has liquidated its national trading company along with unprofitable rice and hotel operations. The President of Tanzania, where "African socialism" proved unsuccessful, has declared that state enterprises will henceforth have to operate without government subsidy, often a step toward private ownership.

Summary

The Commission has approached each of the areas of government activity addressed in this report with a firm commitment to improve services to the American people. The Commission received extensive evidence of difficulties in the current delivery of services, heard testimony that more effective alternatives are available through the private sector, and found convincing evidence that some government actions impede development of private alternatives (and obstruct improvements in public services). In many of these cases the Commission recommends a renewed reliance on the talents and ingenuity of private citizens to develop better ways to accomplish what is now government's business.

Chapter 2

Low-Income Housing

The overall condition of American housing has improved dramatically since World War II, as the percentage of housing rated inadequate on the basis of U.S. Census statistics has declined from more than 40 percent to less than 5 percent. From 1950 to 1979, the average number of square feet of a new U.S. home doubled.[1] The success story of U.S. housing has been a product largely of private market forces, supported by federal tax advantages and federal assistance in housing finance.

There have always been some Americans, however, for whom the housing market does not work well. Some of these citizens live in crowded and deteriorated housing much below national standards. Others live in acceptable housing, but pay so much for it that their ability to buy adequate food, transportation, and other necessities is endangered. The Department of Housing and Urban Development (HUD) estimates that in 1983 about 47 percent of very low-income renters were paying over half their incomes for housing.

The best known form of government housing assistance for low-income people has been the direct construction of new public housing. Following authorization of the public housing program in the Housing Act of 1937, the rate of completion of public housing varied widely by year, but averaged almost 20,000 units annually, resulting in the construction of 440,000 units by 1960.[2] The 1949 Housing Act promoted new construction of public housing by establishing a national goal of "a home and suitable living environment for every American family." During the Eisenhower administration public housing was deemphasized but new construction picked up again in the mid-1960s. Another sharp cutback in new construction occurred under the Nixon administration, followed by encouragement during the Carter years, and then cutbacks again under the Reagan administration. Today, public housing represents about 5 percent of all rental housing in the nation and up to 15 percent in several major cities.[3]

Because of the substantial lags in construction, each administration tends to inherit a backlog from its predecessor. Hence, as shown in table 1, the early 1980s were a period with a high rate of completion of public housing, even while authorization of future units was declining. For fiscal year 1988, Congress authorized expenditures of $340 million, sufficient to build 5,000 units of public housing.

TABLE 1.—*Construction of Public Housing Units, by Year*

Year	Public Housing Units Completed
1940	34,308
1945	2,080
1950	1,255
1955	20,899
1960	16,401
1965	30,765
1970	70,300
1971	92,000
1973	75,000
1974	36,000
1975	31,000
1976	39,000
1977	24,000
1978	15,000
1979	15,000
1980	25,000
1981	32,000
1982	38,000
1983	35,000
1984	29,000
1985	24,130
1986	18,800
1987	18,113

SOURCE: For 1940 to 1965, *The Report of the President's Committee on Urban Housing, A Decent Home* (Washington, D.C., 1968); for 1970 to 1987, figures supplied by the Department of Housing and Urban Development.

Under the public housing program, as created in the 1930s, the capital costs of public housing were paid by the federal government and the costs of operation by resident rents. However, over time the residents of public housing tended to come more and more from the poorest segments of American society. These low-income residents found it difficult to cover operating costs. Under pressure to assist them, Congress in 1969 enacted the so-called Brooke Amendment, limiting rent payments to 25 percent of resident income and committing the federal government to pay any operating subsidies that became necessary. In so doing, Congress formally acknowledged that the public housing program had become an important part of the national welfare system.[4]

Seeking to rely on private management skills, while still providing financial assistance to low- and moderate-income households, Congress in the 1960s adopted new housing programs to subsidize mortgages for privately built rental housing. In return for the mortgage subsidy, the builder was required to price the housing at a level affordable by low- and moderate-income groups.

The first of the major housing subsidy programs was created in 1961 under Section 221(d)(3) of the National Housing Act. Pressures soon arose, however, to devise an alternative because Section 221(d)(3) mortgages were provided directly by the government and the full mortgage amount showed up at the point of issuance as a federal budget outlay.

Section 236 of the National Housing Act was enacted in 1968 partly to address this Congressional concern about the direct loans of earlier programs. Under Section 236 government outlays would be limited to annual subsidy payments made to the developer, who would obtain the mortgage from a private source. The government was permitted to pay subsidies up to an amount sufficient to bring the developer's interest rate down to 1 percent. A similar program, Section 235, was also created in 1968 to provide interest subsidies for the purchase of new and existing homes. As shown in table 2, new construction of subsidized housing under Section 235 and Section 236 peaked in the early 1970s.

Widely publicized scandals and other problems led President Nixon to suspend new construction under all the housing programs in 1973. Following the recommendations of a task force assigned to conduct a national housing policy review, Congress enacted the Housing and Community Development Act of 1974, which significantly deemphasized the role of mortgage subsidies. Nevertheless, mortgage subsidy programs continued to operate on a lesser scale.

As part of Section 8 of the Housing and Community Development Act of 1974, Congress made a basic change in government housing policy. Critics had long argued that direct financial payments to low-income households would allow available government funds to serve many more low-income families. Under Section 8, low-income households were permitted to rent existing housing in the private rental market. The government would then provide certificates to pay the difference between 25 percent of the household's income and the market rental. Private housing obtained in this way must meet government quality standards and have a market rental no higher than an amount determined by HUD to represent a fair market rent for suitable housing in that locality. The use of Section 8 certificates has grown rapidly since the program was enacted, serving about 800,000 households by 1985.[5]

With Section 8, Congress in effect declared that use of the existing housing stock could also be an important method of providing for the housing needs of low-income households. Residents of public housing and users of Section 8 certificates are treated in much the same way, each

TABLE 2.—*Construction of New Government-Subsidized Housing, by Selected Housing Program and Year*

Year	Number of New Units Completed		
	Section 236	Section 235	Section 8
1970	16,000	21,300	N/A
1971	73,500	153,400	N/A
1972	123,100	156,900	N/A
1973	100,000	98,600	N/A
1974	89,700	27,300	N/A
1975	100,000	15,300	0
1976	81,300	1,000	0
1977	16,900	19,588	25,000
1978	6,600	8,500	53,000
1979	5,900	11,200	125,000
1980	3,700	13,300	150,000
1981	1,200	67,400	135,000
1982	217	38,800	107,500
1983	0	12,800	80,000
1984	N/A	2,000	60,000
1985	N/A	4,900	35,500
1986	N/A	5,205	11,500
1987	N/A	1,900	21,000

SOURCE: Department of Housing and Urban Development.

paying up to 30 percent of their income, while the government pays the remainder of the housing costs.

Section 8 also contained other provisions that sharply altered the operation of the programs for privately built but government-subsidized housing. Instead of mortgage subsidy payments, the government would now provide builders with tax advantages and guarantees of future streams of rent payments from low-income residents. As shown in table 2, completions of new and rehabilitated housing under Section 8 subsidies exceeded 100,000 units per year from 1979 through 1982. By 1987, more than 800,000 subsidized housing units had been constructed or rehabilitated under Section 8.

By 1987, there were a total of 1.3 million units of public housing, 1.9 million units of private housing built with federal subsidies, and 900,000 units of housing for which the federal government made a direct payment to cover some share of the rental. The total number of people living in these forms of government-assisted housing approached 10.6 million, about 5 percent of the U.S. population.[6]

Problems of Government Housing Programs

Reinforcing the findings of previous study groups, the Commission heard testimony that the cost per unit of constructing new housing today continues to be much higher than the cost of providing vouchers to rent existing housing units. Table 3 shows recent Office of Management and Budget estimates of the cost per unit of providing low-income housing under various programs. Construction of new public housing currently costs about two and one half times the cost of providing housing through existing rental markets; new subsidized housing costs about twice the existing market cost. On a monthly basis, new construction of public housing currently involves a cost per unit of almost $700 per month, compared with typical costs of about $300 per month for units obtained with vouchers.

TABLE 3.—*Costs of Providing Government Housing Assistance, by Program*

Program	Twenty-year Cost
Voucher	$27,892
Section 8 Certificate	27,955
Farmer's Home Section 515 (new construction loan subsidy)	35,210
Rental Housing Development Grant (new construction loan subsidy)	53,500
Section 8/292 Elderly Housing (new construction loan subsidy and rental subsidy)	53,575
Public Housing (new construction loan subsidy and rental subsidy)	69,863

SOURCE: *Federal Housing Policy and Opportunities for Privatization*, report submitted to the Commission by the Office of Management and Budget, October 20, 1987, p. 32.

NOTE: Comparisons are based on discounted present value for new units constructed today or new rental subsidies issued today.

The high cost of government-assisted housing is partly a consequence of government rules and regulations. Under the Davis-Bacon Act, for example, builders of public housing must follow rigid union work rules and pay the prevailing union wage in the construction industry, often significantly higher than other builders are paying. The Commission heard testimony from Professor Richard Muth of Emory University that new housing built by local government agencies is "incredibly expensive," partly because these agencies do "not feel the competitive pressure for efficiency that private producers do." [7]

Given the high costs, the continued use of government funds for new housing construction creates some major social inequities. John Weicher of the American Enterprise Institute testified to the Commission that

> Because new housing is so expensive, housing is unique among our benefit programs for the poor. It is not an entitlement; instead it's a lottery. In every other program—AFDC (Aid to Families with Dependent Children), Food Stamps, Medicaid—anybody who is eligible is entitled to benefits. In housing, you have to take your chances. A few people—about a quarter of the poor—"win big" in the lottery; they get a very large subsidy to live in very good housing. Most poor people—equally poor and as far as we know, equally deserving—get nothing.[8]

With many more eligible households than units of public housing available, long waiting lists have developed at some of the more attractive projects. In a few cities, waiting periods have reached 11 years, causing managers to stop accepting applications. The average wait nationwide is 13 months and at 9 percent of public housing authorities the wait exceeds 3 years.

Another major problem with construction of new government-assisted housing is the racial and social segregation of the residents that results. Where whole projects are occupied predominantly by households on welfare, the social problems of these households have frequently been exacerbated. Some projects are not able to maintain even minimum requirements for a satisfactory living environment such as the assurance of personal safety and enforcement of law and order. It is reported that Newark, New Jersey, is planning to demolish almost a third of its existing public housing because of poor conditions.

Public housing also limits low-income families in the locations and types of housing they can obtain. There may be no housing project, for example, located near a promising source of employment. Like other families, low-income households will have varying preferences in the layout and design of housing, preferences that may not be satisfied by uniform government housing specifications. If employment or family circumstances change, it may be difficult for a low-income household to obtain another housing unit that would be better suited to its new circumstances. The range of consumer choice in public housing is necessarily restricted.

As economic conditions change, some public housing units may come to occupy urban sites with high commercial or other use values. Sale of appropriately selected housing projects could improve the overall efficiency of land and also generate substantial additional government funds that would be capable of assisting many more low-income households. In general, because decisions concerning public housing are largely removed from the influence of market incentives, socially beneficial responses to economic and other pressures for change occur slowly.

Reflecting all these concerns, the President's Committee on Urban Housing in 1968 and the President's Commission on Housing in 1982 both recommended against construction of new housing as the basic long-run strategy for providing government housing assistance.[9] Arthur Solomon, a former Director of the Harvard-MIT Joint Center for Urban Studies, stated in 1974 that

> A history of federal policies for housing the urban poor would chronicle a succession of programs, each in its turn, oversold to the public only to become sadly mired down in its operation, leaving the central dilemma—millions of families trapped in squalid living conditions—as unresolved as ever. The causes of disappointment have varied with circumstances: in most cases, a host of unanticipated costs, red tape and local political conflicts (over building codes, tenant selection, lending practices, and site location) have combined to frustrate congressional intent; in a few dramatic cases, exposes of windfall profits, shoddy construction practices, and other more or less familiar forms of human venality have culminated in outright congressional hostility. It is symptomatic of our political system's indulgence that these programs have long outlived their fall from favor and have been quietly pensioned off on a token annual appropriation rather than administered a surgical and final *coup de grace.*[10]

The public housing program was initiated in the depression years as a public works project whose main purpose was to stimulate the construction industry and to create jobs, a linkage that has persisted ever since. As Solomon wrote in 1973, "Far too often these programs have been designed to stimulate the construction industry, despite the rhetoric of legislative preambles couched in terms of eradicating blight, providing low- and moderate-income housing and revitalizing older neighborhoods."[11] The managers of public housing projects have come to represent another important constituency with an interest in maintaining public housing programs.

The most influential factor in housing availability for low-income households is not the level of construction of public housing, but the zoning and other regulatory policies adopted by suburban municipalities.[12] The nation has been unable or unwilling to open up more suburban land for development, which has raised land and housing prices for all concerned, but adversely affected the poor most of all. In some central cities, rent controls have had similar effects on the supply and price of housing available to new entrants in the housing market. Anthony Downs of the Brookings Institution believes that a main underlying purpose of public housing programs has actually been to serve as a kind of salve for the national conscience, relieving well-to-do suburbanites and other citizens of the burden to help the poor in more effective ways—but ways that also might infringe significantly on their own comforts and prerogatives.[13]

Housing Vouchers

Although Congress has continued to provide funds for new construction of low-income housing, it heeded many criticisms in enacting the Section 8 certificate program of the Housing and Community Development Act of 1974. However, the Section 8 program itself had some significant design flaws.[14] By fixing an allowable rent ceiling in each locality, the legislation simply encouraged landlords to raise the rent to the maximum amount allowed by HUD. Moreover, low-income recipients may have little incentive to search for a better housing bargain, because their housing payment is fixed at a maximum of 30 percent of their income in any case. Savings achieved by a lower rental would largely accrue to the government, not the Section 8 recipient. Recipients of Section 8 certificates also are not allowed to purchase higher quality housing if rent exceeds the HUD ceiling, even when they are willing to make the financial sacrifice.

The Housing Voucher Program avoids these problems. Similar in some ways to food stamps, the amount of the housing voucher varies with the income of the recipient. Recipients of vouchers can spend as much as they want for housing, supplementing the voucher payment with their own funds, if they choose. They can also spend less, retaining a portion of the voucher payment for other uses.

Vouchers have already proven a workable means of providing assistance to the poor. A large-scale HUD demonstration project was carried out with successful results in the 1970s. Since receiving Congressional authorization in 1983, a voucher program has been established by HUD that is now serving more than 100,000 households.[15] The value of the voucher is set at the difference between the HUD-determined local fair rent and the recipient's expected contribution, normally 30 percent of net income or at least 10 percent of gross monthly income. The recipient has the freedom to choose rental housing of any quality or price, provided it meets HUD minimum standards.

In 1987, HUD issued the first in a series of reports, as part of a 3-year study of its voucher demonstration program. The preliminary report found that, on average, 60 percent of voucher recipients succeeded in finding suitable housing within the 90 days allowed for their search.[16] All available vouchers were eventually used by some household. Some families, however, did not find suitable quarters after searching more or less diligently, while very large families and those with a history of eviction sometimes find private markets inhospitable. In urban areas where vacancy rates are low, there is a concern that vouchers might merely drive up rentals, rather than providing low-income housing, creating a windfall for landlords. The National Governors' Association testified to the

Commission that, partly for this reason, it did not regard vouchers as the entire answer to the need for low-income housing programs.[17]

According to the Arlington County, Virginia, Department of Management and Finance, voucher-type assistance administered under the county's Housing Grants Program works well even in a market with traditionally low vacancy rates, as long as the turnover rate remains high. Under this program, Arlington County subsidizes half of the difference between the actual rent and 80 percent of the household's gross annual income. The HUD-measured fair market rent serves as a cap to limit the county's subsidy.[18]

Congress provided permanent authorization for vouchers in the Housing and Community Development Act of 1987. This legislation also contains a nondiscrimination clause to be used against anyone refusing to rent an available dwelling unit at the HUD fair market rent. An important advantage of vouchers is the potential—supported by some evidence to date—to achieve greater integration, as compared with government-constructed projects.

The Commission concludes that vouchers are a workable and preferable means of assisting low-income households to obtain housing. Because vouchers cost much less per household than construction of new public housing, their benefits can be extended to many more households for a given level of federal housing expenditure. Vouchers do not segregate low-income households, most of them receiving welfare payments, in isolated projects, but instead allow voucher recipients to enter into broader communities of the working poor. Vouchers generally offer much greater mobility, allowing low-income families to respond to changing circumstances in their choice of housing. By subjecting the housing decisions of low-income families to market incentives, vouchers also enhance the efficiency of land and housing markets.

These features make vouchers a superior mechanism for providing governmental assistance to low-income Americans in obtaining housing. Accordingly, the Commission recommends:

Recommendation (1)

As an alternative to furnishing public housing accommodations, the government should provide housing assistance to low-income households by giving subsidies (vouchers) to eligible households to select and rent acceptable private housing in the marketplace at a price that is within their voucher-augmented means.

Management of Existing Housing Units

Even if construction of new government-assisted housing stopped today, there would still be a large stock of existing housing to be managed. Some of this housing might best be sold to project residents, while the conditions of other public housing could be significantly improved by a greater private sector involvement in its management.

The physical design, quality and other characteristics of public housing units vary greatly across the United States, ranging from rural single family homes to multi-story apartment housing clustered in large complexes in some central cities. Government policies for the management of existing public housing need to be closely tailored to suit the widely varying circumstances of individual housing projects.

Sale of Small Scale Units to Residents

Ownership by residents of their public housing units would have many advantages. Residents would have the flexibility and incentives to reduce significantly the costs of operations and maintenance—perhaps doing much of the work themselves.

In some cases residents have lived in the same public housing units for many years. Selling the unit to these residents would in effect acknowledge the de facto permanency of resident occupancy. However, the government would benefit from the ending of its operating subsidies and from a reduced administrative responsibility in the future while residents would benefit from the possession of a valuable capital asset that could be sold for retirement or for other needs. Where new economic circumstances might warrant a whole new use of a project site, freedom of project residents to sell would facilitate needed transitions in land use.

Sales of public housing to residents have proven successful in Great Britain. As of 1987, more than one million housing units had been sold, representing more than 15 percent of all British public housing existing in 1979. Sales are to residents who have lived in public housing for at least 2 years, at prices discounted 30 to 60 percent below market value. There are no restrictions on resales, although the discount is recaptured according to a sliding scale that requires 100 percent repayment in the first year and declines 20 percent per year thereafter.

The opportunity for successful sale of public housing has been greater in Britain, because public housing has constituted a much larger share of the national housing stock, and many occupants of public housing have been from the middle classes. There have also been more single-family homes and public housing of newer vintage in Britain. Nevertheless, the gains achieved suggest that similar results might also be achieved in the United States in appropriate circumstances.

In June 1985, HUD announced the Public Housing Homeownership Demonstration (PHHD), attempting to extend homeownership to low- and moderate-income families.[19] The sale terms of these units require HUD's continued payment of the debt service, but all operating costs must be borne by the resident-purchasers. Several conditions must be met for a sale to be completed:

- Properties transferred to residents must be in good condition prior to sale.

- Public housing authorities (PHAs) cannot involuntarily displace a resident who does not want to, or is financially unable to, participate in the homeownership demonstration.

- Resident-buyers usually may not profit from the resale of these units before 5 years of ownership.

- Resales must be structured to serve lower income families through income ceilings.

By February 1988, 184 units had been sold to residents under the PHHD program, including 43 sales at 6 of the 11 single-family demonstration sites (at an average unit price of $30,158) and two multi-family sales at two sites (at an average price of $38,180). Resident annual incomes for those units when sales have been closed have ranged from $7,900 to more than $26,000 with an average of $17,026.[20] Congress recently permitted HUD to continue the PHHD but limited any expansion.

As some Commission witnesses noted, HUD's efforts to promote home-ownership have been hindered by a lack of residents with the financial resources to purchase their units. According to estimates made by the Congressional Research Service, 9 percent of all public housing households might have sufficient income to purchase public housing without excessive financial strain.[21]

The Commission concludes that ownership of public housing units will encourage greater resident pride and a sense of responsibility for the maintenance of the unit. Ownership provides the resident with a valuable long-term asset, while saving the government the burden of current operating subsidies. Resident ownership makes future housing decisions more responsive to the incentives of the market. Accordingly, the Commission recommends:

Recommendation (2)

For public housing in good condition and consisting of detached one-family houses, duplexes and row houses, Congress should pass legislation authorizing and directing HUD to sell these units aggressively to tenants at a discounted price, with no further government expenditures for upkeep or debt service, while providing vouchers to tenants that freely elect to vacate.

Sale of Larger Projects to Tenant Management Organizations

The sale of public housing to residents may also be feasible for some large-scale projects. The most promising possibilities exist where residents have already shown the capacity to manage the project through successful tenant management organizations. As shown in table 4, a variety of forms of resident involvement already can be found in public housing projects.

Although there are only a limited number of tenant management organizations in large public housing projects, the successes of several of them have attracted national attention.[22] The Commission heard testimony concerning "several spectacular successes" at such projects:

> The best examples are programs initiated by HUD and the Ford Foundation in 1976: the Kenilworth-Parkside Project in Washington, D.C., and the Cochran Project in St. Louis, managed by Bertha Gilkey. Three years ago, Kenilworth was plagued by arson and drugs and had no heat or hot water. Since tenant management was initiated, utilities have been repaired, and crime, teenage pregnancy, and welfare dependency have decreased. Rent collections have risen 105 percent. In 1976, the Cochran Project had 250 vacant units out of 800, graffiti and gangs. Today, there are no vacant units, all units have been renovated and townhouses, playgrounds and a community center have been built. Other examples are the B.W. Cooper Project, New Orleans, where 3,000 requests for maintenance have dropped to zero and the A. Harry Moore Project in Jersey City, where vacant units have been cut from 20 percent to 2 percent.[23]

Under successful resident management, vacancies have been reduced, rent receipts increased and residents hired to perform maintenance, custodial, and security work formerly done by nonresident PHA employees. The extra revenues have gone to raise the level of service and to fund resident enterprises. PHAs continue to pay all debt service charges and ongoing utility costs as well.

In 1987 Congress enacted legislation allowing resident management corporations to earn the opportunity to buy their projects, once they have demonstrated successful management for 3 years. Proposals that would guarantee a resident's "right to buy" have also been introduced in Congress, although there is some question concerning the power of the federal government to require a local housing agency to sell a project. Conversion of a housing project from resident management to actual ownership could be accomplished as either a cooperative or a condominium. In a cooperative, tenants can screen prospective owners closely and supervise present owners. A condominium emphasizes individual ownership and responsibility, advantages that may prove more important over the long term.

The sale of large projects to resident organizations is not without risk. Some residents may find their financial means stretched to the limits and some defaults are likely. The government should also be prepared to provide training and other assistance to resident groups, both in planning sales and in subsequent management.

TABLE 4.—*Resident Participation in Public Housing: 1986*

PHA Size	Percent PHAs With Tenant Councils	Percent PHAs with PHA-Resident Agreements		
		Management	Maintenance	Services
Small	15.0	1.3	1.3	1.3
Medium	17.1			
Large	50.9		3.8	3.8
Very Large	71.8	7.9	13.2	15.8
Largest 14	100.0	25.0	33.3	25.0
All Respondents	38.8	3.2	5.6	5.6

SOURCE: National Association of Housing and Redevelopment Officials 1986 Housing Survey.

KEY: Small   = 1–500 public housing units
        Medium   = 501–1,250 units
        Large   = 1,251–2,500 units
        Very Large   = 2,501 or more units—excluding the largest 14

Sales of public housing to resident organizations would generally require a discount below market value. The residents would have to have sufficient income to cover the operating costs. Since some residents could not meet this requirement, they would not be able to remain in the project. Any such residents should be provided with vouchers or other assistance to ensure that they can afford to remain in the project or obtain satisfactory alternative housing.

The Commission concludes that the residents of public housing have the greatest stake in the quality of maintenance and management. Where resident management groups have already shown an ability to manage a project successfully, the government and the residents would both benefit from the sale of the project to the residents. The residents would acquire a valuable asset and, as owners, would have a strong incentive to ensure effective management. The government, by selling at a discounted price, would receive some sales revenue and would no longer bear maintenance and operations costs. Accordingly, the Commission recommends:

Recommendation (3)

Where a multi-family public housing project is in satisfactory physical condition and is under successful tenant management, sale to tenant cooperatives at a discount should be encouraged, but only with the clear understanding that no operating subsidy will be provided and no further capital investment, not even for debt service on the original construction, will be made by the government after the sale.

In making its recommendations to sell certain public housing units, the Commission clearly intends that alternate housing be provided for those who need it through vouchers. This housing stock should not be replaced by new government financed public housing construction.

Contracting Out of Public Housing Management

Many resident groups may not have the financial resources to pay even a discounted price to buy their housing project and cover the operating costs as well. A more limited step would be for the housing authority to sign a contract with the residents to manage the project. If this is not feasible, contracting out to a private management firm is another alternative.

To promote resident management, HUD is currently requiring PHAs to give residents information about their PHA's operating policies and assistance in forming resident organizations. HUD has published regulations to allow PHAs to waive competitive bidding requirements in contracting directly with resident management organizations. A further incentive for resident organizations provided for in the 1987 housing bill is to allow them to invest some or all of the savings they achieve in further building improvements.

Recently, the accounting firm Coopers and Lybrand conducted an analysis of resident management operations at Kenilworth-Parkside, a 464-unit public housing project in southeast Washington, D.C.[24] This analysis identified the following benefits:

- A 77 percent increase in rent receipts per unit-month from 1982 to 1985, adjusted for the actual number of occupied units at the site;

- A 70 percent increase in project income resulting from a reduction in the vacancy rate;

- A reduction in the cost to the District government for dependence on public assistance;

- An increase in District income tax payments associated with converting persons from welfare to gainful employment;
- A higher level of public service provided at the project.

Even under conservative assumptions about the costs of establishing the Kenilworth-Parkside resident management corporation, the analysis estimated net benefits to the District of Columbia government of $4.5 million (actual and projected) for the 10-year period 1982–1991.

Resident management organizations are not always successful. In the past decade, three of five such organizations failed in St. Louis. The residents may not have the substantial leadership and management skills required and some local housing authorities have sought to impose a new set of bureaucratic rules on tenant organizations, defeating much of their purpose.

Where residents may not have the skills and capabilities for successful management of a project, private management firms may be able to supply them. The private sector contains many firms that specialize in the management of residential and commercial facilities. Putting the experience of these firms to use would offer the prospect of more effective management of public housing projects.

The Commission concludes that in many cases large public housing projects could be managed more successfully by private property management firms and/or by the residents themselves. Because private firms would be held accountable for their performance, and could be replaced if necessary, private firms would be more responsive to the needs of government and residents alike. Where feasible, the best management might be provided by the residents themselves, the group that has the greatest interest in achieving successful management. Accordingly, the Commission recommends:

Recommendation (4)

To the maximum feasible extent, management of large public housing projects that are in satisfactory physical condition should be contracted out. This should be done by competitive bidding. Contractors would be either property management firms or tenant management organizations. It is recognized that the latter may be able to make a significant contribution to the effective management of public housing projects.

Closing of Public Housing Projects

The stock of existing public housing is aging rapidly. More than 400,000 units of public housing were built prior to 1960. Fully 34 percent of public housing buildings are today more than 25 years old. Portions of this housing have been subject to regular abuse and mismanagement that have left them well below government quality standards. Some unoccupied buildings lack even basic requirements such as heating and plumbing.

According to Commission witness Rene Henry, Jr., of the National Institute of Building Sciences, one study has shown that ". . . $9.5 billion is required just to make necessary repairs." Henry said, "If other important work, such as energy conservation, abatement of the hazards of asbestos and lead-based paint . . . and redesign of units, is implemented, the price tag is $21.5 billion." [25]

Indeed, some public housing projects have passed beyond the point where they can be salvaged by good management—resident or otherwise. Some of these projects have been allowed to deteriorate to the point that resident health and safety is endangered. Others may require very large expenditures to bring them up to an acceptable standard of quality. Bringing these projects up to standards would involve a cost per resident significantly greater than the cost of providing vouchers to rent private market housing.

There are also cases where deteriorated public housing occupies high value urban sites. If the projects were sold, revenues could be used to assist many more low-income families to obtain adequate housing elsewhere. Existing residents should be guaranteed receipt of vouchers and relocation assistance to find other housing accommodations.

The Commission concludes that it no longer makes sense to maintain public housing at some sites. Demolition of some projects will save the government unacceptably high future costs of rehabilitation. In some cases, sale of deteriorated projects in high-value urban areas may yield significant government revenues. The use of new revenues to provide housing vouchers would allow the government to assist a larger number of low-income households. Accordingly, the Commission recommends:

Recommendation (5)

For public housing that is in poor physical condition and requires extensive repairs and modernization, public housing authorities should be granted the flexibility to give vouchers to current tenants to enable them to obtain equal or better housing. The properties can then be vacated and sold for private use, with or without demolition, to the highest bidder.

Government-Subsidized Private Housing

Public housing was the first of the major federal housing assistance programs and remains the one most familiar to the public at large. However, a higher total number of units have been constructed under the several programs that have subsidized the private construction of housing, providing mortgages to builders at below-market interest rates or other forms of subsidy. At present, there are a total of 1.9 million housing units that were constructed under the various subsidy programs.

Many of the past subsidized projects contained provisions in their contracts for an initial term, after which renewal was optional with the developer. During this initial term—typically 15 years or more—the developer was required to offer housing at below-market rentals. At the end of the term, however, the developer could pay off the project and convert it to ordinary private rentals at market rates. The General Accounting Office recently estimated that from 240,000 to 890,000 units might be withdrawn in this fashion from the subsidized housing stock by 1995.[26]

Congress has expressed concern over this potential decline in the supply of government-assisted housing for low- and moderate-income groups. Recently enacted legislation contains procedures designed to restrict and delay prepayment of mortgages or other changes in the status of the contractual agreement between HUD and the private owners. Under this legislation incentives to continue the contract might be offered by HUD to the owner. If the private owner still seeks to pay off the mortgage, HUD must find that implementation of the action plan would not create hardships for current tenants or displace them when comparable and affordable housing is not generally available.

The Commission concludes that the government should not abrogate contracts that had been entered into to subsidize private mortgages. However, such contracts are an inefficient use of federal funds. The poor in need of housing can be more effectively assisted with housing vouchers. Accordingly, the Commission recommends:

Recommendation (6)

Contracts for private housing built with government subsidies should not be renewed, provided that no owner's right to renewal shall be abrogated. Vouchers shall be issued to eligible tenants who cannot afford the new market rents.

NOTES FOR CHAPTER 2

1. *The Report of the President's Commission on Housing* (Washington, DC: U.S. Government Printing Office, 1982), p. 4.

2. *The Report of the President's Committee on Urban Housing, a Decent Home* (Washington, DC: U.S. Government Printing Office, 1968), p. 61.

3. Raymond J. Struyk, *A New System for Public Housing:* Salvaging a National Resource (Washington, DC: The Urban Institute, 1980), p. 14.

4. John C. Weicher, *Housing: Federal Policies and Programs* (Washington, DC: American Enterprise Institute, 1980), p. 35.

5. *Federal Housing Policy and Opportunities for Privatization*, report submitted to the Commission by the Office of Management and Budget, October 20, 1987, p. 30.

6. Supplementary material to testimony of Carl D. Covitz, Department of Housing and Urban Development, submitted to the President's Commission on Privatization, Hearings on Housing (hereinafter cited as Hearings on Housing), October 20, 1987.

7. Testimony of Richard F. Muth, Emory University, Hearings on Housing, October 21, 1987.

8. Testimony of John C. Weicher, American Enterprise Institute, "Private and Public Roles in Housing Policy," Hearings on Housing, October 21, 1987.

9. *The Report of the President's Committee on Urban Housing* (1968), p. 71; and *The Report of the President's Commission on Housing* (1982), p. 18.

10. Arthur P. Solomon, *Housing the Urban Poor: A Critical Evaluation of Federal Housing Policy* (Cambridge, MA: The MIT Press, 1974), p. 1.

11. Ibid., p. 7.

12. Testimony of Rene A. Henry, Jr., National Institute of Building Sciences, Hearings on Housing, October 21, 1987.

13. Anthony Downs, *Neighborhoods and Urban Development* (Washington, DC: The Brookings Institution, 1981), pp. 116-17.

14. Weicher, pp. 74-81.

15. Covitz testimony.

16. Abt Associates, Inc., report prepared for the Department of Housing and Urban Development, *Report of First-Year Findings for the Freestanding Housing Voucher Demonstration*, June 1987, p. 5.

17. Testimony of Richard B. Geltman, National Governors' Association, Hearings on Housing, October 21, 1987.

18. Letter to the Commission staff from Mark Jinks, Budget Director, Arlington County, Virginia, Department of Management and Finance, January 22, 1988.

19. William M. Rohe, Michael A. Stegman, Raymond J. Burby, and Roberto Quercia, *Public Housing Homeownership Demonstration Assessment, Background Program Report*, draft report prepared for the Department of Housing and Urban Development, September 1987.

20. Supplementary material of Carl D. Covitz.

21. Morton J. Schussheim, Senior Specialist, Congressional Research Service, "Update of Study on Selling Public Housing to Tenants," in memorandum to U.S. Congressman Jack F. Kemp, April 24, 1986, p. 2.

22. Testimony of Stuart M. Butler, Heritage Foundation, Hearings on Housing, October 20, 1987, and Henry testimony.

23. Henry testimony.

24. National Center for Neighborhood Enterprise, "Cost-Benefit Analysis of the Kenilworth-Parkside Public Housing Resident Management Corporation—Executive Summary," Washington, DC, May 1986.

25. Henry testimony.

26. U.S. General Accounting Office, *Potential Reduction in Inventory for Federally Assisted Rental Housing*, June 16, 1986, p. 11.

Chapter 3

Housing Finance

Federal government policies to support financing of homeownership date back to 1932, when Congress established the Federal Home Loan Banking System and 1934 with the creation of the Federal Housing Administration. Since then, the federal presence in mortgage financing—the complex process through which housing loans are bought, sold, and insured on the open market—has grown enormously. This growth has dramatically increased the availability of capital to support homeownership.

Although the government has long encouraged homeownership, there is strong evidence that federal policies have created agencies that may now compete unfairly with the private sector. Critics also charge that the financial exposure and risk of federal agencies involved in mortgage financing have increased markedly in recent years, and that this situation could lead to substantial losses to taxpayers in the event of a collapse in housing prices.

The federal government encourages homeownership by easing the flow of capital into housing. This policy is implemented through various programs of federal and quasi-federal agencies, and through the deductibility of mortgage interest and property taxes from income that is subject to federal income taxes.

To understand the role of government and quasi-government agencies, it is useful to begin with a brief description of the mortgage finance system in the United States,[1] as it applies to one- to four-family homes. (This is the housing discussed in this chapter.) The process begins when a home buyer obtains a loan, called a mortgage, to buy a house. The lender, who originates the loan, may be a savings and loan association or a savings bank (together these two types of lenders are usually referred to as the thrift industry, or "thrifts"), or the lender may be a mortgage banker, a commercial bank, or some other source of funds.

The lender, seeking to reduce the risk that the borrower will default, may require the borrower to obtain insurance against that possibility; such insurance may be obtained from private mortgage insurers (PMIs) or, if the borrower qualifies, from the Federal Housing Administration or the Veterans Administration.

The lender generally sells the loan in the secondary mortgage market; the loan may appear in that market individually as a whole loan, or, alternatively as part of a pool of mortgages that serve as backing for mortgage-backed securities (MBSs). MBSs are issued by private banking institutions, by the Federal National Mortgage Association (Fannie Mae), and by the Federal Home Loan Mortgage Corporation (Freddie Mac). Some MBSs have a guarantee that increases their marketability.

The original lender may continue to service the loan or sell the servicing to another entity. Servicing consists of collecting monthly payments from the borrower; forwarding the proceeds to investors who have purchased the loan; maintaining escrow accounts for payment of taxes and insurance; acting as the investors' representative in case problems arise with the loan; and counseling borrowers when necessary.

The Federal Government's Role

Mortgage finance activities are conducted by the following agencies and corporations with ties to the federal government:

The **Federal Housing Administration** (FHA), which is part of the Department of Housing and Urban Development (HUD), insures mortgages for one- to four-family dwellings.

The **Veterans Administration** (VA) provides a federal guarantee to mortgage loans for homes purchased by veterans and, in certain instances, their dependents.

The **Farmers Home Administration** (FmHA), which is part of the Department of Agriculture, lends money to home buyers in rural areas and guarantees home mortgage loans.

The **Government National Mortgage Association** (Ginnie Mae), which is part of HUD, guarantees securities backed by FHA-insured and VA-guaranteed mortgages. When lenders assemble pools of such mortgages and issue mortgage-backed securities, Ginnie Mae enhances the appeal of these securities to investors by adding another tier of insurance, guaranteeing the timely payment of principal and interest. Ginnie Mae in effect connects mortgage markets with the broader capital markets, so that funds can flow more easily from the latter into the former.

The **Federal National Mortgage Association** (Fannie Mae), which was created in 1938 as a federal agency to buy, sell, or hold FHA-insured loans, is now a privately held corporation, but it retains important federal ties. Fannie Mae buys conventional mortgages, as well as those insured by FHA and guaranteed by VA to hold in portfolio or pool in support of MBSs. It issues mortgage-backed securities that it holds in portfolio or sells in secondary mortgage markets.

The **Federal Home Loan Mortgage Corporation** (Freddie Mac) performs activities similar to Fannie Mae but unlike Fannie Mae, it does not have a large portfolio operation.

These agencies support three major activities: home loans (FmHA), mortgage insurance (FHA, VA, FmHA), and secondary mortgage markets (Fannie Mae, Ginnie Mae, Freddie Mac).

With respect to home loans, FmHA lends money directly to would-be home buyers in rural areas, a function that is also performed by private mortgage lenders.

With respect to mortgage insurance, FHA, VA, and FmHA all provide mortgage insurance or guarantees; that is, they protect private lenders against the risk that borrowers will not be able to meet their mortgage payments. About one-fifth of the dollar volume of housing loans is insured by these agencies, but PMIs handle a comparable volume. In fact, PMIs generally insure more mortgages than do the federal agencies.

With respect to the secondary mortgage markets, Fannie Mae and Freddie Mac purchase mortgages and issue MBSs, while Ginnie Mae guarantees MBSs that have FHA- and VA-insured mortgages as collateral. Together these agencies establish a secondary market for mortgages, making it easier for investors to buy guaranteed mortgages. But private investment banking firms also pool mortgages and issue MBSs.

None of the federal or quasi-federal credit institutions performs a unique role in mortgage finance. Government-related agencies and private sector institutions perform similar functions and therefore compete for the home loan, mortgage insurance, and secondary mortgage market business. When government and private organizations compete, the former have certain inherent advantages—such as implied government guarantees on obligations—and some exemption from regulations by other government agencies. As a result, a bias is introduced in favor of an expanded government role and a reduced private role. The government should take steps to put government and quasigovernment agencies on an equal footing with their private competitors. Therefore, the President's Commission on Privatization recommends:

Recommendation (1)

The federal government should adopt a more neutral position with respect to direct housing finance programs, such as the Farmers Home Administration, Government National Mortgage Association, Federal Home Loan Mortgage Corporation, Federal National Mortgage Association, Federal Housing Administration, and Veterans Administration.

TABLE 1.—*Mortgage Loans Originated Annually for One- to Four-Family Houses, 1972–1986*

[In millions of dollars]

Year	FHA-Insured	PMI-Insured	Total Mortgage Loans
1972	8,456	9,158	75,864
1973	5,185	12,627	79,126
1974	4,532	9,220	67,508
1975	6,265	10,024	77,913
1976	6,998	14,600	122,785
1977	10,469	21,595	161,973
1978	14,581	27,327	185,036
1979	20,282	25,327	186,595
1980	14,958	19,035	133,765
1981	10,538	18,097	98,212
1982	11,482	18,753	96,951
1983	28,753	42,363	201,863
1984	16,600	63,405	203,205
1985	28,436	50,475	243,076
1986	62,038	46,138	454,055

SOURCE: Data for 1972 to 1984 from HUD, *Report of the FHA Task Force*, January 1987, p. 6; supplementary data for 1985 and 1986 were supplied by HUD.

Mortgage Insurance

FHA, the oldest federal credit agency dealing in mortgage insurance, was created during the Depression. Previously, private financial institutions typically made loans requiring a 50-percent down payment and 10-year, interest-only payments, leaving the buyer with a "balloon" payment at the end. Relatively few persons qualified for these loans. FHA offered longer term, low-down-payment, self-amortizing loans, and it insured such mortgages against default.

The private mortgage insurance industry had collapsed during the Great Depression, but later revived under strict state regulation. By 1972, PMIs were issuing more mortgage insurance than was FHA. A comparison of FHA-insured versus PMI loan originations for the period 1972 through 1986 is shown in table 1. The table indicates that although most mortgages are not insured, PMIs recently have provided almost twice as much insurance as FHA overall and had exceeded the FHA total in every year prior to 1986. In that year, FHA insured 26 percent of all mortgage originations for newly built homes, compared with 12 percent underwritten by PMIs.[2] By the end of 1986, FHA had outstanding loan guarantees on $224 billion worth of home mortgages, corresponding to 6 million properties.[3]

The markets served by PMIs and FHA overlap substantially. Table 2 shows the characteristics of borrowers whose loans were within FHA limits. Inspection of the table reveals that a significant fraction of FHA mortgage insurance is for loans above $60,000, goes to borrowers with incomes above the median, goes to investors as distinguished from owner-occupants, is used to refinance homes, and goes to higher income borrowers who make minimal down payments despite their higher incomes. FHA even insured some borrowers who had annual incomes greater than $100,000.[4]

TABLE 2.—*Selected Characteristics of FHA- and PMI-Insured Loans, Various Years*

	FHA-Insured	PMI-Insured
Loan-to-value ratio (1985)	89	91
Percentages of loans greater than $60,000 (1982-1986)[a]	43	31
Percentage of borrowers with incomes above 120% of local median incomes (1986)	60	76
Percentage of borrowers with incomes greater than $40,000 (1982-1986)[a]	35	38
Percentage of loans to first-time home buyers (1981 and 1983)	63	53
Percentage of loans for refinancing (1986)[a]	25	17
Percentage of loans for investment properties (1985)[a]	11	3
Percentage of loans for investment properties to borrowers with incomes greater than $60,000 (1986)[a]	52	57
Percentage of low-down-payment loans (less than 10% down) to borrowers with incomes greater than $60,000 (1985)[a]	11	8

SOURCES: HUD, *Report of the FHA Task Force*, January 28, 1987; Temple, Barker, and Sloane, Inc., *Comparison of the Markets Served by Private Insurers and the Federal Housing Administration*, report prepared for the Mortgage Insurance Companies of America, Boston, MA, November 19, 1987; Mortgage Bankers Association, material submitted to the Commission.

[a] For loans within FHA limits.

Several witnesses recommended to the Commission that FHA's efforts be rechanneled, restricted, or both. Gregory Barmore, President of Mortgage Insurance Companies of America, said that FHA-insured loans to low-income borrowers should be risk-free to the lender, but those to higher income borrowers should require that lenders be coinsurers with FHA. Furthermore, he said, at least 25 percent of Ginnie Mae pools should be reserved for low-income borrowers. Barmore added that the recent dramatic expansion in FHA coverage has not extended the affordability of homeownership to a previously unserved market segment, but instead has taken a market share that the private sector is well prepared to serve.[5] On the other hand, Warren Lasko, Executive Vice President of the Mortgage Bankers Association, suggested that private markets should seek ways to be more effective instead of focusing on what they term FHA's "unfairly" competitive activities.[6]

FHA loans carry a greater risk of default than do loans insured by private institutions. For example, the current default rate nationwide among loans insured by a major PMI (General Electric Mortgage Corporation) is only 1.1 percent, versus 1.9 percent for FHA.[7] Some analysts are pessimistic about FHA's ability to withstand a collapse in the residential housing markets. One observer regards FHA's recent growth in coverage as a "fiscal time bomb":

> In the past year [1985], the FHA has accommodated the surge in home-ownership by more than doubling its credit ceiling, from $57 billion to a record level of $132 billion. The frightening aspect of this growth in FHA credit is that the agency is failing to take prudent measures to protect itself, and thus the American taxpayer, against the huge contingent liability the agency carries. Should the economy slide into a deep recession the FHA could easily be facing multi-billion-dollar losses.[8]

Although FHA has undertaken activities virtually indistinguishable from PMI activities, a HUD task force concluded that it is impractical to try to sell FHA to the private sector,[9] and no Commission witnesses advocated such a sale. Moreover, in the 1987 Housing and Community Development Act, Congress reaffirmed its fundamental support for FHA's underlying mission by authorizing permanent insuring authority for FHA. Nevertheless, there is no need for FHA to compete with PMIs and a recent HUD report concluded that FHA's efforts could be redirected to provide a greater distinction between the clients served by FHA and those served by PMIs.[10] Accordingly, the Commission recommends:

Recommendation (2)

The Federal Housing Administration should reduce its mortgage insurance activity so that it does not compete as directly with private mortgage insurers. It should direct its efforts toward that market not served by private insurers, that is, toward buyers who have been turned down by private mortgage insurers.

FHA should refocus its efforts in order to subsidize primarily those who are unable to obtain mortgage insurance without such assistance. Better targeting of FHA and less overlap in markets served adequately by PMIs could be achieved by restricting FHA from serving any or all of the following categories of borrowers: upperincome persons, buyers of vacation homes, borrowers who want to insure large mortgages, borrowers who want to refinance mortgages on their present homes, nonoccupying investors, and persons who are not first-time home buyers. Guidelines can readily be developed to define these categories in an operationally useful manner. Additional policy changes to achieve these objectives would be to impose partial co-insurance requirements on lenders who want borrowers to obtain FHA insurance, and to charge premiums that are comparable to those needed for a PMI to meet regulatory requirements and to obtain a higher rating from credit-rating agencies.

The Commission is aware that its recommendation would mean a cutback in FHA's business in the more profitable, higher income market, and that greater concentration on lower income borrowers involves greater risk of default. Such targeting, however, would also have the effect of revealing the extent of the current subsidy.

Secondary Mortgage Markets

Fannie Mae was created in 1938 as a wholly owned government corporation, intended to "provide supplementary assistance to the secondary market for home mortgages by providing a degree of liquidity for mortgage investments, thereby improving the distribution of investment capital available for home mortgage financing." [11] In 1954, it was partially privatized in response to concern about its competing with traditional mortgage lenders. As a result, Fannie Mae was restricted to a supplementary role.

Originally the only truly national purchaser of home mortgages, Fannie Mac was further privatized when it became a federally chartered, wholly shareholder-owned, private corporation in 1968. Because it maintains important ties to the federal government, however, Fannie Mae can obtain credit at rates significantly lower than private firms have to pay. Moreover, its federal charter fosters a sense of government involvement and responsibility that capital markets recognize in ascribing "agency status" to Fannie Mae.[12] In effect, this means that the corporation's operations are subject to less market discipline, and Fannie Mae can operate at a lower capital-asset ratio than the private market would require.

The factors that give Fannie Mae agency status include the following:

Treasury link—Fannie Mae can borrow $2.25 billion from the Treasury, and its debt issues require Treasury Department approval.

Security—Depository institutions can use Fannie Mae securities as collateral, and the Federal Reserve accepts them as equivalent to Treasury bonds.

Tax exemption—Fannie Mae is exempt from state and local taxes.

SEC exemption—Fannie Mae securities are exempt from registration requirements of the Securities and Exchange Commission.

Board of Directors—5 members of Fannie Mae's 18-member board are appointed by the President.

HUD oversight—The Department of Housing and Urban Development has general oversight authority over Fannie Mae.

Charter limitations—Fannie Mae's charter limits it from expanding into fields other than real estate.

Freddie Mac is a publicly chartered corporation whose stock is owned by thrifts and savings banks that belong to the Federal Home Loan Banking System. The latter was established by Congress in 1932 to supervise federally chartered savings and loan associations and to provide a credit facility for thrift institutions.

Before Freddie Mac was created, there were significant regional differences in the availability (i.e., price) of capital for investment in conventional mortgages.[13] Similar in purpose to Fannie Mae, Freddie Mac was created in 1970 to bring about the same "coast-to-coast leveling" for conventional loans that Fannie Mae accomplished for FHA- and VA-backed mortgages.[14]

Federally sponsored credit plays a dominant role in housing finance, as is shown in table 3. Loans guaranteed directly or indirectly by the federal government totaled $862 billion at the end of fiscal year 1987; they constituted 42 percent of all housing credit and 66 percent of all federal credit.

The situation shown in table 3 resulted from the rapidly growing popularity of mortgage-backed securities. The process of converting mortgage loans or other illiquid assets into instruments acceptable to capital markets, known as securitization, has been popularized by Ginnie Mae and, later, Freddie Mac and Fannie Mae. In 1982, Freddie Mac initiated the guarantor swap program to exchange securities for large portfolios of existing mortgages held by thrift institutions. In 1983, Freddie Mac created collateralized mortgage obligations or "mortgage by the slice."[15]

Table 4 compares the volume of federal and nonfederal mortgage-backed securities collateralized by loans on one- to four-family houses. As this table shows, federally sponsored issues—especially Ginnie Mae issues—have dominated the MBS market. Private sector financial institutions began issuing conventional MBSs in 1977. Between 1977 and 1981, their share grew to 26 percent of the total dollar value of MBSs issued. When Fannie Mae began issuing MBSs, however, the private sector share of the market dropped sharply, although its dollar volume grew. By 1985, market share was down to 7 percent of the total; 93 percent of all MBSs are backed directly or indirectly by the federal government.

TABLE 3.—*Volume of Credit Outstanding in the United States,*
Fiscal Year 1987
(estimated at year end)

[In billions of dollars]

Credit for Housing		$2,033
Federal		862
Ginnie Mae	292	
Fannie Mae	220	
Freddie Mac	217	
Federal Home Loan Banks	106	
FmHA	27	
Other Housing		1,171
All Other Credit		6,347
Federal	449	
Other	5,898	
Total Credit		8,380
Federal	1,311	
Other	7,069	
Federal credit as a percentage of all credit		15.6
Housing credit as a percentage of all credit		24.3
Federal housing credit as a percentage of all federal credit		65.8
Federal housing credit as a percentage of all housing credit		42.4

SOURCE: Supplement to HUD testimony, "Growth of Federal and Private Credit," November 1987, from *Economic Report of the President, 1987* and *Special Analysis F*, Budget of the U.S. Government, 1988.

On the other hand, it is not entirely accurate to conclude that the government tilts the playing field in the secondary mortgage market completely in favor of federal agencies. Dale P. Riordan, Vice President of Fannie Mae, pointed out to the Commission that "all financial institutions—including banks, thrifts, and credit unions—have significant ties to the government." [16] The thrifts receive federal support through Federal Savings and Loan Insurance Corporation (FSLIC) deposit insurance and the banks through Federal Home Loan Bank Board advances and Federal Deposit Insurance Corporation guarantees.

Today, Fannie Mae has almost $100 billion in assets with $131 billion in additional off-book guarantees, making it the third-largest corporation in the United States. It is the largest quasi-governmental borrower in the

TABLE 4.—*Issues of Mortgage-Backed Securities Collateralized by Loans on One- to Four-Family Houses, 1971–1985*

[In billions of dollars]

Year	Ginnie Mae	Fannie Mae	Freddie Mac	Private	Total[a]
1971	$2.7 (98%)		$0.1 (2%)		$2.8
1972	2.5 (89%)		0.3 (11%)		2.8
1973	2.7 (87%)		0.4 (13%)		3.1
1974	4.3 (99%)		0.1 (1%)		4.4
1975	7.2 (83%)		1.5 (17%)		8.7
1976	13.1 (88%)		1.8 (12%)		14.9
1977	16.7 (77%)		4.6 (22%)	$0.2 (1%)	21.6
1978	14.6 (67%)		6.2 (28%)	1.1 (5%)	21.9
1979	24.0 (77%)		4.5 (15%)	2.8 (9%)	31.3
1980	19.7 (72%)		2.5 (9%)	5.3 (19%)	27.5
1981	13.3 (56%)	$0.7 (3%)	3.5 (15%)	6.3 (26%)	23.9
1982	14.8 (26%)	14.0 (24%)	24.2 (42%)	4.4 (8%)	57.3
1983	48.4 (55%)	13.3 (15%)	19.7 (22%)	7.5 (8%)	88.9
1984	26.4 (39%)	13.5 (20%)	18.7 (28%)	8.7 (13%)	67.4
1985	44.6 (39%)	23.6 (20%)	38.8 (34%)	7.8 (7%)	114.8

SOURCE: HUD, *Report of the FHA Task Force*, January 28, 1987, p. 11.

NOTE: Data for 1981–1986 include swap-type portfolio transactions.

[a] Numbers do not add due to rounding.

capital markets—a federally chartered, private corporation owned by 35,000 shareholders whose stock is traded on the New York Stock Exchange.

The Commission received contradictory testimony expressing concern about the rapid growth and sheer size of Fannie Mae, HUD's failure to conduct adequate oversight of the corporation, Fannie Mae's apparent reluctance to assume risk by increasing its loan activity as housing starts decline, its "crowding out" of other capital investment, and the increased risk of losses should interest rates rise substantially for a sustained period of time.

The General Accounting Office (GAO) analyzed Fannie Mae's role in recent years and the inherent risk to the federal government if Fannie Mae continues to grow. GAO concluded that, in 1985, many of the loans in Fannie Mae's portfolio carried interest rates below levels required to refurbish its capital, a major ingredient that contributed to Fannie Mae losses in 1981, 1982, and 1984.[17] To alleviate this problem, Fannie Mae has tried to achieve a better match, of both interest rates and maturity dates, between its assets and its liabilities, that is, its mortgages and its securities.

The Commission also heard testimony strongly urging limitations on Freddie Mac's competitive advantages over savings institutions, by establishing higher capital requirements and more substantial user fees.[18] Representatives of savings institutions are vocal in their opposition to the growth of Fannie Mae, Ginnie Mae, and Freddie Mac. The Commission heard testimony that the market share of residential loans going through the three corporations now exceeds 68 percent, a spectacular increase since 1980—when their share was 20 percent.[19] What happened, essentially, is that the thrift institutions, which hold mortgage loans in their portfolios, lost market share to the federal agencies, which issued MBSs. From the point of view of federal credit and interest subsidies, the difference between the thrifts and the agencies is modest, as the thrifts are also beneficiaries of federal programs, through Federal Savings and Loan Insurance Corporation (FSLIC) insurance and through Federal Home Loan Bank Board advances.

A persuasive argument, frequently heard, is that because of their quasi-government status, the agencies can borrow preferentially at lower rates than they would otherwise have to pay. As a result, they "crowd out" other borrowers. The net effect to society is an inefficient allocation of capital, as these agencies are subsidized at the expense of other borrowers.

On the other hand, a witness from Fannie Mae maintained that "crowding out" due to borrowing by, or credit enhancement of, Fannie Mae and Freddie Mac has never been proved and, in any case, has no effect on the funds available or on borrowing rates. In the statement the witness stressed that since the creation of the two corporations, homeownership has increased from 50 percent to 65 percent of the population. This increase is, he contended, a direct result of Fannie Mae's obligation to funnel revenues into the secondary market for home loans. Because Fannie Mae's implicit subsidy permits it to borrow money less expensively than it could otherwise do, removing its agency status would mean higher interest rates.[20]

The growth of Ginnie Mae, Freddie Mac, and Fannie Mae has been accompanied by a steady increase in the individual loan ceiling; the limit on the size of loans that these agencies can purchase is set by statute at $168,700. A witness representing savings and loan associations contended that each agency should be limited to loan levels at the low end of the market to reduce unfair competition with private savings institutions. Limitations should be designed to curb the growth of Fannie Mae and Freddie Mac, such as an annual ceiling on total assets and guarantees, substantial user fees, and minimum capital equity requirements.[21]

In support of the need to reassess Fannie Mae, HUD reported, with respect to Fannie Mae's portfolio operation, that the importance of Fannie Mae's agency status to the mortgage market has decreased to the point where it is no longer justifiable in terms of public policy objectives.[22]

With respect to Fannie Mae's MBS operation, the HUD report states that

> . . . a Federal presence in the MBS market is no longer justified by the need to support the development of pass-through securities. Termination of agency status for FNMA's (Fannie Mae's) and FHLMC's (Freddie Mac's) MBS programs could lead both organizations to continue as private MBS issuers with greater flexibility than they have now. Other private issuers of MBSs, now unable to compete in the portion of the market dominated by FNMA and FHLMC, would likely grow. However, another possible outcome is that investor confidence in MBSs would decrease, causing a decline in the market and reduced availability of mortgage funds. The likelihood of such an adverse effect depends on investor confidence, the nature of which is not fully known. There is also some concern about the ability of private firms to respond quickly enough to avoid credit availability problems during the transition to a system without agency status. If these transition problems could be surmounted, a market without agency status should become more competitive, and by implication, more efficient.[23]

The Commission advocates continuing the process of privatization that Congress has steadily pursued for Fannie Mae and Freddie Mac. It finds no compelling reason to justify the special advantages the two corporations continue to enjoy over private sector institutions engaged in similar activities. These advantages result in implicit interest subsidies for government-sponsored borrowing and higher interest rates for private borrowing.

Several plans have been proposed to carry out the privatization of these agencies, but the Commission considers it outside its scope to prescribe either specific steps or a specific schedule. Accordingly, the Commission recommends:

Recommendation (3)

The Federal National Mortgage Association and, by extension, the Federal Home Loan Mortgage Corporation, should be fully privatized on an appropriate schedule and with an announced transition period. This full privatization would entail the elimination of all federal benefits and limitations. During the scheduled transition to full privatization, they should pay fees for their federal attributes, increase their equity-to-assets ratios, and satisfy Securities and Exchange Commission registration requirements, among other steps.

Government agencies historically have played an important role in encouraging homeownership among Americans by popularizing mortgage insurance, various mortgage instruments, and mortgage-backed securities.

The private sector, however, can play a larger role in the mortgage finance marketplace. Unfortunately, private firms have been hampered by competition from federal agencies that can borrow at interest rates that are artificially low, subsidized by private borrowers.

The Commission's recommendations call for changes that would create more equitable conditions so that private sector institutions could compete for a greater share of business in secondary mortgage markets. Adopting these recommendations would lead in time to a more efficient allocation of capital for mortgage finance.

NOTES FOR CHAPTER 3

1. Mortgage Bankers Association of America, *Preserving and Building the American Dream*, February 1987.

2. U.S. Office of Management and Budget, background material submitted to the President's Commission on Privatization, Hearings on Mortgage Finance (hereinafter cited as Hearings on Mortgage Finance), October 21, 1987.

3. U.S. Department of Housing and Urban Development, *Report of the FHA Task Force*, January 1987, p. 5. Preliminary data for 1987 indicate that the FHA insured close to the same volume of mortgages as in 1986 and that its market share was virtually unchanged. Much of this rise in FHA volume since 1986 has been in the form of refinanced mortgages.

4. Temple, Barker, and Sloane, Inc., *Comparison of the Markets Served by Private Insurers and the Federal Housing Administration*, report prepared for the Mortgage Insurance Companies of America, Boston, MA, November 19, 1987.

5. Testimony of Gregory T. Barmore, Mortgage Insurance Companies of America, Hearings on Mortgage Finance, October 21, 1987.

6. Testimony of Warren Lasko, Mortgage Bankers Association, Hearings on Mortgage Finance, October 21, 1987; and Dale Riordan, Federal National Mortgage Association, Hearings on Mortgage Finance, October 20, 1987.

7. Barmore testimony.

8. Heritage Foundation, "How Congress Can Defuse the Federal Housing Administration Time Bomb," *Backgrounder*, No. 528, July 1986, p. 1.

9. U.S. Department of Housing and Urban Development, *Report of the FHA Task Force*, p. 28.

10. Ibid., p. 23.

11. Federal National Mortgage Association Charter Act, 12 U.S.C. 1716 et seq.

12. Lasko testimony.

13. Testimony of Lee Holmes, Federal Home Loan Mortgage Corporation, Hearings on Mortgage Finance, October 21, 1987.

14. Ibid.

15. Lasko testimony.

16. Testimony of Dale Riordan, Federal National Mortgage Association, Hearings on Mortgage Finance, October 20, 1987.

17. U.S. General Accounting Office, *The Federal National Mortgage Association in a Changing Environment*, GAO/RCED–85–102, April 15, 1985, pp. 38, 53, 94.

18. Testimony of Dennis Jacobe, U.S. League of Savings Institutions, Hearings on Mortgage Finance, October 21, 1987.

19. Ibid.

20. Riordan testimony.

21. Jacobe testimony.

22. U.S. Department of Housing and Urban Development, *1986 Report to Congress on the Federal National Mortgage Association*, pp. viii, ix.

23. Ibid., p. 8.

Chapter 4

Federal Loan Programs

The single largest commercial activity of the United States government is lending money. The federal government lends more funds each year than any other financial institution in the world. In fact, its $250 billion loan portfolio exceeds in value the combined loan assets held by the nation's two largest commercial banks.[1] In addition, the federal government currently guarantees $450 billion worth of outstanding loans issued by private lenders. Approximately 15 percent of all credit originated in the United States between 1981 and 1986 was either issued, or insured, by the federal government.[2]

The objective of federal lending is to provide subsidized credit to classes of borrowers or economic activities that Congress considers underserved by private credit markets. Over the past three decades, Congress has created more than 100 separate federal loan programs to accommodate a diverse assortment of credit seekers: farmers, college students, home buyers, military veterans, local governments, foreign governments, utility companies, small businesses, and even some Fortune 500 companies.[3]

The government's lending activities were initiated to achieve certain nationally established social policy objectives. For example, the federal government established the loan programs of the Rural Electrification Administration to bring electricity to rural America in 1935, when fewer than 15 percent of all farms had access to electricity.[4] Similarly, homeownership has been directly encouraged by the availability of federal mortgage guarantees and low-interest housing loans.

There is broad agreement, however, that the federal lending agencies have been ineffective as loan managers. The federal government's performance has lagged behind private sector standards in three areas: loan collection procedures, loan management practices, and accounting treatment of loan programs.

Loan Collection Procedures. The delinquency rate on federal loans is 8 percent, almost three times the rate on private sector loans (3 percent).[5] Some individual loan programs within the Small Business Administration (SBA) have recorded delinquency rates of well over 20 percent, while an estimated 50 percent of the Farmers Home Administration's (FmHA) current farm loan portfolio is in danger of default. In total, the federal government is now owed $24 billion in nontax delinquent debt. The Guaranteed Student Loan Program alone is projected to be holding $12 billion worth of defaulted loans by 1990.[6]

Loan Management Practices. Over the past 10 years, the U.S. General Accounting Office (GAO) has released more than 40 reports urging reforms in federal credit management practices.[7] A 1986 report charged: "GAO's financial statement audits, as well as inspector general reviews, have consistently disclosed serious weaknesses in agencies' systems that account for and control receivables. These problems include understating the amount of delinquent debt, not establishing allowances for loan losses, and the inability to promptly record amounts due and to reconcile account balances."[8] A subsequent GAO review of the loan management performance of the Department of Housing and Urban Development (HUD) Multifamily Housing Loan Program revealed that 20 percent of the agency's sampled loan files were either "completely missing [or] missing key documents such as the mortgage contracts."[9]

Nor do federal agencies acknowledge the reduced value of their loan portfolios by systematically writing off bad loans. The Office of Management and Budget (OMB) reports, "The FmHA holds in its portfolio, at their full nominal value, several billions of dollars of loans that are delinquent by more than a year."[10] The Export-Import Bank still carries on its books, at full face value, $89 million worth of loans made to Cuba in the 1950s.

Accounting Treatment of Loan Programs. The budgetary treatment of federal loan programs misstates the actual cost of lending activities to the government. These accounting procedures have encouraged policymakers to divert federal resources into the credit portion of the budget so as to minimize the perceived effect of their actions on the budget deficit. As Representative Willis D. Gradison, Jr. (R-OH), a principal architect of a credit reform package currently before the House of Representatives, as reported in the *Washington Post*, concedes, loan programs have become "a technique used during a period of budget stringency to do good things where the cost does not show up until later."[11]

The root of the problem is the government's cash-flow budgeting system, which is ill-equipped to capture the full fiscal effect of federal loan programs. Federal direct loans are treated as assets at full face value on the federal agency balance sheet, regardless of the degree of taxpayer subsidy made to the borrower. In the private sector it is considered good banking practice to account immediately for the expected future losses from new loans. As a net result of its unconventional accounting treatment, the government has no accurate measure of the true value of its $250 billion in loan assets.

Accounting for federally guaranteed loans has become an even more refined form of budgetary distortion. Loan guarantees, because they do not involve an immediate cash payment, are treated as if they were free to the taxpayer, even though they place a sizable contingent liability on the taxpayer's shoulders. Carol Cox, Executive Director of the Committee for a Responsible Federal Budget, concluded that federal credit programs are "the real last wilderness of federal budgets and accounting systems." [12]

With an eye toward remedying these three costly aspects of federal loan programs, the President's Commission on Privatization has investigated such privatization options as selling federal loans, purchasing reinsurance for federal loan guarantees, and adopting private sector loan collection techniques.

A 20-Year Expansion of Federal Credit Activities

In 1986 more than $1 trillion worth of outstanding loans carried some form of direct or indirect federal assistance.* The federal government makes credit available through two principal channels. First, federal agencies make direct loans. In this case, the federal agency assumes the role of a bank; it disburses the cash to the borrower and engages in all the activities associated with loan management. Table 1 breaks down the amount of outstanding federal direct loans by the type of economic activity assisted. Roughly half of all direct loan funds issued in fiscal year 1986 went to support farmers. [13]

The second form of federal credit assistance is provided through the guarantee of loans issued by private lenders. The purpose of government loan guarantees is to encourage banks to lend to categories of borrowers, such as certain foreign governments or college students, who, because of the lack of an established credit history or other factors that increase the risk of a loan, would have to pay interest rates Congress considers excessive. Frequently, the government agency provides a 100-percent guarantee on such loans. This guarantee means that, if the borrower defaults, the government will pay the private lender the full amount owed and will assume ownership of the loan. One of the best-known government loan guarantee programs is the Guaranteed Student Loan Program, which insures about $9 billion annually in private loans to college students. Table 1 shows the activities assisted by federal loan guarantees.

---

*This figure includes the $450 billion in lending activities of the so-called government-sponsored enterprises (GSEs). These five quasi-government institutions—the Federal National Mortgage Association, the Federal Home Loan Banks, the Federal Home Loan Mortgage Corporation, the Student Loan Marketing Administration, and the Farm Credit System—direct credit into areas such as housing, education, and agriculture. The securities of the GSEs are not government-insured, yet the agencies enjoy special government benefits, such as a direct line of credit with the federal Treasury, that are not available to private financial institutions.

TABLE 1.—*Direct and Guaranteed Federal Loans Outstanding, by Type of Activity Assisted, through Fiscal 1986*

[In millions of dollars]

Activity	Direct loans	Guaranteed loans
Housing	15,855	373,864
Business	80,759	25,641
Agriculture	135,555	10,043
Education	17,047	37,482
All Other	2,378	2,778
Total Loans Outstanding	251,594	449,808

SOURCE: Joseph R. Wright, Office of Management and Budget, testimony before the President's Commission on Privatization, November 9, 1987.

Over the past 20 years, both these forms of federal lending have risen sharply. The $41 billion lent directly by federal agencies in 1986 constituted a threefold increase in federal lending since 1970 but was slightly down from the peak year (1985), when the federal government lent $50 billion. But the real growth area of federal credit has been in loan guarantees. The dollar amount of loans receiving federal guarantees on an annual basis climbed from $25 billion in 1970 to $80 billion in 1980 and to $159 billion in 1986. It is estimated that total outstanding loans with federal guarantees will exceed $700 billion by 1991.[14]

This steady increase in federal lending activities is cause for concern because taxpayer losses on loan programs have risen correspondingly. On the basis of estimated default rates, OMB projects that the federal government's direct loans and loan guarantees originated in 1987 alone will eventually cost the U.S. Treasury almost $18 billion.[15]

Accounting for Federal Loans

The Congressional Budget Office (CBO) states that the purpose of the U.S. budget is to "provide a framework for debate and decision about the appropriate size, financing, and allocation of the federal government's fiscal resources. . . . If the budget is incomplete in coverage or if the costs of an activity are otherwise misstated, decisions may be biased toward activities with excluded and understated costs and away from those with overstated costs." In 1984, CBO estimated that the budget miscalculates the cost of federal loan programs by approximately $20 billion each year.[16]

Budgetary Treatment of Direct Loans

In the case of direct loans, which involve an immediate cash disbursement, current-year federal outlays are increased by the amount of the loan. However, federal lending agencies employ two bookkeeping conventions that disguise the cost of their direct loans. First, many of the lending agencies have established revolving loan funds, whereby the agency finances a large portion of its new lending activities with the revenues collected from the repayment of previous loans.[17] This practice is misleading because the repayment of loans outstanding is entirely irrelevant to the cost of new loans. This procedure also empowers the agency to make loans without having to seek congressional appropriations each year. Revolving loan funds are thus partially exempt from annual budget decisionmaking.

A second anomaly in direct loan program accounting procedures is that the agencies carry loans on their balance sheets as assets at full face value. This practice disguises the assortment of implicit subsidies the government extends to the federal borrower, including (1) lower interest rates than a private bank would charge, (2) longer maturities than commercial loans offer, (3) waiver of loan origination fees, (4) generous forbearance provisions, and (5) less stringent credit risk threshold requirements than are customarily imposed by private lenders. The FmHA's Rural Housing Loan Program, for example, extends what is known as "interest credit" to its borrowers. If a borrower's income level falls by more than 20 percent in a year, the borrower has the right to reduce the interest rate payments on the loan to 1 percent; if income falls by more than 30 percent, the borrower qualifies for a 2-year moratorium on loan repayments.[18] As a result of such generous loan terms, OMB estimates the present value of federal subsidies on $41 billion of 1986 direct loans to be $7.7 billion.[19]

Consider the case of the Rural Electrification and Telephone Revolving Loan Fund. Congress created the fund in 1973 to make 35-year, low-interest loans to rural electric cooperatives. Marvin Phaup, CBO Financial Analyst, investigated the agency's bookkeeping records and found that "during the 1979 to 1983 period, while the fund was providing more than $20 billion in subsidized credit to cooperatives, its government equity, or net worth, increased by $882 million."[20] The agency arrived at this favorable bottom line budget surplus by offsetting its sizable loan commitments against previous loan repayments and other sources of revenue. Unfortunately, the agency's stated financial well-being differed radically from its actual financial condition. In fact, in 1984—the year after the agency's 5 years of purported fiscal health—emergency legislation was introduced in Congress to pump billions of additional dollars into the fund.[21]

Budgetary Treatment of Loan Guarantees

Federal accounting of loan guarantee programs also creates budgetary distortions. Because loan guarantees involve no immediate withdrawal of cash from the Treasury, they have an invisible effect on the current year's budget deficit, even though the government assumes a contingent liability. When a federally guaranteed loan goes into default, the agency that guaranteed the loan reimburses the lender and records the loan as an asset at full face value, even though the probability of full payback on a defaulted loan is extremely low.

Consider, as an example, the budgetary treatment of Federal Housing Administration (FHA) mortgage insurance, the government's largest loan guarantee program. When the FHA insures a new home mortgage, the transaction appears to reduce the budget deficit because the FHA collects an up-front fee from the homeowner. This fee is then offset against federal spending.

This accounting practice can transform a taxpayer subsidy into a federal asset, as occurred during the final budget negotiations for fiscal 1987. To comply with the Gramm-Rudman-Hollings Deficit Reduction Act, Congress authorized the FHA to raise its overall credit ceiling by $57 billion, and then counted the $700 million to be collected in additional fees as deficit reduction. Yet, many of these insured home loans will eventually go into default, at which time the mortgage holders will demand payment from the government. The current budget treatment of loan guarantees fails to reflect in any way these future losses.

There is mounting evidence that Congress increasingly relies on this form of subsidy as an alternative to grant programs, whose costs appear on the budget immediately. Between 1976 and 1986, federal loan guarantees grew at an annual rate of about 20 percent, well over twice the 8.6 percent growth rate of federal domestic spending as a whole.[22] The record $159 billion worth of new loan guarantees issued in 1986, a year of supposed budget austerity, prompted the *Washington Post* to observe, "What the right hand taketh away in budget cuts, the left hand giveth in loans."[23]

Federal Credit Reform

One of the main goals of credit reform is to provide Congress with accurate information about how much individual federal credit programs ultimately cost the taxpayer. Credit reform proposals provide for immediate scoring of the budget cost of loan subsidies, thus reducing the incentive to provide credit assistance because the costs are either hidden or pushed off into the future. Carol Cox stresses that credit reform would prod Congress to "make decisions as to how we finance federal activities based on

efficiency and . . . on what's going to work the best, not based on what's
going to show up cheapest on the budget." [24]

Many of the techniques underlying credit reform—including loan sales
and purchasing private reinsurance of federally guaranteed loans—require
the participation of the private sector. These are called "market valuation" plans because they establish a fair market value of federal direct
loans and a market cost for federal loan guarantees. The President's Commission on Privatization favors this approach and recommends:

Recommendation (1)

> The federal government should develop a market valuation
> method of identifying the subsidy cost of its credit pro-
> grams. This would enable policymakers to more accurately
> weigh the costs and benefits of direct loan and loan guaran-
> tee programs.

This policy was first endorsed 20 years ago by President Lyndon Johnson's Commission on Budget Concepts, which recommended that, for
budgetary purposes, all loan subsidies should be "capitalized at the time
the loan is made."

The Sale of Federal Loans

Selling federal loans is a key component of the market valuation approach to credit reform. Selling loans would also yield other advantages
to the government, such as improvements in loan management and
collection.

A Brief History of Loan Asset Sales

Selling loans is a common practice in the banking industry today. Commercial lenders normally group their loans into packages that can be con-
veniently sold to investors. This practice of pooling similar loans and
selling them as a tradeable security is known as "securitization." By selling loans, the lender takes an up-front profit equal to the spread between
the amount of cash received for the securitized loans and the amount of
cash paid out to make the loans. The lender then can use the cash to issue
new loans. In 1986, for instance, it is reported that General Motors Acceptance Corporation (GMAC) sold more than $3 billion in automobile
receivables to private investors to improve the company's liquidity and to
avoid having to borrow funds.

The federal government, too, has been selling loans for many years.
The Government National Mortgage Association (GNMA) has purchased
and then resold more than $30 billion worth of private mortgages since
the program began in 1968. [25] Similarly, the Veterans Administration has

been selling portions of its vendee loan portfolio for over 10 years. In both cases, however, the federally owned loans were sold with federal guarantees, that is, "with recourse."

Another type of loan asset divestiture is the sale of loans without federal guarantees, that is, "without recourse." In fiscal 1987, Congress first sanctioned nonrecourse sales on an experimental basis.* Sales of seasoned loans having a face value of $9 billion generated $6.4 billion in government receipts.* * [26] In its fiscal 1988 budget proposal, the Administration suggested further sales of the existing loan portfolio and recommended adoption of a comprehensive credit reform package for new loans.

Except for minor problems primarily attributable to the newness of the endeavor, the loan divestitures launched to date have proved the technical feasibility of nonrecourse loan sales. In late 1987, the FmHA conducted sales from two of its loan portfolios: community program loans, which are used primarily by rural towns to build water and sewer plants, and rural housing loans, which provide housing assistance to low-income rural residents. These sales generated approximately $2.8 billion in receipts. According to the testimony from former Salomon Brothers Vice President Miner Warner, the rural housing loan sale was "the largest credit insured issue ever done in the United States capital markets."[27] A few weeks later, the U.S. Department of Education sold college housing loans with a face value of $237 million for $121 million.

A model loan divestiture was the sale of approximately $1.8 billion worth of community program loans to bond investors in September 1987. First, FmHA hired Manufacturers Hanover Trust to serve as a financial adviser to the sale and to assemble extensive information on the credit worthiness of the program's borrowers. As with private sector loan sales, the next hurdle involved securitizing the debt instruments by fixing a common interest rate and maturity on more than 7,700 loans. Manufacturers Hanover then arranged a form of self-insurance, commonly known as "overcollateralization." This process involved setting aside a pool of junior securities that can only receive payments after the holders of senior loan-backed securities are paid in full. Packaged in this manner, the senior loan securities received an AAA rating from Standard and Poor's and were purchased by investors almost immediately, despite a relatively weak

---

*In 1982 the FHA sold for $131 million, without recourse, defaulted mortgages having a face value of $235 million. In the same year, the Economic Development Administration sold for $2 million, without recourse, defaulted loans with a face value of $14 million. However, both of these loan sale initiatives were subsequently discontinued.

**About half of this revenue came from actual nonrecourse loan sales. The source of the remaining revenues was loan prepayments in which borrowers were permitted to pay off their loans to the government in advance. In most cases the borrowers did not incur a prepayment penalty.

bond market. The sale of these community program loans generated just over $1 billion in federal receipts.

Officials from OMB and members of the financial community told the Commission they are confident that future sales will be even more successful.[28] Their optimism is based on two factors. First, the pilot sales have blazed a trail for other agencies, which can avoid the learning mistakes made in these initial transactions. Second, investor participation in these loan sales is expected to rise as the financial community grows more familiar with the quality of federal loans and as Congress demonstrates a long-term commitment to the loan sale concept.

The Goals of Federal Loan Sales

Loan sales need not diminish the federal role in making loans to achieve public policy objectives. Frederick Wolf, Director of GAO's Accounting and Financial Management Division, told the Commission: "Loan programs are a means to achieving policy or program goals, as opposed to being ends in themselves. If the federal government sells to the public all or a part of a loan portfolio, this does not mean that its role in providing loans, for example, to students is at an end. . . . Even if we sell all loans, we will continue to make new loans in the future."[29] Congress has repeatedly made clear its intention to continue federal lending activities. Loan sales would directly affect federal loan making only to the extent that they provide accurate information to taxpayers and federal policymakers about what contemplated future loan commitments will ultimately cost the government.

Nor will loan sales significantly reduce the federal budget deficit. Loan divestiture might provide minor relief to the long-term budget deficit, because the efficiency gains of private ownership normally generate higher receipts than the present value of the receipts collected from the loan under continued government ownership. This budget impact, however, is a benign by-product of selling loans rather than an overriding goal of the initiative. Frederick Wolf of GAO put the point this way: "If somebody were to say we ought to sell loan assets because it will reduce the deficit, I'd say you're barking up the wrong tree." [30]

Counting all the cash proceeds from a loan sale as deficit reduction overstates the economic benefit of the transaction, because when an agency sells a loan it forfeits a future stream of income that could be used to retire government debt in later years.* [31] However, the receipts collected from federal loan sales cannot be ignored. When the federal government sells loans without recourse, its immediate borrowing needs are

---

*In September 1987 an amendment was attached to the Debt Extension Act forbidding Congress from counting the revenues from loan sales as deficit reduction for the purpose of reaching Gramm-Rudman-Hollings deficit reduction targets.

reduced by the amount of cash generated by the sales. For this reason, it may be appropriate to count these sales receipts as a form of deficit reduction, so that the annual deficit figure matches the federal government's total amount of borrowing during the year.

The situation is entirely different, however, when loan sales are made with federal recourse. Both OMB and CBO agree that selling federal loans with recourse has the same fiscal impact as simply issuing additional Treasury securities to finance the deficit, because the loans would be backed by the full faith and credit of the U.S. government. Hence, recourse sales do not reduce the government's total borrowing.

In sum, the Commission disapproves of the use of loan sales as a device to reach deficit reduction goals but recognizes that, in keeping with the principles of a cash-flow budget, sales receipts from nonrecourse sales must be counted. The Commission therefore recommends:

Recommendation (2)

The receipts from loan asset sales should only be counted as deficit reduction if they are sold without recourse—that is, if the federal government faces no future liability after the sale. Furthermore, none of the receipts from loan asset sales—whether with or without recourse—should be counted in attempts to reach mandated annual deficit reduction goals or targets.

The Commission views loan sales as containing public policy goals completely separate from their effect on the deficit. Loan divestiture would, at least in part, remedy each of the three deficiencies in federal loan programs identified earlier.

Loan sales would enhance federal loan collection. Turning ownership of federal loans over to private investors responsible for collection could lead to sharp reductions in delinquency and default rates on these loans. When private sector investors purchase federal loans, they attempt to maximize the return on their investment, and they systematically seek full payback on the loan. Federal agencies do not share this incentive, which explains in part why the delinquency rate on federal loans is three times higher than the rate on private loans. The private sector also has greater resources, experience, and management expertise for effective credit collection.[32]

Loan sales would improve the management of federal loans. When the federal government sells loans without recourse, it transfers the loan management function to the private sector. The purchaser of government loans not only obtains the revenue-producing financial assets; it also assumes all the related responsibilities of administering the loans.

The three loan sales completed in 1987 have already spurred improvements in federal loan management. As preparation for future sales, OMB reports that lending agencies are improving their loan documentation to bring their standards closer to private sector requirements.[33]

Loan sales also are encouraging agencies to reevaluate their loan contract policies and adjust them to conform with private sector standards. When the Export-Import Bank loan portfolio was examined for sales purposes in 1986, private investors discovered that for years the bank had permitted borrowers to prepay their loans at any time with no penalty. As a result, businesses that had received loans in the early 1980s at subsidized interest rates of 10 percent were able to prepay their loans with no penalty and refinance them in the private sector at 7 percent. The government, in contrast, which had to borrow in the early 1980s to make the funds available to Export-Import Bank borrowers, must continue to pay its debts at double-digit interest rates. Miner Warner told the Commission that prepayment without penalty "doesn't happen in the private sector, but there had been no incentive to focus on that provision before the loan asset sales. . . . Now, for the first time in years, the Ex-Im Bank direct loan documentation calls for a [loan] prepayment penalty."[34]

Loan sales would identify the subsidy cost of federal credit programs. If the federal government were to sell federal loans immediately after issuing them, the federal subsidy to the borrower would be revealed as the difference between the face value of the loan and the sales price. CBO determined, from the receipts collected in the 1987 sale of the FmHA community program portfolio, that the subsidy value of these loans was, on average, 44 percent of their face value.[35] Congress and federal agencies can now incorporate this information into budget decision-making.

Sale of Newly Originated Federal Loans

Efficiency gains are likely to be higher for the sale of new loans—because management improvements can be exploited fully from the first day the loan is made—than for existing loans. William Inglehart, President of GC Services Corporation, the nation's largest private debt collection agency, describes new loans as "a very saleable product," in contrast to seasoned loans, which "grow more and more worthless over time"[36] because of poor federal management.

But some federal loan portfolios may not be appropriate candidates for loan sales. For instance, the State Department oversees programs that lend money to foreign countries; in such cases, foreign policy considerations could preclude a sale. Other federal loan portfolios, such as the government's holdings of defaulted student loans, may be of such poor quality that private sector interest in purchasing them is minimal. An oversight agency such as OMB could prepare a list of agency exemptions from loan sales.

A second critical issue is the timing of loan sales. Under ideal circumstances, all loans would be sold in the same fiscal year that they were issued so that, for budgetary purposes, the cash disbursement could be offset against the revenue from the sale. Requiring loans to be sold immediately, however, might be an unnecessarily rigid policy, forcing loan sales in an unreceptive market. Certainly, financial prudence would argue against selling federal loans in a very weak bond market or during an economic slump. Private sector lending institutions that sell commercial instruments are responsive to such market conditions, and the government should be, too.

Although adverse market conditions might be reason for delaying a loan sale, these conditions should not relieve agencies of their obligation to obtain appropriations for their loan programs. Each year, lending agencies should be required to seek appropriations based on the expected subsidy component of new loan originations. Once the loans are sold, if the original subsidy estimates are discovered to be off-target, the agency should be required to obtain additional appropriations to compensate for any shortfall. This policy would protect against agencies' systematically underestimating the cost of their loan programs. The Commission therefore recommends:

Recommendation (3)

The federal government should phase in a loan asset sale program, requiring lending agencies to sell all newly originated loans. These sales should take place as soon after loans are issued as is practicable, given market conditions. The Office of Management and Budget should develop loan asset guidelines that would exempt certain agencies from this requirement for particular policy reasons. Agencies should be required to obtain appropriations for the loans they make, and these appropriations should be adjusted upward or downward once the revenues from agency loan sales have been received and the government's cost of these loans is fully determined.

Should Loans Be Sold with Federal Guarantees?

When a loan is sold with recourse, the holder may return it to the seller for payment if the borrower defaults. Hence, selling federal loans with recourse creates a contingent liability for the government. When the loan is sold without recourse, the federal lending agency transfers all the risk of carrying the loan to the private sector investor.

Proponents of selling federal loans with recourse maintain that by offering a federal guarantee, the government will be assured of receiving top dollar for the loans. GAO has consistently held this position. In a report titled "OMB Policies Will Result in Program Objectives Not Being Fully Achieved," GAO warned: "We believe that, because the OMB guidelines require that loan asset sales be made without future recourse to the government, the net proceeds from the sales will not be maximized." GAO's study concluded that even over the long run, net sales receipts would be generally higher with recourse sales than with nonrecourse sales.[37]

Recourse sales, however, conflict with several goals of the asset divestiture program. If loans are sold with federal guarantees, calculating the implicit subsidy from the sale becomes impossible, because the price investors would be willing to pay for the loans would be based in part on their evaluation of the guarantee. But the guarantee has nothing to do with the loan's market value.

One of the primary advantages of selling federal loans is that private investors employ innovative collection techniques to maximize their return on the loans. If these loans were federally guaranteed and investors were confident they would receive full payment regardless of default, the incentive for aggressive collection would be reduced. Furthermore, if loans carried guarantees, administrative savings would be lessened, because all the problem loans would be returned to the government, and most of the loan portfolio management costs are associated with delinquent loans. OMB Deputy Director Joseph Wright insists that, if loans are sold with any form of recourse, "the private sector would skim the cream and send the junk right back to us. We would then have real budget problems 5 years down the road."[38]

Some types of insurance place no contingent liability on the federal government and are thus fundamentally different from recourse sales. An example is the overcollateralization FmHA used in selling its community program loans. As long as the government divests itself of all claims on the assets in the pool—including both the junior and senior securities—it incurs no contingent liability. For budget scorekeeping purposes, the average price received for the junior and senior securities would be the loan sale price.

The Commission recommends:

Recommendation (4)

Federal loans should not be sold with any type of recourse that would create a future liability for the government. Overcollateralization and other types of insurance that place the risk on the private sector underwriter are acceptable.

Loan Sales as a Vehicle for Achieving Federal Credit Reform

One of the central objectives of loan sales is to measure accurately the subsidy component of credit programs. The difference between the face value of a loan and its sales price would approximate the taxpayer's subsidy to the borrower. For instance, if the federal government made a 10-year, $10 million college housing loan at 5 percent interest and then immediately sold the loan for $8 million, the implicit subsidy to the university borrower would be $2 million. This process is called the "market value" approach; the actual value of a loan is determined by the amount the private sector is willing to pay for it.

An alternative credit reform proposal that has won the approval of the Senate Budget Committee is called the "cost-to-government" approach. Under this plan, the federal lending agency would estimate its loan subsidies on the basis of three factors: the interest rate subsidy (i.e., the difference between the government's cost of borrowing and the interest rate on the loan), loan administrative costs, and historical default rates.[39] The lending agencies would then be required to obtain appropriations for new loans equal to this cost estimate. Loan sales would be *permitted* for purposes of more precisely estimating subsidy costs, but would not be *required*. Advocates of this approach contend that it obviates the need for selling loans or purchasing reinsurance for loan guarantees, thus eliminating the transaction costs associated with the market value methods.

The cost-to-government approach may be an improvement over the status quo, but it is less desirable than the market value approach. The Senate Budget Committee plan may understate the cost of loan programs because it calculates the interest rate subsidy on a federal loan by examining the spread between the interest rate on the loan and the rate on Treasury bills—in contrast to the market interest rate for such loans. The logical extension of this costing method is that because the government can borrow at a lower interest rate than the private sector, economic gains could be realized if the government were to issue all credit. But the government can borrow for less than the private sector only because it spreads the risk of its borrowing over all taxpayers. According to OMB Deputy Director Joseph Wright, the Senate Budget Committee plan ignores these social costs of government borrowing.[40]

The cost-to-government approach can also lead to perverse policy recommendations. Consider a case in which the federal government can borrow at 7 percent, the market interest rate is 9 percent, and the federal government lends money to a business at 8 percent. According to the Senate Budget Committee credit reform proposal, this loan is not only free to the government, it is actually a moneymaker, because the government borrows at a lower interest rate than it lends. If this conclusion were valid, the federal government could eliminate the budget deficit by rushing out into the credit market and offering borrowers loans at 8 percent interest. The business community would enthusiastically accept these terms, because this interest rate is less than the market rate. In contrast, under the market value method, investors will gauge the value of federal loans according to the rate of interest on alternative investments of similar risk.

Another shortcoming of the cost-to-government approach is that it depends on the federal agencies having accurate information on the historical default and loss rates of their loan programs. However, reviews of the agencies' loan portfolios indicate that they lack this information. Without precise historical loan data, the cost-to-government calculation is little more than an unscientific guess as to the loan subsidy.

A final drawback of the Senate Budget Committee proposal is that it precludes one of the primary advantages of selling loans: improving loan collection and management by employing the specialized skills of the private sector. For these reasons, the Commission rejects the cost-to-government approach to credit reform and recommends:

Recommendation (5)

Selling newly originated loans should be employed as a tool to identify the subsidy cost of federal direct loan programs. The subsidy is equal to the difference between the loan amount and the sales price.

The Sale of Seasoned Loans

Unlike the sale of new loans, the sale of a seasoned loan portfolio cannot, in most cases, be used as a device to identify loan program subsidies. The discount on the portfolio is at least partially attributable to changes in economic and financial conditions between the time the loans were made and when they were sold.[41] Also, some loans will have been prepaid and some will have defaulted.

The purpose of selling existing loans is to move the government out of the loan management business. The Commission believes there is no compelling reason why the government should engage in the commercial activities of a private bank. Selling seasoned loans would foster efficiency in administering and collecting the government's $250 billion loan portfolio.*

Opponents of selling the federal loan portfolio charge that the government is unlikely to receive a fair price for its assets. Many fear that government loans will be purchased at "fire sale" prices.[42] The CBO found

---

*The Congressional Budget Office has estimated that the market value of the entire $250 billion federal loan portfolio is about 50 cents on the dollar, or $125 billion.

that the three large loan portfolios sold in 1987 were bought by the private sector at discounts ranging from 49 percent to 40 percent off their face value.[43]

A discounted price does not necessarily imply that the lender is losing money by selling its loans. For example, to improve its financial standing, GMAC sold its $3.2 billion worth of automobile receivables to private investors at a discount. Government loans must be sold with especially heavy discounts because they carry borrower subsidies and because they have high risks of default. Those subsidies and default risks are sunk costs to the government; they can neither be avoided by selling the loans nor recaptured by holding onto them until maturity.[44]

In any determination of whether the government is receiving top dollar, the relevant comparison is not the face amount of the loan versus its selling price, but rather the value of the loan to the government versus the loan's value to the private sector as reflected in its selling price. Given the problems federal agencies have experienced in servicing loans, it is highly doubtful that the government is a more efficient loan manager than the private sector. William Niskanen, a former member of President Reagan's Council of Economic Advisers, in fact, endorses selling loans with the heaviest discounts first. He advised the Commission: "Don't be scared by high discounts in the sense that those high discounts are the loans that are most likely to reflect differences in the efficiency of loan management by the federal government and the private sector."[45]

The Commission therefore recommends:

Recommendation (6)

The federal lending agencies should divest themselves of their seasoned loan portfolios over a 5- to 10-year period, subject to favorable market conditions and the ability of the financial markets to absorb the sales. This requirement should apply to all agencies except those that hold loans that warrant an exemption due to foreign policy concerns or where divestiture might conflict with program objectives.

Loan Sales and Revolving Loan Funds

One of the common criticisms of loan sales is that the divestitures will deplete revolving loan funds of their future streams of income. Dennis Cullinan, spokesman for the Veterans of Foreign Wars of the United States (VFW), testified before the Commission:

> The VFW clearly recognizes that the sale of loans would have disastrous consequences for the VA home loan program and we adamantly oppose its implementation. In our view, forcing the VA to sell off all or a large portion of its vendee loan portfolio would be nothing other than a short-term fiscal fix which would completely deprive the VA home loan

program of the assets necessary to generate revenues on its own in future years.[46]

This fear is misplaced. As long as the revenues from the loan sales are captured by the revolving fund or are identified in an account with the Treasury Department, these lending agencies will be no better off financially if they hold their loans and collect the streams of income over time than if they sell them today and invest the sales receipts in new loans or in an interest-bearing account, regardless of whether the sales price lies above or below the loans' par value. Loan sales may even enhance the financial condition of revolving loan funds, because if debt collection and management improve under private ownership, a portion of these efficiency gains should be passed on to the lending agency in sales prices. The Commission recommends:

Recommendation (7)

Loans should be sold from revolving loan funds, but all of the revenues from the sales should be filtered back into the revolving funds to keep them financially solvent, or should be transferred to a central Treasury fund which would account for the inflows and outflows of cash for each revolving fund.

Protecting the Rights of Federal Borrowers

The federal government traditionally has adopted a policy of leniency toward delinquent borrowers. A GAO investigation found that agencies often "modified loan terms or extended repayment periods for some types of loans whose borrowers experienced difficulties in meeting their payments."[47] These policies contribute in part to the high delinquency rate on federal loans.

The rights of borrowers should be protected if federal loans are sold. The results of the loan sales completed to date are reassuring. Harold Wilson, Executive Director of the Housing Assistance Council, a nonprofit organization that deals with the housing problems of low-income, rural residents, told the Commission: "The plan adopted by the Farmers Home Administration and the underwriters does protect the borrowers' rights. We were very pleased to see that they responded so forthrightly to the concerns of the borrowers."[48] These sales conformed to the official OMB loan sales policy that states, "Nothing in the loan sales program in any way reduces the legal and contractual rights of the borrower."[49]

These guidelines, although appropriate, may not go far enough in preserving the rights of federal borrowers. Borrowers enter into federal loan contracts with the understanding that the lending agency's servicing and collection policies also apply to their loans. Therefore, the Commission believes that explicit agency loan policies should transfer with ownership of the loan in the same way that explicit contractual rights of the borrower transfer. If indulgent agency collection policies are contrary to the interests of the taxpayer, policies should be changed. In selling their loans, agencies should not be released from unduly restrictive collection policies. The Commission believes that selling loans is one method of exposing costly and unnecessarily indulgent loan payback policies and that in the future, all borrower rights should be made explicit in federal loan contracts to avoid this problem. Therefore, the Commission recommends:

Recommendation (8)

The legal and contractual rights of the borrowers should be protected when federal loan assets are sold; in addition, the private sector owners should be required to abide by the stated collection policies that are used by the agency that makes the loan.

Privatizing Federal Loan Guarantees

Federal loan guarantees have become an increasingly popular form of subsidy in an era of budgetary stringency. Evidence of this trend is the 20-percent annual growth rate in loan guarantees since 1975. Because the budgetary cost of insuring privately issued loans is pushed off into future years, loan guarantees can be used as a device to evade deficit reduction ceilings and thereby thwart federal efforts to balance the long-term budget deficit.

These incentives could be corrected if the federal agencies were required to purchase private reinsurance for the credit they guarantee. The cost of the loan guarantee subsidy would be the price of the reinsurance. Under this plan, the federal government would incur the cost of providing the loan guarantee in the same year that it made the guarantee.

Although the Commission endorses the general concept of reinsurance, it is particularly concerned about the question of whether an adequate private sector market exists to provide this reinsurance. Joseph Wright of OMB warned the Commission that currently "the insurance industry does not have the capability of handling [government] guarantees."[50] But economist William Niskanen counseled the Commission: "We should be careful not to be swayed by the argument that private institutions do not exist to manage some of these portfolios. It's a chicken and egg problem. . . . So don't accept the argument that there are no private organizations out there yet that could manage these loan portfolios or loan guarantees, because I have every reason to believe the institutions will arise."[51] The Commission recommends:

Recommendation (9)

The federal government should phase in, over a 5-year period or for as long as it takes for a mature loan insurance industry to develop, a policy of purchasing reinsurance for all loans it guarantees. This insurance should be purchased immediately after the loan guarantee is issued, and the agencies should be required to obtain annual appropriations to pay for the reinsurance.

Methods of Improving Federal Debt Collection

Although loan sales could contribute substantially to reducing the delinquency rate on federal loans, this $24 billion problem warrants further corrective measures.

As a general principle, the federal government should adhere to the practices of the private sector in its efforts to improve debt collection. For federal loans that are never sold, lending agencies should employ debt collection tools such as hiring private debt collectors and turning over delinquent account information to private credit bureaus.

Hiring Private Debt Collection Agencies

The use of private debt collection agencies to collect delinquent and defaulted debt is standard procedure for private lenders. Private lenders typically turn debt over to collection agencies 90 to 180 days after it becomes delinquent. Federal lending agencies received statutory authority to employ private collection agencies with passage of the 1982 Debt Collection Act. The General Accounting Office concluded in a 1986 report that few agencies have chosen to adopt this measure.[52] To counteract this federal agency resistance, the Commission recommends:

Recommendation (10)

It should be made mandatory for federal lending agencies to hire private debt collection agencies to pursue delinquent debtors—except when the Congress or the Office of Management and Budget determines that there are unique characteristics of the loan program which mitigate this approach.

The General Accounting Office has previously endorsed this policy proposal.[53] The recommendation would give statutory authority to OMB Circular A–129, which requires agencies to turn their debt over to debt collectors once it has become 6 months delinquent.* In making this rec-ommendation, the Commission is reassured that federal borrowers would be extended the full legal safeguards provided under the federal Fair Debt Collection Practices Act, as well as additional regulations on private sector collection procedures that have been enacted in 32 states.

Reporting Delinquent Borrowers to Private Credit Bureaus

Referring delinquent loan accounts to credit bureaus is also a common practice in the private sector. Privately originated loans normally are re-ported to credit bureaus immediately after they are made; then the status of the account is updated every 30 days. Under the Debt Collection Act, the federal agencies were granted the authority to report delinquent debt to credit bureaus, but agency personnel have not made use of this authority.[54]

The GAO has found that the only agency that has informed private credit bureaus of delinquent debtors is the Department of Education. GAO's investigation into federal debt collection policies concluded that the initiative has been highly successful: "(U.S. Department of) Education officials consider credit bureau reporting one of the most useful collection tools available to government agencies. Although they cannot specifically measure the effects in terms of higher collections, officials stated that Education's three regional collection offices receive an estimated 75 to 100 calls a week from borrowers who have had their credit records affected by adverse credit referrals."[55]

The GAO has consistently favored a statutory requirement mandating that federal agencies report delinquent debtors to credit bureaus. The Commission agrees with this policy and recommends:

Recommendation (11)

Federal lending agencies should report delinquent borrow-ers to credit bureaus after attempts have been made to col-lect through the normal debt collection procedures of the agencies.

Summary

The federal government has been lending money for over 50 years to achieve national policy goals. Most federal loan programs are likely to

---

*OMB circulars are presidential policy directives that apply to executive branch federal agencies. However, OMB circulars lack the force of law and thus are not always enforceable. A GAO report on federal debt collection procedures has con-cluded: "We believe that Circular A–129, by itself, will not provide a sufficient basis for agencies to take action to improve debt collection procedures."

continue well into the future. But in attempting to service and manage a
$250 billion loan portfolio, the federal government has taken on all the
commercial activities normally reserved for private banks and investment
firms. The Commission maintains that these activities are appropriate candidates for privatization.

Early in this chapter three weaknesses were identified in the oversight
of federal loan programs: (1) loan collection efforts are inadequate,
(2) loan programs are poorly managed, and (3) improper accounting and
budgetary treatment of loan programs encourage a misallocation of resources. The recommendations formulated by the Commission are designed to redress each of these problems.

Selling federal loans immediately after they are issued would, in effect,
transfer loan management to professionals in the private sector. Private
owners, attempting to maximize the return from these loans, would have
a strong incentive to manage loans carefully; such incentives are absent in
the federal bureaucracy.

Selling federal loans might also reduce the extremely high delinquency
rate on federal loans to rates typical of private loans. Once federal loans
are placed in private hands, the talents and resources are available in the
private sector to assure prompt and full payback on these loans. Even in
cases where the federal government continues to hold loans, employing
private debt collectors and reporting delinquent debtors to private credit
bureaus are techniques the government can no longer afford to ignore.

Finally, the budgetary treatment of federal credit activities needs to be
overhauled. The government cannot continue to provide more than
$40 billion in loans each year and more than $150 billion in loan guarantees
without knowing how much these actions cost the taxpayer. The best and
most honest method of identifying the cost of credit activities is a market
value approach: selling new loans and purchasing private reinsurance for
loan guarantees. This approach would place credit programs on a level
budgetary playing field with other forms of federal spending. By exposing
the subsidy cost of loan programs, policymakers will, for the first time,
have the information to weigh the costs and benefits of federal lending
activities accurately. The Commission is convinced that performing this
cost-benefit analysis is essential to sound economic policy.

NOTES FOR CHAPTER 4

1. U.S. Office of Management and Budget, "Federal Credit Programs," *Budget of the United States Government, Fiscal Year 1988, Special Analysis F*, p. F-3.

2. Ibid., p. F-31.

3. Ibid. A complete rundown of federal spending on all federal credit programs can be found on pp. F-56 to F-71.

4. U.S. Office of Management and Budget, *Major Policy Initiatives, Fiscal Year 1987*.

5. U.S. General Accounting Office, *Debt Collection: Information on the Amount of Debts Owed the Federal Government*, December 1985.

6. U.S. General Accounting Office, *Debt Collection: Billions Are Owed While Collection and Accounting Problems Are Unresolved*, May 1986, p. 27.

7. Ibid., appendix 2.

8. Ibid., p. 4.

9. Testimony of Frederick D. Wolf, U.S. General Accounting Office, "An Assessment of the Government's Loan Asset Sales Program," before the Subcommittee on Legislation and National Security, Committee on Government Operations, U.S. House of Representatives, March 26, 1987.

10. U.S. Office of Management and Budget, "Federal Credit Programs," p. F-39.

11. Quoted in Judith Havemann, "Uncle Sam's Math: 2 + 2 = 5?" *Washington Post*, April 19, 1987.

12. Testimony of Carol Cox, Committee for a Responsible Federal Budget, before the President's Commission on Privatization, Hearings on Federal Loan Programs (hereinafter cited as Hearings on Federal Loan Programs), November 10, 1987.

13. Ibid.

14. U.S. Office of Management and Budget, "Federal Credit Programs," p. F-20.

15. Ibid., pp. F-35 to F-37.

16. Congressional Budget Office, *New Approaches to the Budgetary Treatment of Federal Credit Assistance*, March 1984, p. xi.

17. Testimony of Joseph R. Wright, Office of Management and Budget, Hearings on Federal Loan Programs, November 9, 1987.

18. Testimony of Marvin Marcus, Kidder Peabody & Co., Hearings on Federal Loan Programs, November 10, 1987.

19. U.S. Office of Management and Budget, "Federal Credit Programs," p. F-35.

20. Marvin Phaup, "Accounting for Federal Credit: A Better Way," *Public Budgeting and Finance* (Autumn 1985), p. 32.

21. Ibid.

22. U.S. House of Representatives Committee on the Budget, "Federal Credit Reform," minority staff working paper, 1987, p. 1.

23. Havemann, "Uncle Sam's Math."

24. Cox testimony.

25. Congressional Budget Office, *New Approaches*, p. 69.

26. Congressional Budget Office, *Loan Asset Sale Update*, Issue No. 4, November 1987, p. 12.

27. Testimony of Miner Warner, Hearings on Federal Loan Programs, November 10, 1987.

28. Warner testimony and Wright testimony.

29. Testimony of Frederick D. Wolf, U.S. General Accounting Office, Hearings on Federal Loan Programs, November 10, 1987.

30. Ibid.

31. Ibid.

32. Testimony of William Inglehart, GC Services Corporation, Hearings on Federal Loan Programs, November 9, 1987.

33. Wright testimony.

34. Warner testimony.

35. Congressional Budget Office, *Loan Asset Sale Update*, p. 6.

36. Inglehart testimony.

37. U.S. General Accounting Office, *OMB Policies Will Result in Program Objectives Not Being Fully Achieved*, September 1986, p. 4.

38. Wright testimony.

39. Wolf testimony, November 10, 1987.

40. Wright testimony.

41. For a thorough discussion of this issue, see Wolf testimony, November 10, 1987.

42. Testimony of Dennis Cullinan, Veterans of Foreign Wars of the United States, Hearings on Federal Loan Programs, November 10, 1987.

43. Congressional Budget Office, *Loan Asset Sale Update*, p. 1.

44. Testimony of Vance L. Clark, Farmers Home Administration, Hearings on Federal Loan Programs, November 10, 1987.

45. Testimony of William Niskanen, the Cato Institute, Hearings on Federal Loan Programs, November 10, 1987.

46. Cullinan testimony.

47. U.S. General Accounting Office, *Debt Collection: Billions Are Owed*.

48. Testimony of Harold O. Wilson, Housing Assistance Council, Hearings on Federal Loan Programs, November 10, 1987.

49. U.S. Office of Management and Budget, *Loan Asset Sale Pilot Program*, June 18, 1987, p. 3.

50. Wright testimony.

51. Niskanen testimony.

52. U.S. General Accounting Office, *Debt Collection: Billions Are Owed*, p. 4.

53. Ibid., p. 5.

54. Ibid., p. 4.

55. Ibid., p. 75.

Chapter 5

Air Traffic Control
And Other FAA Functions

As airline deregulation moves into its second decade in the United States, the national air transportation system faces tremendous challenges. Dissatisfaction over consumer service is apparent in the record number of complaints received by the U.S. Department of Transportation (DOT), the flurry of news media attention recently directed toward American aviation, and the voluminous aviation legislation introduced in Congress during 1987. Three major commercial aviation accidents in the last 5 months of 1987—although apparently not traceable to systemic causes—have contributed to the public perception of turmoil in the nation's airspace.

In 1986 Congress created the Aviation Safety Commission (ASC). With a chairman appointed by the President, the ASC is charged with investigating aviation safety and recommending necessary reforms. Testimony before the President's Commission on Privatization by 23 witnesses, as well as analysis of literature compiled for the record, indicates that the controversies surrounding U.S. aviation extend beyond the scope of safety into the efficient management of resources. During the Commission's hearings, witnesses with a wide range of expertise confirmed that a variety of difficulties and deficiencies seriously impair efficient operation of the system. The continued high growth in air travel projected by the Federal Aviation Administration (FAA) increases the urgency of improving system efficiency.[1] The Commission therefore studied opportunities to make air transportation more responsive to the dynamic demands of its markets.

Effects of Deregulation

With the deregulation of air carriers, new firms entered the commercial air transportation market, increasing the number of companies in the industry from 40 to more than 200 in 1986. The entry of new carriers, which has since been followed by a period of consolidation, was accompanied by a shift in air traffic patterns within the national airspace. Instead of "point-to-point" routes, some innovative carriers established "hub-and-spoke" systems, whereby an airline would pick up passengers at several different points along the "rim" of its route structure, fly them to a "hub," and then transport them to their destinations along the rim. Whereas point-to-point systems prospered by encouraging large aircraft operations at extended intervals between different points, hub-and-spoke systems require the ability to land many, usually smaller, airplanes in a limited time, shift passengers between aircraft, and then fly them on to their destinations.

Deregulation had profound effects on rate and route structures, the uses of equipment, and the numbers of passengers served. From 1981 to 1986, air carrier fleets have grown from 4,074 to 4,909 aircraft. Since 1978, passenger enplanements rose from 278 million to 445 million during 1987. Since the economic recovery of 1983, when there were 83 million operations (takeoffs at airports or movement through an en route sector) at FAA air traffic control centers and towers, total operations grew to more than 92 million in 1986 and 95 million in 1987.[2]

Overview of the FAA

This phenomenal growth in air travel has had enormous consequences for the management of the national airspace system. Although safety statistics show improvement and consumer benefits have risen into the billions of dollars,[3] the Commission's hearings demonstrated that the challenges of growth are seriously straining the resources of the system's manager, the FAA. With 46,000 employees, the agency regulates air transportation and operates various support services. Aircraft certification, airport security, maintenance inspection, pilot licensing, and related safety functions are the responsibility of the FAA Office of Aviation Standards, which approves standards used throughout aviation and monitors and enforces system safety performance.

The FAA Office of Development and Logistics is responsible for developing and maintaining system equipment, including radars, communications devices, weather systems, and computers. Nearly 9,000 maintenance technicians provide services used primarily for the air traffic control system equipment. The FAA Airports Office allocates airport construction and development grants and assists with some airport planning initiatives.

Air traffic control—by far the largest FAA function—employs more than 26,000 people, of whom more than 15,000 are air traffic controllers. Other workers include flight service station personnel, supervisory personnel, and support staff. The air traffic control organization develops procedures to move aircraft through the nation's airspace, coordinates approval of these procedures with other offices and system users, and operates the system on a daily basis.

The air traffic control system is composed of three segments: flight service stations, airport traffic control towers, and en route air traffic control centers. Flight service stations provide weather briefings and other information about the airport and airways system and assist with filing flight plans. Airport towers provide different levels of service to aircraft, ranging from Level 1 (fewer than 200,000 operations per year) through Level 5 (nearly 800,000 operations per year).

The FAA's 20 en route centers in the continental United States manage the flow of air traffic between the airports in the system. Once a flight leaves the airport departure area, tower controllers "hand it off" to the centers. Flights are monitored through the more than 600 sectors of the national airspace system, with controllers required to keep a minimum distance of 5 miles between aircraft flying on the same airway and at least 1,000 feet of vertical separation between aircraft. Controllers must make adjustments for intersecting flight paths of different aircraft and for aircraft moving in the system at different speeds.

Management of the National Airspace System

Two former FAA Administrators testified before the President's Commission on Privatization that micromanagement of FAA operations by DOT, the Office of Management and Budget (OMB), the Congress, and other government entities constitutes a significant impediment to system efficiency. One former FAA Administrator, J. Lynn Helms, noted that in the appropriations process during 1987, congressional committees mandated the installation of more than 30 pieces of equipment that had neither been authorized by Congress nor requested by the FAA.[4] Representative Guy V. Molinari (R-NY) admitted, "Unfortunately, sometimes when we act, we wait so long we have a tendency to overreact and we go too far."[5] Helms also maintained that he was hampered during his tenure at the FAA by "little or no experience by junior OST (Office of the Secretary of Transportation) staff personnel to render decisions or even serious judgment" and "an insufficient depth of experience at the senior levels to recognize the impact of this projected management style."[6]

Other witnesses agreed that scrutiny of FAA operations imposes an inordinate burden on senior FAA personnel. J. Donald Reilly of the Airport Operators Council International (AOCI) observed, "It is not uncommon to have 20 simultaneous investigations of FAA activities" by the General Accounting Office (GAO), the DOT Inspector General, OMB, and the Office of Technology Assessment, or to "have more people investigating a project than there are working on it productively."[7]

Witnesses also testified extensively about the personnel problems that impede effective FAA management of the national airspace system, in particular, the inflexibility of federal personnel regulations. William Bolger, President of the Air Transport Association (ATA), and John Thornton, National Coordinator of the National Air Traffic Controllers Association (NATCA), agreed that the civil service system provides no incentives for controllers to move to busier, understaffed facilities. Said Bolger, "They need to be able to recruit people, move them through training fast, compensate them properly, . . . [and] move them to centers that they can't move them to today." [8] Thornton also suggested that the personnel system be made flexible enough to move controllers between different levels of air traffic density, and thereby avoid putting undue pressure on controllers assigned to busier facilities. [9]

The appropriate number of air traffic controllers needed to operate the system has been a subject of debate for some time, but a GAO representative, Kenneth Mead, told the Commission, "FAA's current staffing standards fall short of accurately reflecting controller staffing needs, especially in providing sufficient staff to cover peak traffic periods and maintain an adequate training pipeline." [10] Mead concluded, "Until valid staffing standards are in place, FAA will not know how many controllers it needs." [11]

Controller staffing is not the only personnel problem. Mead also noted, "Attrition of FAA's maintenance staff has resulted in critical technician vacancies across the country, and this shortage could become much more acute." [12] Representative Molinari agreed, adding that he had found the number of aviation safety inspectors to be seriously inadequate. [13] Across the board, the Commission heard testimony alleging personnel deficiencies in nearly every aspect of the FAA's system operations.

Procurement

Many witnesses also observed that the government's regulations are too cumbersome to procure the technology needed to improve the system as it becomes available. Although one witness viewed the installation of the new Host air traffic control computer system as a sign of progress in this area, [14] another pointed out, "It often takes 9 to 12 months to process and award even small and simple procurements." [15] Again, critics of the system were supported by GAO testimony on the National Airspace System (NAS) Plan,* which has been plagued by project delays: "FAA underestimated the complexity of these systems, the time needed to develop software, and the interdependency among the different systems." Moreover, as Mead testified for GAO, "Factors like these, not funding shortages, were what caused the NAS plan delays." [16] The testimony before the Commission indicates that procurement procedures are of

---

*The NAS Plan was authorized by the Airport and Airway Improvement Act of 1982. The FAA proposed the NAS Plan as a package of modernization projects for air traffic control equipment, including airport radars, navigational aids, aircraft electronics, and computer services at en route centers. The first computer enhancement was named the Host computer because it would "Host" existing en route center computer system software in new hardware, then provide capacity for further refinements of the programs. The NAS Plan was initially promoted as a 10-year, $11.7 billion program that would lead to automated air traffic control, but is now anticipated to require longer development time and involve additional expenditures.

significant concern to most system users. Observations at three FAA facilities reinforced this testimony. At the Leesburg, Virginia, en route center, for example, air traffic controllers rely on vacuum tube technology that is inadequate for current operations.

Trust Fund and Airport Development

Many complaints regarding the management of the national airspace system centered on two interrelated issues—the Airport and Airways Trust Fund and airport development. The Trust Fund has accumulated an unobligated balance of approximately $5.6 billion, and several witnesses advocated using this surplus for system development, as intended by Congress. In the words of former FAA Administrator Helms, "The Administration and the Congress have abdicated their firm commitment of 1982" to use the Trust Fund "as needed to modernize the air traffic control system and the national integrated airport system."[17]

The Airport and Airway Improvement Act provides that Trust Fund support shall emphasize airport construction and development grants, FAA research and development, and the purchase of facilities for the FAA. FAA operational revenues (i.e., funding for the bulk of air traffic control services, including the systems maintenance and flight service station functions) are derived primarily from general revenues.

Pointing to the Trust Fund surplus, those who support elements of current privatization proposals, as well as former Administrator Donald Engen, expressed confidence that needed operations could be supported by revenues generated by the Trust Fund tax sources, without relying on general revenues to the current extent. A 1986 GAO study projected that, under then-current policies, the balance would rise to $12.4 billion by 1990.[18]

Congress and the Administration continually blame the existence of this unobligated balance on each other. Precise allocation of the balance is complicated by a "penalty provision" included in the 1982 airport and airway reauthorization legislation. Congress adopted the penalty provision to discourage the Administration from using the Trust Fund for operations rather than for system development. Under the terms of the penalty provision, Trust Fund allocations to the FAA are reduced proportionately whenever facilities and equipment appropriations fall below authorized levels. The FAA still receives its full appropriation; however, the funds are drawn from general revenues rather than from the Trust Fund.

Although the Administration has argued that as much as 85 percent of total FAA expenditures should be paid from the Trust Fund, Congress has consistently rejected this level of Trust Fund support for FAA operations. Trust Fund revenues are derived from two sources, user fees and interest on securities held by the Trust Fund (paid from the General Fund into the Trust Fund). As indicated in table 1, that interest payment has become an increasing component of Trust Fund revenues in recent years.

TABLE 1.—*Sources of Trust Fund Revenues*

[In billions of dollars]

Source	1982	1983	1984	1985	1986	1987
Taxes/User Fees	0.133	2.165	2.499	2.851	2.736	3.060
Interest	0.541	0.533	0.546	0.747	0.829	0.880
Total	0.674	2.698	3.045	3.598	3.565	3.940

Total Trust Fund income for 6-year period: $17.520
Total tax/user fee contribution: $13.444
Total interest accumulated from General Fund: $4.076

SOURCE: Office of Management and Budget, January 21, 1988.

Table 2 shows the portion of total FAA expenditures borne by the Trust Fund and the General Fund during the 6 years from 1982 to 1987.

TABLE 2.—*FAA Revenues*

[In billions of dollars]

Source	1982	1983	1984	1985	1986	1987
Trust Fund	1.593	2.805	2.007	3.720	2.532	2.585
General Fund	1.541	1.464	2.644	1.635	2.340	2.361
Total	3.134	4.269	4.651	5.355	4.872	4.946

Total FAA spending, 1982–87: $27.227
Total Trust Fund revenues to FAA, 1982–1987: $15.242
Total General Fund revenues to FAA, 1982–1987: $11.985
Portion of Trust Fund derived from General Fund: 30.3%

SOURCE: Office of Management and Budget, January 21, 1988.

NOTE: These figures include funds for the Metropolitan Area Airports (removed from the FAA by Congress in 1987) and for support of the loan-guarantee program, which were not included in the calculation of the $26.7 billion spending figure in OMB Associate Director Carol T. Crawford's testimony of December 1, 1987.

These tables demonstrate that, to the extent that the Trust Fund is derived from interest paid from the General Fund, the figures understate the portion of FAA expenditures borne by the General Fund by 30.3 percent of the contribution attributed to the Trust Fund.

Testimony submitted to the Commission indicated that some portion of aviation funding should continue to come from general revenues. This portion would probably include the 15 percent commonly attributed to public agency (including the military) use of the airspace, as well as the 13 percent of FAA expenditures that can be attributed to regulatory costs for functions that would likely remain with the government under the current proposals for change. This analysis indicates that if current levels of aviation spending and current levels of service are to be sustained in the face of an elimination of subsidies from the General Fund, user fees would have to increase by about $1.4 billion per year.

Potential Management Solutions

Proposals to reform the management of the national airspace system fall into three categories. The first, which currently enjoys the most congressional support, would remove FAA from DOT and restore it as an independent agency. Several witnesses endorsed this idea as an effective way to free the FAA from the potential for DOT micromanagement. Others argued that this would do little to address the perceived problems of oversight by other government organizations—or any other difficulties.

A second category of proposals, advanced by the ATA, would create a government corporation to manage the national airspace system. Such an entity would be exempt from federal personnel and procurement requirements and would manage the Trust Fund more efficiently by applying user fees directly for system improvements. Despite these theoretical benefits, the government corporation idea has been criticized both by those who think it goes too far and by those who think it does too little.

The third category includes a proposal for more extensive privatization of the system. Developed by Robert W. Poole, this plan would transfer responsibility for the system to a nonprofit, user-owned corporation. Airport towers and landing slots would be turned over to the airport owners, who would be free to charge market prices to sustain the system. These revenues would obviate the need for the Trust Fund, the funds from which could be reinvested in the system. Supporters believe that this method of privatization is the only way to reduce the political interference that is a disruptive factor in contemporary American aviation. This proposal enjoyed the support of several witnesses, some of whom pointed out the need for further study of the consequences of privatization.

A number of witnesses argued that the current system provides substantial benefits to a full range of system users and that the various reform proposals do not address crucial operational concerns. Former Administrator Helms likened any attempt to separate the system's different functions to trying to unscramble an egg. The Department of Defense (DOD) opposed privatization on the grounds that a high degree of coordination now exists between it and the FAA, which might not be the case under a private system. Other witnesses, including those representing NATCA and the American Federation of Labor-Congress of Industrial Organizations (AFL–CIO), expressed reservations that a private system would become dominated by the biggest users of the system—the large air carriers.

Former Administrator Engen observed that the current air traffic control system was a result of more than 50 years of experience, with each part grafted on to respond to a specific need. The system's coordination needs extend beyond the FAA to the manufacturers of equipment, owners and operators of airports and airplanes, and those who develop and implement operating procedures linking people and equipment. The testimony delivered to the Commission demonstrated a need for further studies of operational procedures before implementing proposals to reorganize or privatize the FAA's functions. There was general agreement that the airspace is one of the few resources that must be treated as a "natural monopoly," because price competition within the same airspace would be impracticable. William Kutzke, President of Air Transport Holdings, pointed out myriad technical difficulties to be resolved before privatization could be achieved, but he concluded that these constituted a reason to begin planning rather than an argument to reject private sector initiatives.

Management

The Commission's recommendations indicate broad policy directions. They do not endorse any specific reform plan or operational guidelines. Instead, the Commission surveyed many discrete functions now performed by the FAA and considered methods by which they might be improved through increased private sector involvement. With regard to general policy, the Commission recommends:

Recommendation (1)

For reasons of safety, public service, and efficiency, there is a strong public need for the foreseeable future for the FAA to regulate the national airspace system. However, portions of that system can and should be considered for private operation or for contracting, when such options would improve air commerce.

This recommendation reflects the Commission's opinion that for the foreseeable future the FAA should maintain ultimate responsibility for system regulation and safety oversight, even as specific portions of the system should be scrutinized for incremental privatization opportunities.

Witnesses who opposed changes in the current system structure were skeptical about the feasibility of having an integrated national resource broken up and operated by different entities. These witnesses advocated continued FAA management of the entire system, although some favored removing the agency from the DOT. Among reform proponents, even the strongest advocates of system privatization testified that, in the near future, a residual FAA should continue to serve as safety watchdog. The Commission supports that premise.

Trust Fund Allocations

Admiral Engen, the most recent former FAA Administrator, testified that the system could operate on revenues from the Trust Fund, "and without cost to the general taxpayer."[19] Other witnesses, such as Representative James L. Oberstar (D-MN), showed reluctance to fund FAA operations from the Trust Fund, expressing a "philosophical problem about a user paying to be regulated in the way that such a system might envision."[20] Although most users agreed that money from the Trust Fund should be spent for its original purpose, witnesses differed over how to correct the Trust Fund's deficiencies. Some suggested abolishing it, whereas others suggested taking it out of the general budget. OMB Associate Director Carol T. Crawford expressed the Administration's opposition to the latter proposal, pointing out that Trust Fund expenditures would still be subject to annual appropriations by Congress. She also maintained that the unobligated balance can be reduced only by eliminating the controversial penalty provision.[21] Rather than eliminate the penalty provision, however, Congress amended it in 1987 to restrict even further the FAA's ability to use Trust Fund revenues for its operations.

Most witnesses also spoke of the need to increase airport capacity to meet the growth in air travel. The Trust Fund is directed toward the development of airports as well as airways. Over the years, funding for airports has increased and become more broadly distributed around the nation. Under the 1982 authorizing legislation, more than 3,200 airports participate in the National Plan of Integrated Airport Systems. The systems concept encourages consideration of airports in relation to the varieties of airspace system requirements—general aviation, commuter aviation, air cargo transport, business aviation, and training facilities—in addition to the needs of commercial air carriers. By developing airports to serve a variety of needs, system planners may be able to design methods of diverting smaller, less sophisticated aircraft from airports and airways used by larger, high-performance aircraft.

Revenues for the Airport Improvement Program (AIP) are derived from the Trust Fund and allocated by formula. Within categories, the FAA Administrator and the Secretary of Transportation retain some discretion among grant applicants. Obligations on airport grants were limited to approximately $800 million annually from 1982 to 1987. In 1987 Congress authorized the program at $1.7 billion per year for fiscal years 1988 through 1990, and at $1.8 billion for fiscal 1991 and 1992.

Despite the demand for increased airport capacity and the economic benefits that communities derive from airports, airports cannot be easily expanded because of property taxes on the extensive land holdings required for airport operations and community groups opposed to airport operations for noise and environmental reasons. Many witnesses advocated increasing airport operators' authority to seek their own revenues for capacity improvements. They encouraged alternative means of airport development financing and favored allowing airport pricing arrangements that would have users pay more directly for system improvements.

A more privatized system could provide a variety of fee-for-service arrangements—including charges for weather briefings, peak-hour pricing at airports, passenger facility charges, and others—to secure reimbursement from users. Supporters of market pricing contend that charging fees is the surest method of defining the value that users put on the system. They also argue that it is the most efficient method of directing resources to points of greatest demand. Former Administrator Helms noted, however, that the passenger ticket tax and aviation fuel charges are administratively easy to collect and obviate the need for new collection and accounting procedures that would have to be developed under private systems or a system comparable to that used in Europe, where the air traffic control system identifies aircraft as they use the system and periodically bills owners (usually air carriers).

Recognizing that, as a general rule, user fees are an excellent means of allocating resources, the Commission recommends:

Recommendation (2)

The portion of national airport and airway expenditures borne by users through direct charges should be increased.

Although debate on this issue centered on the specific types of direct charges, such as peak-hour pricing at congested airports, and their potential for enforcement, the Commission makes this recommendation as a general policy guideline, to inject a measure of flexibility into the airport and airway funding system. The Commission views flexibility as an integral part of market systems and recognizes the need for periodic changes in pricing systems in response to changing use of the system.

Airport Development

Airport development has many benefits for communities. Former Administrator Helms discussed the revenues generated near airports and the businesses and jobs created by aviation activities. Spencer Dickerson of the American Association of Airport Executives testified that the existence of an airport traffic control tower enhances safety, attracting corporations to communities that have one. However, many airports are closing, especially those near major metropolitan areas, because of tax, noise, and environmental issues.

Some believe that an airport should be able to generate the revenues to pay for operation at the level that consumers and the local community demand. Through a variety of pricing mechanisms—such as peak-hour pricing, passenger facility charges, rents from airport tenants, and baggage and freight handling charges for shippers using airport facilities—resources could be directed to active airports. Those airports that did not generate the activity to support development would see it go elsewhere.

For example, revenues from a passenger facility charge (which would generate most revenue at airports used by bigger, occasionally noisier, jets) could support noise abatement programs. Similarly, peak-hour pricing arrangements could provide airport services to passengers willing to pay higher fees at busy times and encourage other passengers to take advantage of off-hour discounts. Witnesses testified that some combination of these pricing elements would allocate airport resources more rationally than the current political mechanisms, and without holding the threat of federal preemption of the noise issue over local airports, as was advocated by several other witnesses. On the basis of these and other arguments, the Commission recommends:

Recommendation (3)

The federal government should reduce its direct role in the development of airports by encouraging each airport to develop its own sources of funding from the full range of beneficiaries of aviation services.

Recommendation (4)

Airport operators should be allowed to charge peak-hour takeoff and landing fees to alleviate congestion. These fees would allocate scarce resources in the most equitable manner possible. Users who value peak takeoff and landing slots would pay a market-based premium for their use, while users whose demand for peak travel is less would choose to fly at cheaper, less congested times.

Recommendation (5)

Airport operators should be allowed to charge passenger facility fees as a means of generating revenues to support the airport locally. These charges provide one of many pricing mechanisms for directing resources to airport needs without subjecting aviation issues to political interference.

In making these recommendations, the Commission endorses the concept of greater flexibility and local airport discretion about appropriate funding systems. In the Commission's view, airports currently remain tied to the federal grant system largely because of restrictions imposed by the government when it grants federal funds to airports.

Again, as with recommendation (2), discussion among the Commissioners centered on whether peak-pricing policies could be enforced, especially when applied to general aviation. The Commission concluded, however, that enforcement methods should be based on experience; they are administrative, rather than policy, questions.

Air Traffic Control Functions

Air traffic controller staffing has been one of the most contentious issues facing national aviation policymakers during the 1980s. Since the 1981 strike by the Professional Air Traffic Controllers Organization (PATCO)—which resulted in the firing of more than 11,400 controllers, many of them qualified at full performance level (FPL)—the FAA has attempted to recruit, hire, train, and certify a new controller work force. Congress has conducted hearings assessing the numbers of controllers, established legal requirements for the portion of them who should be FPLs, investigated hiring and training programs, and reviewed performance at specific facilities. The FAA has conducted extensive training in human resources management programs for controllers and supervisory personnel. Despite this effort, the controllers voted for a new union, the National Air Traffic Controllers Association, in 1987.

The FAA has extensive training and certification programs for its controller work force, and the agency operates an Air Traffic Control Academy in Oklahoma City to train controllers. For every 100 controllers who enter the training program, 40 fail to complete the course. Controllers who qualify for the en route center option (usually the best performers in training) get added radar training at the Academy before being assigned to a center. For controllers in the tower, professional advancement consists of a series of moves from lower activity airports to busier airports, with training at each step. A controller rated FPL at a Level 2 tower, for example, would be eligible to bid on job vacancies at Level 3 towers. If selected for a Level 3 tower position, the controller would revert to developmental status until fully certified at the new facility.

Controllers' skills and pay levels vary according to the level of activity and equipment at their facility. Staffing levels for all facilities are defined according to FAA's air traffic controller staffing standard and are based on activity at the center or the airport during the previous 2 years. These procedures make it difficult to adjust the rating of particular facilities as air traffic patterns change. For example, Dulles International Airport outside Washington, D.C., has experienced tremendous growth in activity during the past 2 years, but only recently was changed from a Level 3 to a Level 4 airport.

En Route Centers

One witness proposed the creation of a private, not-for-profit corporation to operate the en route air traffic control centers, which now guide aircraft along airways in the continental United States and in adjacent oceanic airspace. Recognizing that this service appears to be naturally monopolistic (no one envisages competition among firms to offer different air traffic control services in the same airspace), supporters of this plan believe, however, that a private entity could better manage the en route system by directing resources to busier airspace sectors according to the demands of the market. Others expressed scepticism as, internationally, only Switzerland offers comparable private air traffic control services. Former Administrator Helms testified that, in his view, the Swiss service was inadequate to meet the requirements of the U.S. national airspace.

Other witnesses opposed changes in the structure of the national en route system for reasons of national security. Lloyd Mosemann, a Deputy Assistant Secretary of the Air Force representing the Department of Defense, stressed the military's close relationship with the FAA in the use of the system. Mosemann suggested that this coordination might be jeopardized by attempts to privatize the system, and argued that the military could not and should not be treated as "just another system user."[22] Fred Smith of the Competitive Enterprise Institute, however, termed this a "red herring," saying that a transition to private system operation ". . . need not change any of those cooperative procedures."[23] Although OMB maintained that "the function of controlling en route air traffic is not inherently governmental,"[24] other witnesses testified that the en route activities of the FAA are clearly within the domain of interstate commerce and that they have developed through historical experience in response to a variety of system requirements.

The Commission agrees with this basic assessment and recommends:

Recommendation (6)

The FAA should retain authority over the en route centers, but some of the activities should be subject to contracting out.

The recommendation is closely related to Recommendation (1), in that it would maintain the FAA as the ultimate overseer of system operations and safety but allow room for improvements within the system. It reflects the basic view of most witnesses that the en route system is a tightly integrated national structure that should be kept intact for now.

The Commission considered making no recommendation on the en route centers, but decided that such a vote might be interpreted as an endorsement of the present system. The foregoing recommendation reflects the Commission's recognition of the need for en route center improvements coupled with the Commission's belief that no current proposal adequately addresses all the technical, legal, and financial concerns that would be involved in transition to a private system. The Commission recognizes, however, that some functions within the en route centers—such as computer maintenance and weather briefings for air traffic controllers—might be contracted out rather than provided by FAA itself.

Airport Traffic Control Towers

The FAA operates 416 airport traffic control towers throughout the United States. Critics of the system believe that rigidities such as restrictive personnel regulations obstruct airport and aviation development. Under the present system, an airport operator does not have the flexibility to hire additional controllers if he wishes to extend the airport's operating hours, contract with an air carrier to establish a hub, or expand activity in other ways. Moreover, if a carrier moves its hub operations from one airport to another, controllers will remain at the first airport long after flight activity decreases. Such rigidities in federal personnel procedures are alleged to restrict system development.

Even those critical of the current system agree that the FAA should establish standards for controller performance and airport and airways operations, but they maintain that—much as it licenses pilots who fly for commercial air carriers—the FAA can regulate the system without operating it. Proposals have been advanced to turn airport traffic control tower operations over to airport operators, who could charge fees for their services. Fees would vary according to demand, size of aircraft, and other performance criteria. These fees would direct resources to busier airports, facilitating the rapid response to market conditions.

These analysts also believe that the private sector can be more flexible in personnel requirements than the public sector. The FAA, for instance, does not hire former military controllers as controllers if they are over 31 years of age, thus limiting the pool of controller applicants. A private firm following similar practices not only would be liable for age discrimination litigation, but usually would be eager to hire controllers who, by virtue of their military experience, would need less training than an inexperienced applicant. FAA also prohibits fired PATCO controllers from reinstatement, although some believe that PATCO controllers could bring needed skills back to air traffic control facilities and shorten the training time required for the FAA to certify new controllers. The Administration has strongly opposed any reinstatement of controllers who went on strike in 1981, citing the principle that strikes against the government are illegal and emphasizing that reinstatement might impair morale among the controllers who remained on the job.

Proposals to privatize airport traffic control towers received little unqualified support from aviation professionals during the Commission's hearings. William Kutzke of Air Transport Holdings, who supported such an initiative, emphasized that many operational details would have to be addressed before such a program could be implemented.[25] The two former Administrators of the FAA who testified strongly supported the integrated nature of the airport and airways system, and expressed grave reservations about the potential for diverse standards and operating procedures creeping into a fragmented system.

Other witnesses supported expansion of the FAA's contract tower program, under which it currently authorizes local governments to establish their own towers or to hire private firms to operate them. These witnesses, however, advocated private airport traffic control towers as a means of expanding the current system to include additional airports, assuming that once the activity level rose, airport traffic control operations would be taken over by FAA personnel.

The Commission believes that there is significant potential for increased private operation of airport traffic control towers and therefore recommends:

Recommendation (7)

FAA should move to a system of private airport traffic control towers, but this move should be made incrementally. First, FAA should develop controller skills at smaller airports, gradually privatizing larger, more sophisticated facilities as the work force of private sector controllers increases.

The Commission agreed with witnesses who proposed the expansion of private air traffic control operations. It was the view of the Commission that the goal need not be solely to expand the system but also could serve to increase gradually the portion of the system operated by the private sector.

Flight Service Stations

Since the adoption of the National Airspace System Plan in 1982, the FAA has been automating flight service station facilities throughout the United States and closing selected facilities that still rely on older equipment. Flight service stations provide a range of services, primarily to general aviation. They issue weather briefings, file and record flight plans, issue Notices to Airmen (information on runway closings, new airport openings, and changes in approved traffic patterns surrounding airports), and provide in-flight services, primarily by radio contact. The FAA estimates that more than 95 percent of flight services are provided by phone, a practice that weighed heavily in plans to automate and consolidate these facilities. Table 3 indicates the decline in flight services provided by the FAA's flight service stations during the years since consolidation began.

TABLE 3.—*Flight Service Station Activity*

Year	1983	1984	1985	1986
Flight Services (thousands)	56,186	54,684	51,705	48,702
General Aviation Flight Hours (millions)	31,048	31,510	30,590	30,361
Number of Flight Service Stations	315	312	294	274

SOURCE: FAA, Office of Management Systems.

The flight service station automation/consolidation program has experienced many difficulties. Written testimony submitted by the National Association of Air Traffic Specialists (the union representing flight service specialists) recognizes that Congress has been heavily involved in selecting sites for facilities, reversing FAA decisions to close facilities, mandating equipment requirements, and determining staffing levels within the system specialist work force.

A GAO study pointed out some early difficulties involving the quality of service provided with some of the automated equipment, although these have since been resolved, and the contractor developing new equipment for the automated flight service stations has had difficulties delivering on schedule.[26] The FAA's plan for future research and development within the national airspace system anticipates the development of private contractors who would provide many of the same services as flight service stations on a fee-for-service basis.[27] The FAA is developing computer capability for Direct User Access Terminals (DUAT) that would enable pilots to file flight plans through their home computers. Some providers have begun offering weather briefings and other information to pilots. The State of Wisconsin, for example, has developed a program to provide weather briefings at airports through computers. However, there are a limited number of such facilities within the state, and they do not yet help pilots file flight plans.

Supporters of the FAA's flight service station program recognized the difficulties in the current automation and consolidation program but maintain that FAA is taking the first steps toward an integrated system. Former Administrator Engen testified that instituting charges for weather information would encourage some pilots to fly without getting the information—exposing themselves and perhaps others to unnecessary risk in order to save the expense.

The Commission found that flight service stations provide an essential service and should be operated as efficiently as possible. The Commission recommends:

Recommendation (8)

The FAA should contract out the operation of its flight service stations with the understanding that individual pilots should not be charged a fee for the information supplied to them.

The Commission concluded that the private sector could provide flight service station activities more efficiently than the government. Debate among the Commissioners focused on whether pilots would be willing to pay for flight services previously provided at no charge. The Commission believes that, to minimize the chance that pilots will use flight service station services less, the government should continue to pay for such services. The Commission also strongly recommends that during the flight service station privatization process, the interests of all flight service specialists should be taken into consideration.

Air Traffic Control Systems Maintenance

Under the current system, the FAA has a work force of slightly fewer than 9,000 airway facilities technicians stationed at airports and en route centers around the country. Each technician is expected to be capable of maintaining a range of equipment at a given site when fully trained, a process that requires as long as 6 years.

There are serious problems involving the systems maintenance work force. The airway facilities work force is aging (the median age of fully certified technicians is now near 50), and much of the equipment that these technicians maintain is being replaced as the NAS Plan is implemented. FAA is short of maintenance technicians, especially if it continues to require technicians to be trained on a variety of equipment at each facility.

Some claimed that it is impossible to separate operations and maintenance from the highly integrated equipment of the national airspace system. They cite the dedication of the airway facilities work force, observe the potential for labor disputes involving contractors, and question whether a contractor could deliver the maintenance services as required by the system.

Others, however, noted that the efficiencies of greater specialization are readily available and that, by relying on contractors to develop new equipment, the FAA could save substantial funds. In response to questions after the Commission's hearings, GAO stated that contracting could speed the training of systems maintenance technicians.

Having weighed these views, the Commission recommends:

Recommendation (9)

The FAA's system maintenance service should be privatized. Current conditions—the simultaneous aging of the facilities maintenance work force and the replacement of a great portion of system equipment—present a unique opportunity to FAA. The agency should seize this opportunity incrementally to contract out the maintenance of new facilities and equipment as they are introduced into the system.

In making this recommendation, the Commission found that the introduction of new equipment would allow the FAA to reduce its requirement for individual technicians and increase its reliance on contractors—probably trained by the manufacturers of the new equipment. The Commission believes this offers a more efficient method of replacing the technician work force than the current system does.

Summary

The Commission recognizes the major implications for change in national airspace system operations that would result from these recommendations. The system was developed over a 50-year period and has changed incrementally in response to the changing needs of the American people. The recommendations discussed here support that trend of incremental development, even though they point in the direction of greater private sector responsibility for the system's performance.

A more extensive involvement of the private sector in the management of the delivery and maintenance of air traffic services would improve their effectiveness, safety, and cost. The role for the private sector needs to be increased to bring more creativity and ingenuity to the maintenance of these facilities. Regulations and policies governing consistent, standardized procedures and communications would remain the responsibility of the federal government. The FAA would remain an integral part of the system in establishing policies and standards, but there is great opportunity for the private sector to carry out many of the agency's current operations and systems maintenance functions.

Effective implementation depends on experimentation within the current system to develop methods to make it work better than it does. The Commission is confident that the private sector will afford a better route to future aviation progress.

NOTES FOR CHAPTER 5

1. FAA estimates that U.S. commercial air carrier passenger enplanements will rise by an annual average of 4.5 percent through 1998. See Federal Aviation Administration, *FAA Aviation Forecasts, 1987–1998*, February 1987, p. 42.

2. Unless noted otherwise, data used in this chapter were supplied by the Office of Management Systems, Federal Aviation Administration.

3. A 1986 Brookings Institution study found that travelers had saved $6 billion annually through lower fares and better service. See Steven Morrison and Clifford Winston, *The Economic Effects of Airline Deregulation* (Washington, DC: Brookings, 1986). For safety statistics, see *Heritage Foundation Backgrounder*, No. 545, "What Deregulation Has Meant for Airline Safety," November 12, 1986.

4. Testimony of J. Lynn Helms, former Administrator, Federal Aviation Administration, before the President's Commission on Privatization, Hearings on Air Traffic Control (hereinafter cited as Air Traffic Control Hearings), December 1, 1987.

5. Testimony of Representative Guy V. Molinari, Air Traffic Control Hearings, December 2, 1987.

6. Helms testimony.

7. Testimony of J. Donald Reilly, Airport Operators Council International, Air Traffic Control Hearings, December 2, 1987.

8. Testimony of William Bolger, Air Transport Association, Air Traffic Control Hearings, December 2, 1987.

9. Testimony of John Thornton, National Air Traffic Controllers Association, Air Traffic Control Hearings, December 2, 1987.

10. Testimony of Kenneth Mead, U.S. General Accounting Office, Air Traffic Control Hearings, December 1, 1987.

11. Responses of Kenneth Mead, U.S. General Accounting Office, submitted for the record in response to questions by Commissioners, subsequent to Air Traffic Control Hearings, December 14, 1987.

12. Mead testimony.

13. Molinari testimony.

14. Testimony of Jonathan Howe, National Business Aircraft Association, Air Traffic Control Hearings, December 2, 1987.

15. Reilly testimony.

16. Mead testimony.

17. Helms testimony.

18. U.S. General Accounting Office, *Aviation Funding: Options Available for Reducing the Aviation Trust Fund Balance*, May 1986, p. 44.

19. Testimony of Vice Admiral Donald Engen, Air Traffic Control Hearings, December 1, 1987.

20. Testimony of Representative James Oberstar, Air Traffic Control Hearings, December 2, 1987.

21. Letter from Carol T. Crawford, Office of Management and Budget, to the President's Commission on Privatization, December 11, 1987. Despite the Administration's support for elimination of the penalty provision, the Airport and Airway Safety and Capacity Expansion Act of 1987 maintained the penalty provision.

22. Testimony of Lloyd Mosemann, United States Air Force, Air Traffic Control Hearings, December 1, 1987.

23. Testimony of Fred Smith, Jr., Competitive Enterprise Institute, Air Traffic Control Hearings, December 1, 1987.

24. Background information submitted to the Commission by Carol T. Crawford, Office of Management and Budget, December 1, 1987.

25. Testimony of William Kutzke, Air Transport Holdings, Air Traffic Control Hearings, December 2, 1987.

26. Herbert McClure, "FAA Appropriations Issues," Subcommittee on Transportation of the House Committee on Appropriations, April 21, 1987.

27. "A View of the NAS in 2010," *Federal Aviation Administration Plan for Research, Engineering, and Development*, August 1986, chap. 6.

Chapter 6

Educational Choice

The recent record of educational achievement has fallen far short of the basic goals that Americans set for their schools. In 1983, the National Commission on Excellence in Education issued a report, *A Nation at Risk*, describing a "rising tide of mediocrity" in education. Despite substantial public spending on education—at all levels of government—the nation's schools were not producing commensurate results. Average scores earned on Scholastic Aptitude Tests (SATs) by high school seniors seeking admission to college began a steady decline in 1963, but those scores indicated only the surface of the problems.

Similar results on other educational report cards have turned the 1980s into a decade of dissatisfaction with schools. In view of the disappointing standardized test results reported through the National Assessment of Educational Progress (NAEP), other tests of basic skills widely administered to children in primary grades, and the poor results registered in the first NAEP evaluation of historical and literary knowledge,[1] a consensus has developed that the nation needs better results from its educational institutions. Although SAT scores improved during the early part of this decade, average SAT scores remain 74 points below the 1963 peak. For many reasons, the demand for education reform persists.[2]

Academic Achievement in the Public Schools

Dissatisfaction with the performance of United States educational systems has regularly been registered in public opinion polls. Each year for the past 18 years, the Gallup Poll has surveyed American attitudes toward education. When people were asked to rate their *local* community schools on the four-point scale commonly used for academic purposes, their schools' grades declined from 2.63 (B—) in 1974 to 2.12 (C) in 1983. The average grade for the *nation's* schools has increased slightly, from 1.94 (D+) in 1981 (when the question was first introduced) to 2.13 in 1986.[3] For the 6 years in which respondents were asked to rate schools both locally and nationally, local schools have scored consistently—albeit only slightly—higher than schools in the nation as a whole.

Educational improvements are of vital concern to many Americans, especially when they confront the long-term consequences of failure in the nation's schools. President Ronald Reagan declared in his January 27, 1987, State of the Union Address:

> The quest for excellence into the twenty-first century begins in the schoolroom, but we must go next to the workplace. More than 20 million new jobs will be created before the new century unfolds and by then our economy should be able to provide a job for everyone who wants to work. We must enable our workers to adapt to the rapidly changing nature of the workplace.

Conversion of skills acquired in school to those needed in the workplace has been one of the most pronounced deficiencies of the nation's educational system. Xerox Corporation Chairman David T. Kearns claimed in the fall of 1987, "If current demographic and economic trends continue, American business will have to hire a million new workers a year who can't read, write, or count. Teaching them how, and absorbing the lost productivity while they're learning, will cost industry $25 billion a year for as long as it takes." He added, "Teaching new workers basic skills is doing the schools' product recall work for them—and frankly, I resent it." [4] A report commissioned by the U.S. Department of Labor analyzed future employment trends and concluded:

> As the society becomes more complex, the amount of education and knowledge needed to make a productive contribution to the economy becomes greater. A century ago, a high school education was thought to be superfluous for factory workers and a college degree was the mark of an academic or a lawyer. Between now and the year 2000 . . . a majority of all new jobs will require postsecondary education. Many professions will require nearly a decade of study following high school, and even the least skilled jobs will require a command of reading, computing, and thinking that was once necessary only for the professions.[5]

Funding and Enrollment

Nearly all major educational policy decisions, and the bulk of financial allocations, are made at either the state or the local level. During this century, however, trends in educational financing have shifted away from local governments, and state governments have assumed greater responsibility for educational funding (see table 1). Although federal spending on education has increased throughout much of the century, the portion of educational expenditures derived from federal funds decreased during the 1980s, even though the sums provided continued to increase in real terms.

TABLE 1.—*Sources of Elementary and Secondary School Revenues, 1919–86*

[In thousands of dollars]

School Year	Revenues	Source (%)		
		Local	State	Federal
1919–20	$970,121	83.2	16.5	0 .3
1929–30	2,088,557	82.7	16.9	0 .4
1939–40	2,260,527	68.0	30.3	1 .8
1949–50	5,437,044	57.3	39.8	2 .9
1959–60	14,746,618	56.5	39.1	4 .4
1969–70	40,266,923	52.1	39.9	8 .0
1979–80	96,881,165	43.4	46.8	9 .8
1980–81	105,949,087	43.4	47.4	9 .2
1981–82	110,191,257	45.0	47.6	7 .4
1982–83	117,497,502	45.0	47.9	7 .1
1983–84	126,055,419	45.4	47.8	6 .8
1984–85	137,350,722	44.7	48.8	6 .5
1985–86	149,687,997	43.5	50.1	6 .4

SOURCE: U.S. Department of Education, *The Condition of Education* (Washington, DC: Center for Education Statistics, 1987), p. 36.

NOTE: Revenues represented in current dollars.

During the 1985–86 school year, Americans spent $160.8 billion on elementary and secondary education, with nearly $150 billion of that money derived from governments. Spending for the 39.8 million children attending public schools averaged $3,735 per pupil, while expenditures for the 4.9 million children enrolled in private schools averaged $2,316 per pupil.

Some observers of contemporary education question whether the increased funds were spent well, especially in light of the decline in test scores that coincided with the increase in federal funding. Research evidence supports this concern, as National Center for Education Information Director Emily Feistritzer notes, "There is no hard evidence that there is a correlation between education spending and student achievement in any school."[6]

Since 1970, consistent with demographic trends, the population attending public schools decreased from 46.2 million to 39.7 million in 1983, before rebounding slightly to 39.8 million for 1984 and 1985. Private school enrollment also decreased from 5.7 million students in 1970 to 4.3 million in 1984 before rebounding to 4.9 million in 1985. Private schools have retained slightly more than 10 percent of the elementary and secondary school enrollment, with only minor variations throughout the period. Within the private schools, however, there have been enrollment shifts. Decreases in Catholic school enrollments in the 1970s and 1980s have been offset by gains in other forms of private schooling—both religious and secular. Although the President's Commission on Privatization heard testimony claiming an increase in home schooling, there are few reliable estimates of the numbers of students involved.[7]

Educational Reforms

Since the publication of *A Nation at Risk*, state officials have assumed increasing leadership of educational reform efforts. Different states have proposed experiments with professional career ladders for teachers, merit pay evaluations, changes in teacher certification requirements, open enrollment programs, magnet school initiatives, vouchers both to expand the range of options available at the elementary and secondary levels and to enable advanced students to enroll in colleges, and other options for increasing parental involvement and choice within the public schools.[8] Although most states have confined their experiments with parental involvement and choice to the public schools, the states are clearly inclining toward change in current educational systems. As clear as the call for change is, however, professional and public opinion is widely divided about the form of change that would be most effective for educational improvement.

Despite the wide range of opinions about educational reforms, there is a fairly substantial professional consensus about the characteristics of effective schools. Brookings Institution education analyst John Chubb, on the basis of a study of 10,000 high school students at nearly 500 schools, testified that effective schools are complex organizations characterized by a high degree of autonomy, with "academically focused objectives, pedagogically strong principals, relatively autonomous teachers, and collegial staff relations."[9] For schools to succeed, authority must be placed as close to the building level as possible; the principal must be given considerable discretion to define strong educational objectives, including the authority to hire, train, and replace teachers to develop a faculty that shares those aims. Effective principals also foster a collegial environment emphasizing professional participation in a team.

As presented by John Chubb, however, the paradox of current school reform is that the reforms most likely to provide educational success are politically unpalatable, while the reforms that are most politically adoptable are likely to increase the schools' difficulties.[10] That is, given the complexity of educational challenges and the many indices of school failure, educational policymakers are unlikely to grant the discretion deemed most likely to promote educational effectiveness. Indeed, that distrust of educational discretion extends from local school boards to the Congress of the United States, which restricts 95 percent of nominally "discretionary" funds available to the Secretary of Education under Chapter 2 of the Education Consolidation and Improvement Act.[11] Before legislators are likely to give educational authorities more discretion, something must be done to increase public confidence in the discretion that education policymakers already have.

Choice Programs for the Disadvantaged

The Commission was particularly concerned that educational opportunities for the educationally disadvantaged be increased. Testimony received by the Commission revealed a substantial consensus that choice programs might provide alternative methods of addressing the particular needs of students who are not thriving under current educational practices. Albert Shanker, President of the American Federation of Teachers, proposed, "Let's take the five per cent of the students in this country who are failing on every indicator . . . who can't read, who can't write, who don't come to school a good part of the time, and when they do come are violent a good part of the time . . . and give them free scholarships to private schools, and let's see how the private schools do with them."[12] Douglas Alexander, of Citizens for Educational Freedom, suggested that the Commission take Mr. Shanker up on his proposal; he indicated that some educational research supports the idea that private schools would do better with disadvantaged students than public schools are currently doing.[13]

Since 1965, Chapter 1 of the Education Consolidation and Improvement Act has authorized federal programs targeted toward children with low educational achievement, many of them from low-income families. For eligible students attending private schools (even parochial ones), public school teachers are authorized to provide remedial education services. In 1985, however, the Supreme Court severely limited the use of such funds in parochial schools.[14] Secretary William J. Bennett entered office committed to programs of "Character, Content, and Choice," and the administration proposed The Equity and Choice Act of 1985 (TEACH) as a voucher experiment. Under this proposal, Chapter 1 programs would have been converted to vouchers, with funds going to the parents of eligible students, who could then select the educational institutions they believed most likely to meet their children's needs. The amount of the voucher would have been calculated by dividing the available funds by the number of eligible recipients, a calculation that resulted in estimates of about $600 per eligible child per year.

For a variety of reasons, many voucher proponents reacted lukewarmly to TEACH. Teachers' organizations viewed the proposal as merely a disguise for efforts to reduce education expenditures.[15] Both TEACH and a subsequent voucher proposal for compensatory education programs were rejected by the Congress.

Despite the inability to agree on the specifics of the TEACH legislation, a wide public consensus supports increased efforts targeted toward educationally disadvantaged students. Therefore, the Commission recommends:

Recommendation (1)

The federal government should encourage choice programs targeted to individuals deemed in the lower percentiles of the current elementary and secondary student population. The schools are failing these children now, and alternatives beyond current programs should be explored.

The Commission views this recommendation with a particular sense of urgency about implementing alternative educational programs for students who are failing by all standards in current institutions. As a matter of law, nothing bars the Secretary of Education from promoting choice programs in cooperation with state and local education agencies. The Commission envisages small pilot programs, with incremental development of successful efforts and abandonment of initiatives that do not demonstrate improvement.

Introducing elements of choice into federal programs will require approval that Congress thus far has been unwilling to give. For students who cannot learn in current educational institutions, however, the alternatives appear to be innovative efforts now or remedial programs and diminished earning capacity in the future. Choice today appears to be a better decision.

Vouchers

Chubb concluded from his research that a comprehensive voucher system would be the best way to implement the changes he views as essential to educational success. Such proposals have been part of national policy discussions since 1962, with advocates on the political left as well as on the right. Indeed, one witness submitted testimony claiming that Thomas Jefferson, as Governor of Virginia, advanced an education voucher proposal in 1779.[16]

For many observers of contemporary education, the flexibility essential to improvement is most likely to come through a system of transfer payments—whether labeled vouchers, grants, student assistance, or otherwise—that would finance educational choice. At postsecondary and adult educational levels, the nation has extensive experience with such programs. In 1944, Congress adopted the GI Bill of Rights, which authorized payments to veterans who attended accredited colleges, universities, or vocational schools. Congress adopted similar legislation for needy individuals seeking postsecondary or vocational education. In the late 1950s, Congress authorized National Defense Education Act fellowships to support graduate students and to assist undergraduate students interested in teaching careers. With Basic Educational Opportunity Grants, also known as Pell Grants, people whose family income falls below defined levels can use federal funds to purchase education or training at the institution of their choice. These grant programs are supplemented by a variety of student loan programs enabling students to select the educational program, then pay with federal funds. At the postsecondary or adult education levels, these options are often cited as among the most effective government educational programs.

A great deal of controversy is generated by any proposal to extend such a system of federal financing to elementary and secondary education. Witnesses supporting greater choice in education contended that a full system of transfer payments would be the most effective way to maximize choice, and that the results would be beneficial for education. Under such a program, parents would receive vouchers with which to purchase the educational programs that they decided were most suitable for their children. Supporters believe that such a program would enable students to leave ineffective schools and move to better schools. The resulting competition among schools should introduce incentives to provide innovative programs at minimal cost. Such options are currently available only to parents who can afford to live in exclusive districts or pay private school tuitions.

Voucher supporters believe that a competitive educational choice system would both enable and induce school officials to identify the kinds of education that parents want and to adjust their offerings accordingly. Schools that were unable to attract students would revise their curricula, improve their teaching, develop more effective management, or be taken over by more effective schools.

In current school systems, few of these options are available. Under open enrollment or magnet school programs, for example, parents wanting particular programs can wait in line to get their children into them under the first-come, first-served selection methods commonly used in public schools. Public school officials can adjust curricula in response to high demand but their incentive to do so is limited when parents face few alternatives.

The only school district that has adopted an extensive voucher policy involving elementary and secondary schools (Alum Rock, California) did so as an experiment in the early 1970s, with considerable financial support from the Office of Economic Opportunity, and the National Institute of Education. That experiment was brought to a close after inconclusive results.

Vermont first established a choice system in 1782, which currently operates in rural districts with about 25 percent of the state's population.[17] Technically, however, it is not considered a true voucher program because no paper transfer of funds from school authorities in one district through parents to authorities in another district takes place. Minnesota has enacted a limited voucher experiment emphasizing choice in college classes for advanced high school students, and several other states have used choice programs to encourage dropouts to complete high school.[18]

The Commission was impressed by the consensus about the characteristics of effective schools. At the same time, the Commission recognized the diverse needs of individual students in the nation's schools, as well as the responsibility of government to enhance opportunities for all students. Increasing the range of options available to parents, and thus the incentives for schools to provide high-quality education in a cost-effective manner, appears to be the most effective way to achieve these goals. Accordingly, the Commission recommends:

Recommendation (2)

The federal government has a limited role in education. The federal government should foster diversity to achieve the nation's full range of educational goals. Congress should adopt policies to increase consumer (that is, parental) choice in education at elementary and secondary levels, just as it now fosters choice for adults through GI Bill payments and Pell Grants. The federal government should foster choice options (including vouchers) within national programs, encourage experimentation in educational choice through the Secretary of Education's leadership, and increase research efforts to collect and disseminate information about choice programs conducted by state and local education agencies.

The Commission's deliberations centered on the extent of federal involvement in public school systems, the variety of alternatives that might be encouraged under this recommendation, and the extent to which the recommendation might appear to prompt greater federal involvement in state and local educational policy decisions. The Commission concluded that the federal government properly has a limited role in education, and it does not intend to foster additional programs at the national level.

The Commissioners emphasized that the recommendation should not be construed merely as endorsing vouchers but should be interpreted to include the encouragement of options such as open enrollment, magnet schools, or other choices that might be developed and adopted at different levels of government.

Vouchers for Public and Private Schools

In recent years, the political debate surrounding educational choice has centered on whether public assistance to private schools should be available and in what form at different levels of government. In particular, the Commission considered whether private schools should be able to participate in federal programs providing educational choice to parents. Resolution of those issues is complicated by intense divisions about some basic political principles.

Many parents apparently desire options outside the public school system. In 1982 and 1986, the Gallup Poll asked parents who currently send their children to public schools: "If you had the means, would you send any of your children to a private or church-related school?" In 1982, 45 percent of these respondents indicated that they would choose private schools if they had the means. In 1986, 49 percent of public school parents answered "yes" to the same question.[19]

There also appears to be fairly strong support for some type of voucher system, although the level of support has eroded somewhat in recent years. In a 1983 Gallup poll, 49 percent of respondents indicated support for vouchers, declining slightly to 44 percent in 1987. Support for vouchers appears to be more pronounced among nonwhite respondents—64 percent favored them in 1983—although support has also declined more rapidly—down to 54 percent in 1987.[20]

There are a number of reasons behind the reluctance to experiment with voucher systems that would allow choice among both public and private schools. The nation has extensive capital invested in its school buildings, books, and other physical resources used for education. It has an even greater investment in the education, training, and experience of its current teachers and school administrators. Teachers' organizations not only oppose most educational choice proposals but also have tenure systems providing job security in current schools. In large school systems, teachers often are assigned to particular buildings and cannot easily be removed, even if they disagree with the educational objectives defined by the principal.

More important, there is concern that "adverse selection" would cause the sorting of bright, advantaged students into the best schools, leaving the slower or otherwise disadvantaged students in the poorest schools, arguably worse off than before. There is the additional philosophical objection of many citizens to supporting private schools, especially private parochial schools, with tax dollars.

Even critics of current public school performance are sometimes reluctant to embrace privatization as an appropriate solution to the deficiencies that they see in public schools. Competition does not always promote educational excellence. When differences in the academic caliber of various programs are not readily apparent, students have been known to select schools on the basis of athletic programs, appearance of facilities, or other criteria that are marginally, if at all, related to the caliber of education.

In short, there are a number of reasons for uncertainty about the results of experiments with educational choice. Many people want to be relatively certain of results before embracing substantial policy changes. William Gainer of the General Accounting Office informed the Commission:

> It would be naive to believe that a private school system without regulation or oversight, other than market forces (which we could expect to be imperfect), would provide superior educational services for at-risk youth. To be successful, a carefully crafted accrediting system would be necessary with some form of public involvement. The government entities that provide funding would also need to provide guidelines or standards for educational practice. Finally, some oversight and penalty system for ineffective programs would be needed to assure that consumers were not misled and their children poorly educated by a new, but no more effective, educational delivery system.[21]

In many people's view, any public support for private education threatens the viability of public schools.[22] There are historical reasons, however, to view public schools as seeking monopoly powers that would eliminate private education. University of California law professor John Coons testified that the system of education in the United States should be described as a state-run monopoly, rather than as public schools. He contended, "Tax-supported public schools from the beginning were organized not as open but as exclusive institutions. Access to a government school was based upon residence in a particular area. . . ." As a result of this structure, this witness contended that the state-run schools replicate the class and racial patterns of our society to the disadvantage of the poor and racial minorities. This territorial division of educational markets would be a per se violation of the Sherman Antitrust Act. He further argued, "The history of this curious system is essentially one of aristocratic leaders consciously stripping the family of its authority. . . . The system was adopted with full awareness of the opposite trend in Europe, one emphasizing respect for parental autonomy embodied in a democracy of educational choice."[23]

Public school monopolies were tested early in this century. Oregon, among other states, enacted legislation requiring attendance of students at the state-run schools, measures that would have effectively eliminated private options in education. In striking down the Oregon statute in 1925, the U.S. Supreme Court ruled:

The fundamental theory of liberty upon which all governments in this Union repose excludes any general power of the state to standardize its children by forcing them to accept instruction from public teachers only. The child is not the mere creature of the state; those who nurture him and direct his destiny have the right, coupled with the high duty, to recognize and prepare him for additional obligations.[24]

The deficiencies attributed to public schools often inspire proposals for change, but the National Governors' Association has recognized that support for choice is fully compatible with support for the public schools. The challenge is to develop reforms that address the needs for improvement, while ensuring the availability of high-quality education to all Americans. Therefore, the Commission recommends:

Recommendation (3)

Education benefits all who receive it, therefore private schools should be able to participate in federal programs providing educational choice to parents. In supporting educational choice, the federal government should remain sensitive to retaining the values represented by public schools. Although its educational choice programs should be open to participation by private schools, the full range of civil rights guaranteed by the Constitution should be protected.

The nation has a variety of constitutional guarantees that affect its educational systems. Private schools are guaranteed the right to exist and to operate. Schools accepting government funds are expected to comply with the full range of civil rights guaranteed by the Constitution. The Commission was particularly concerned that this recommendation carry explicit recognition of those civil rights guarantees. During its deliberations, the Commission also expressed its concern to ensure that any system of assistance to private institutions not violate the constitutional clause prohibiting any establishment of religion. If public policies followed this recommendation, the nation might well experience four different types of education: private schools refusing government assistance and regulations (including home schooling), private schools accepting government assistance and related regulations, public schools participating in educational choice programs, and public schools not participating in such programs as a result of local decisions.

Flexibility in Vocational Education

The Commission is also concerned about the role of vocational and adult education programs in preparing students for productive employment. Federal spending on vocational education now exceeds $1 billion per year, but the vast majority of vocational education spending is done by local education agencies. In recent years, the business community has indicated severe dissatisfaction with many vocational education programs.

In a review of research for the Committee for Economic Development, Nathaniel Semple discovered that few workers derived their job skills from vocational education institutions. Many students come to vocational education programs lacking basic skills, and the programs they encounter are often not related to today's workplace. Exploratory programs in industrial arts are often little more than glorified shop—with a smattering of hours devoted to metal working, the printing trades, or technical areas. Unfortunately, despite the prominence of these subjects in vocational curricula, related jobs are disappearing from the marketplace. Semple concluded, "Change is needed. The most important need is to require a minimum level of academic achievement for all students at all levels of elementary and secondary school. A second is to relate vocational education to market needs and a third is to invest in programs that pay off and end those that do not." [25]

More extensive choice programs would introduce elements of market flexibility to improve the process of identifying vocational programs deserving expansion because they lead to productive jobs, and ending those that lead to educational—and employment—dead ends. Vocational and adult education programs might be strengthened by choice experiments that build upon the involvement of the business and education communities.

The Need for Further Initiative

Assistant Secretary Chester E. Finn, Jr., conducted a review of research on choice programs and testified that choice works well for a variety of social and educational goals. He observed:

> Choice favorably affects student achievement. . . . A well-designed choice program is useful in achieving racial desegregation goals; and . . . choice programs appear to improve the vitality of public education. At the same time, the research uniformly fails to support critics' contentions that choice would reduce student achievement, torpedo desegregation goals, or undermine public education. [26]

Given this research base, more effective leadership in support of educational choice is essential. Therefore the Commission recommends:

Recommendation (4)

The Secretary of Education should use discretionary resources to conduct additional research on educational choice. This should include pilot programs, requests for proposals for programs targeted to particular educational needs such as disadvantaged and handicapped students, and other initiatives that might expand the range of educational options for children.

Research should not be limited to gathering information. It should include pilot programs and requests for research proposals of limited scope to reduce the uncertainties that can feed public misgivings. The Department of Education should place high priority on providing full information about effective programs at state levels, including precise discussions about the features that contribute to success in different places. The Secretary has gained considerable notice for publications describing "What Works" in effective schools and substance abuse programs; choice options should be given the same priority.

Summary

The current stalemate in education choice policy is not healthy for the nation's schools and is detrimental to the national interest. The nation is ill-served by a public school system whose teachers and policymakers have so little confidence that policy decisions of many prominent education organizations are dominated by a fear that students would flee if their parents had the resources. Parents are unlikely to remove their children from established institutions until clearly better alternatives are available. Rather than viewing each proposal for greater parental involvement and choice as a threat to public schools, education policymakers would better serve the American public by increasing the options available for the complex task of improving public education. The Commission believes that increased educational choice would enable Americans to chart an incremental path around the current stalemate by building on our highest principles and our best experiences.

NOTES FOR CHAPTER 6

1. Diane Ravitch and Chester E. Finn, Jr., *What Do Our 17-Year Olds Know? A Report on the First National Assessment of History and Literature* (New York: Harper and Row, 1987).

2. Congressional Budget Office, *Educational Achievement: Explanations and Implications of Recent Trends*, August 1987.

3. U.S. Department of Education, *Digest of Education Statistics, 1987* (Washington, DC: Center for Education Statistics, 1987), p. 23.

4. As reported by William Raspberry, "When Industry Gets a Defective Supply . . . of Workers," *Washington Post*, November 20, 1987.

5. William B. Johnston, Arnold E. Packer, et al., *Workforce 2000: Work and Workers for the Twenty-first Century* (Indianapolis: Hudson Institute, 1987), p. 116.

6. Emily Feistritzer, "Public vs. Private: Biggest Difference Is Not the Students," *Wall Street Journal*, December 1, 1987.

7. Patricia M. Lines, "An Overview of Home Instruction," *Phi Delta Kappan*, March 1987.

8. See National Governors' Association, *Time for Results: The Governors' 1991 Report on Education* (Washington, DC: National Governors' Association, 1986), and the follow-up progress report, *Results in Education: 1987* (Washington, DC: National Governors' Association, 1987).

9. Testimony of John Chubb, "Why the Current Wave of School Reform Will Fail," before the President's Commission on Privatization, Hearings on Educational Choice (hereinafter cited as Hearings on Educational Choice), December 21, 1987. This article will be published in a forthcoming issue of *The Public Interest*.

10. Chubb testimony.

11. Paul M. Irwin, *Education Block Grant Reauthorization: Selected Options* (Washington, DC: Congressional Research Service, June 1, 1987), p. 17.

12. Testimony of Albert Shanker, American Federation of Teachers, Hearings on Educational Choice, December 21, 1987.

13. Testimony of Douglas Alexander, Citizens for Educational Freedom, Hearings on Educational Choice, December 21, 1987.

14. *Aquilar* v. *Felton*, 105 S. Ct. 3232 (1985).

15. Testimony of Keith Geiger, National Education Association, Hearings on Educational Choice, December 21, 1987. See also Mary Hatwood Futrell, "Vouchers: The Hoax is Transparent," *Washington Post*, December 15, 1985.

16. See letter to the Commission from David W. Kirkpatrick, dated January 9, 1988. Milton Friedman recommended vouchers for education in *Capitalism and Freedom* (Chicago: University of Chicago Press, 1962). Christopher Jencks, then teaching at Harvard University, was a prominent supporter during the early 1970s.

17. John McClaughry, *Educational Choice in Vermont* (Concord, VT: Institute for Community and Liberty, 1987), p. 2.

18. National Governors' Association, *Time for Results*, pp. 76–77.

19. As reported in *Educational Choice*, September/October, 1986, p. 3.

20. See ibid. for data from 1981 through 1986. The data for 1987 are supplied by Geiger testimony.

21. Testimony of William J. Gainer, Human Resources Division, U.S. General Accounting Office, Hearings on Educational Choice, December 22, 1987.

22. Geiger testimony.

23. Testimony of Professor John Coons, University of California, Hearings on Educational Choice, December 22, 1987. Professor Coons cites a study by Charles Glenn, *The Myth of the Common School* (Amherst: University of Massachusetts Press, in press) to support his historical thesis.

24. *Pierce* v. *Society of Sisters*, 268 U.S. 510 (1925).

25. Nathaniel M. Semple, "Vocational Education: The Missing Link?" background paper for the Committee for Economic Development (1985).

26. Testimony of Chester E. Finn, Jr., Department of Education, Hearings on Educational Choice, December 22, 1987.

Chapter 7

The Postal Service

The government monopoly on the carriage of letter mail has existed in its current form since the private express statutes were adopted in 1845. As our nation grew and pioneers reached out to ever-more-distant frontiers, the postal system helped to bind the nation together. The laws forbidding competition by private express carriers ensured that the government's postal system could sustain itself on revenues from the profitable eastern routes and continue to serve the frontiers.*

The Postal Service continues to provide universal service across the nation, still protected from competition by the private express statutes. But the world today is very different from the 19th century. The telephone has all but replaced the Postal Service as the means of communication between households; only about 8 percent of today's mail is nonbusiness mail.[1] Roughly 40 percent of all mail carried by the Postal Service consists of what is commonly referred to as "junk mail"—direct mail advertising and charitable solicitations. Since 1979, when the Postal Service exempted "urgent mail" from the private express statutes, private express couriers such as Federal Express, Purolator Courier, and DHL have grown dramatically. In the past 4 years, Federal Express alone has grown from handling 42 million pieces per year to 178 million pieces per year. Similarly, private industry now controls more than 90 percent of the parcel market—handling over 2.4 billion packages in 1987. What is more important, the growth of electronic mail, while slower than some had anticipated, threatens to divert a major portion of the mail stream over the next 10 to 15 years.[2]

Many people believe that the quality of service provided by the Postal Service has been declining while costs continued to rise, and that this is the natural result of a government monopoly's lack of incentives to provide competitive quality service at a competitive price.

---

*It should be noted, however, that unlike today, postage rates did vary by distance in the 18th and 19th centuries. Of course, in those times transportation was the major component of cost, whereas today transportation is only 7 percent of postal costs.

In this context, private entrepreneurs, academics, some major mailers, and even members of the Postal Rate Commission, the body that oversees the setting of postal rates, have called for increased private sector participation in the provision of postal services. Depending on the particular point of view, increased private sector participation, or "privatization," can mean anything from contracting out specific functions to lifting the private express statutes altogether.

THE POSTAL SERVICE TODAY

Prior to 1970, mail service in the United States was provided by the Department of the Post Office. In 1970, the Postal Reorganization Act created the United States Postal Service (USPS) that we have today. The U.S. Postal Service is composed of the Postal Service, which collects, sorts, and delivers the mail, and the Postal Rate Commission (PRC), an independent regulatory agency, which is chiefly responsible for setting postal rates. In essence, the U.S. Postal Service functions much like a regulated public utility and the Postal Rate Commission like a public utility commission.

The postal monopoly is protected by the private express statutes—laws that prohibit the carriage of letter mail for hire by anyone but the USPS, with very few exceptions. These laws are found in the *United States Criminal Code*, Title 18, Sections 1693–99. The Postal Service has interpreted "letter mail" fairly broadly to include much direct mail advertising (that which is addressed or targeted to specific households in any way) and even such items as computer tapes. The private express statutes primarily affect first- and third-class mail. Second-class mail, consisting chiefly of periodicals, can be, and often is, delivered by other means, because, as with fourth-class mail, the Postal Service does not consider it to fall under the definition of a letter. In addition to restricting letter carriage, the private express statutes (18 U.S.C., Section 1725) also prohibit the use of mailboxes by anyone other than the Postal Service.

The principal exception to the prohibition on letter carriage appears in the *Code of Federal Regulations* (Postal Code), Title 39, Part 320, and is for "extremely urgent" letters that must be delivered within 12 hours, or letters whose cost is either in excess of $3.00 or twice the going USPS rate for first-class or priority mail, whichever is greater. There is a legal issue as to whether the Postal Service has the authority to issue regulations (as in 39 CFR, Part 320 above) suspending the criminal code. If it does not, then all the private express couriers are in violation of criminal law under Title 18.[3]

The Postal Service processes four major classes of mail. First class is chiefly made up of cards and letters, although larger items also can be sent first class. Second class consists of newspapers, magazines, and other periodicals, and, together with first-class mail, makes up "preferred mail," which is given a higher priority than the other two classes. Third class is made up of catalogs and various forms of direct mail advertising ("junk mail"). Fourth class consists of printed matter, merchandise, and "parcels"; parcel post is a subclass of fourth-class mail. Together, third- and fourth-class mail make up "nonpreferred" or "bulk" mail.

The Postal Reorganization Act of 1970 specifically prohibits cross-subsidization across classes of mail.* Practically speaking, cross-subsidization is likely to occur whenever uniform rates are charged for products that have differing costs of production. However, uniform rates are not a necessary feature for cross-subsidization to occur.

The PRC has typically used, either explicitly or implicitly, a methodology similar to what economists call "Ramsey pricing" as a guide in setting postal rates. Ramsey pricing is a "second-best" solution that is employed when the first-best solution, marginal cost pricing, is not feasible.** Correctly done, Ramsey pricing precludes cross-subsidization, as would competition, because each product bears those costs specific to its production, called incremental costs, and then some share of joint costs. However, the task of separating out the incremental costs specific to each mail class from those costs that are joint is complex and makes it difficult to construct a subsidy-free rate structure in the absence of competitive pressures.[4]

All classes and subclasses of mail are currently required to cover at least 100 percent of their attributed (similar to incremental) costs. However, there is a great deal of variation in the amount of institutional cost covered by each class of mail. A number of mail classes—second-class mail within county, nonprofit, and classroom; third-class nonprofit rate bulk; and fourth-class special rate and library rate—have rates set such that postage revenues cover very little, if any, of institutional cost, as their share of institutional cost is covered by direct, revenue-forgone subsidies from general revenues.***

---

*Cross-subsidization is said to occur in a multiproduct firm when one product is priced below the marginal cost of producing it, while another is priced enough above marginal cost to make up for the other product's losses.

**When a monopoly exhibits economies of scale (or scope), that is, when average costs per unit of production fall as the scale (or scope) of production increases, the firm will be unable to cover average cost at prices set to equal marginal cost. Ramsey pricing is a formula for calculating the percent markup over marginal cost for each product line in a multiproduct firm in a way that minimizes the losses to society from failure to set prices equal to marginal cost.

***The Postal Service received $969.6 million in 1985 in revenue-forgone subsidies (USPS Comprehensive Statement on Postal Operations, 1985). Of this, $140.5 million was a payment for subsidized attributable costs which has been phased out. Budget cuts reduced the revenue-forgone subsidies in 1986 to around $700 million.

The Postal Service contracts out many functions; total contracting out for fiscal 1987 was roughly $3 billion or about one-tenth of the Postal Service budget.[5] Perhaps primary among those functions is virtually all transportation of mail traveling in excess of 600 miles. Roughly 4,500 rural routes out of a total of 42,997 are contracted out to private "star route carriers," who provide delivery and portable retail services (weighing, selling stamps, accepting packages, etc.).[6] These star-route carrier contracts account for about $1.1 billion, one-third the total of contracted services. In addition, the Postal Service contracts out its retail function to roughly 4,000 rural small businesses and has about 8,700 cleaning service contracts.*

In addition to contracting out, a substantial portion of mail sorting is already done by private sector presort firms or mailers themselves. Over half of third-class mail and close to 40 percent of first-class mail is presorted. Presorting of mail down to the five-digit zip code (destination post office) or carrier route saves the Postal Service money, which is reflected in "the presort discount" on postage.

In fiscal 1987, out of 54 billion pieces of first-class mail, roughly 20 billion were presorted, and of those roughly 8 billion, or 37 percent, were presorted by the presort industry. The tremendous rate of growth of this industry, which takes mail from major business mailers, sorts it, and delivers it to the Postal Service, is reflected by the 8.9 percent growth in first-class, presorted mail over fiscal 1986, compared with the 1.8 percent growth in overall first-class mail volume over the same period.**

The USPS is the largest civilian employer in the country, with a labor force of approximately 800,000.*** It is also one of the most labor intensive employers—roughly 83 percent of USPS costs are made up of salaries and benefits—and the most highly unionized of all government agencies. There are seven postal unions with exclusive bargaining rights at the national level. Over 85 percent of postal workers belong to one or more of these unions. In addition, the National Association of Letter Carriers makes up one of the largest Political Action Committees in the country in terms of contributions.

It is now almost conventional wisdom that postal workers receive a wage "premium" relative to the private sector, although the evidence is

*This figure dates back to a 1981 source.

**The incentive for presorting arises from the presort discounts given on postal rates. For example, first-class mail receives a four-cent discount if sorted to the five-digit zip code, and a five-cent discount for sorting to the carrier route. Although the nine-digit or Zip+4 code is a finer breakdown than the carrier route, the presort discount for a nine-digit sort is only four-and-one-half cents because the Postal Service does not have enough Zip+4 coded mail to make it worth sorting on that basis.

***As of October 1, 1987, the USPS labor force was 799,626.

somewhat controversial, in part because of disagreement as to what the standard of comparison should be. In 1984, Jeffrey Perloff and Michael Wachter estimated Postal Service wage rates to be roughly 21 percent higher than the rates in "comparable" private sector jobs.[7] This finding of a wage premium is supported by studies of a more institutional nature that show, for example, long waiting lists for postal jobs and lower-than-average quit rates for the Postal Service.[8]

In a similar study, Martin Asher and Joel Popkin found no statistically significant difference between the wages received by white men in the Postal Service and those received by white unionized men in the private sector.[9] A similar result was obtained in a 1976 study by Sharon Smith, who found a 36 percent wage premium for female postal workers over female unionized workers in the private sector, but no significant difference between the average wage rates of male postal workers as compared with male private unionized workers.[10] Smith did find, however, wage premiums for male postal workers relative to male nonunion private workers of about 25 percent.

Asher and Popkin do not dispute Perloff and Wachter's finding of a large average wage differential between postal and private sector workers, but in their view, the differential is due to wage discrimination against women and minorities in the private sector coupled with nondiscrimination and extensive employment of minorities and women on the part of the Postal Service. However, statistically estimated wage differentials between men and women (or between blacks and whites, etc.) reflect actual discrimination in the marketplace only to the extent that there are no other explanatory factors that have been omitted. Rigorous econometric models such as the ones discussed here naturally try to "control" for all possible factors but are inherently limited by the data. Thus, the extent to which discrimination may explain the postal wage differential is necessarily somewhat speculative.

In sum, there is considerable evidence, based both on econometric studies and the behavior of postal workers and those seeking postal work, of a significant wage premium paid to postal employees. While there are some questions as to *why* the average wage paid to postal employees is higher than for comparable private sector jobs, there is little doubt that the average wage *is* higher.

REPEALING THE PRIVATE EXPRESS STATUTES

The major recurrent postal privatization proposal is to repeal the private express statutes altogether to allow a free market for postal services. The basic impetus for this proposal is the general presumption that competition and private incentives lead to more efficient and better provision of goods and services. In the case of the Postal Service, however, the issue is complex because of the sheer size and complexity of the functions it provides, and the number of people who would be affected.

Benefits of Maintaining the Monopoly

Economies of Scale and Scope

The principal argument raised against lifting the private express statutes is that the Postal Service is a natural monopoly, and therefore the most efficient market structure. If a monopoly were the most efficient market structure, allowing any other market structure, such as competition, would reduce the overall welfare of society, everything else being equal. If the Postal Service were a natural monopoly in the classic sense, it would have nothing to fear from competition, as, being the most efficient producer, it would be able to undercut any entering firms. But proponents of the monopoly argue that the multiproduct nature of the Postal Service leaves it open to "cream-skimming" entry by other firms, and, hence, that it would be unsustainable as a monopoly. Vincent Sombrotto, President of the National Association of Letter Carriers (NALC), expressed this view succinctly before the President's Commission on Privatization:

> Private attempts at mail delivery are not new. In the 1800s, when private express companies were allowed to move mail, they quickly grabbed only the profitable routes within or between urban areas. The resulting imbalance left primarily rural, expensive routes to the Post Office while the private groups skimmed the "cream" off the top. The monetary effects on the public mail system were disastrous, and chaos ensued when many of the private companies failed. *That* is the reality of the Pony Express.[11]

It is unusual, however, for a monopoly to be the efficient market structure *and* to be unsustainable. There is no hard evidence that these conditions hold for the Postal Service.[12] In fact, there is no hard evidence that the Postal Service exhibits significant economies of scale.[13] In response to a question about the Postal Service's concern that cream-skimming would divert the volume needed to maintain its economies of scale, Thomas Gale Moore of the President's Council of Economic Advisers stated:

> I also think the same kind of argument was made by AT&T, when the FCC was considering letting other people into the business. They probably did have a better argument that they had higher fixed costs, but they made the same argument, we need all of this revenue to cover this large fixed cost. And, of course, they seem to have done all right under a competitive system, or more competitive system.[14]

In response to a similar question, Gene Del Polito, Executive Director of the Third Class Mail Association (TCMA), questioned whether the recent increases in volume were helping or hindering the Postal Service:

> . . . in terms of skimming the cream, if you take a look at what kind of service is being provided today, for third-class mail, where the Postal Service meets its service delivery standards 30 percent of the time, not 70, but 30 percent of the time, and where the incidence of nondelivery, nondelivery of properly addressed, properly prepared third-class mail can vary anywhere from 3.5 to 15 percent. . . .
>
> Now there are signs that we think the Postal Service is saying—they are telling us, that perhaps they are in a position now where they can't handle the volume they are currently getting.[15]

Cream-skimming is an expected response to the existence of cross-subsidization if entry is allowed. Cream-skimming is said to occur when a new firm enters the market to supply only that product that is providing the subsidy. That is, if the rate for urban mail is designed to generate revenues *in excess* of those necessary to cover the costs of providing urban mail in order to make up for a shortfall in revenues from rural mail, then there would be room for another firm to enter the market and offer only urban mail—at a lower price. Once this starts to occur, the original firm will have no choice but to eliminate the cross-subsidization in order to match the competition.*

Economic theory predicts that social welfare is enhanced by the elimination of cross-subsidies, because cross-subsidies lead to the misallocation of resources. Similarly, in all but a few unusual cases,[16] monopolies that are unsustainable in the face of competition are inefficient, and the competition will lead to increased social welfare. Nonetheless, there is no hard evidence that the Postal Service is *not* a natural, but unsustainable, monopoly. In this case, there would be social losses incurred from allowing competition to enter—*under the assumption that the natural monopoly was being run efficiently in the first place*. If the postal monopoly is run inefficiently, any efficiency loss from allowing competition to enter would have to be weighed against the efficiency gain from introducing cost-minimizing incentives via competition. Proponents of privatization argue that, although we cannot say for sure that the Postal Service is not a natural monopoly, the evidence from similar industries, such as communications, suggests that there is much to be gained from competition. In his testimony before the Commission, Douglas Adie of Ohio University noted:

> The Postal Service, like AT&T, has argued that it is a natural monopoly, and that competition would yield a less efficient system. Historic evidence, however, suggests that local telephone exchanges that are still protected may never have been natural monopolies at all, and that

---

*Economic theory suggests that removing legal barriers to entry would mean the end of cross-subsidization whether or not the monopoly is sustainable. This is because, if the monopoly is to sustain itself in the face of competition it will be forced to eliminate the cross-subsidies, and if it is unsustainable, the cross-subsidies will be eliminated by the competitive process. (See Owen and Willig, "Economics and Postal Pricing Policy.")

competition improves service, reduces prices, and encourages technological improvements.
   The same evidence has been presented with cable companies in various areas and even with electric power companies.[17]

Of course, statements such as the foregoing do not reassure those who
have relied upon being cross-subsidized. The critical point is that
economic theory also predicts that it is generally more efficient to subsidize directly. In other words, cross-subsidies going from, for example,
urban dwellers to rural dwellers will consist of (1) transfers from urban
dwellers to rural dwellers, which reflect no change in the welfare of society
as a whole, and (2) costs to society in the form of misallocated resources resulting from distorted prices. Direct subsidies, in contrast, are
merely transfer payments and do not add other costs to society by distort-
ing prices. Thus, it should be cheaper for society to subsidize rural dwellers directly with funds from general revenues than it would be to support
the postal monopoly in order to ensure continued cross-subsidization.

The most likely effect of allowing free entry into the market for postal
services would be to render any cross-subsidization infeasible, and, at the
same time, to eliminate any monopoly profits. This would have two immediate implications. First, those services formerly receiving subsidies
would no longer receive them, and their prices would rise to reflect actual
cost. At the same time, of course, those services formerly providing the
subsidies would experience a fall in price. Second, revenues to USPS
would fall, making it likely that it would be forced to substantially revise
its labor contracts.

Postal Workers: The Cost of Transition

The second major issue in a discussion of lifting the private express statutes is what would happen to the people whose livelihood depends on
USPS? Because of the explicit and implicit contracts between postal labor
and USPS, it is clear that action of this magnitude would have to be
phased in with careful consideration for the Postal Service employees. As
noted earlier, there is some evidence that postal employees receive
roughly a 21 percent wage premium over comparable private sector workers—and they receive very generous retirement and health benefits. A
competitive postal service would be unlikely to be able to remunerate its
workers at the current level. Even if a free market for postal services
would be efficient and even though private firms would doubtless be willing to hire postal workers at the competitive wage, the issue of how to
compensate the 800,000 postal workers for the loss of the wage premium
that they now receive would remain.*

---

*This problem is further complicated because the skills acquired by postal work-
ers (other than clerical) are not readily transferred. It reportedly takes up to a

Cross-Subsidized Groups

Assuming cross-subsidization is taking place now, the third major issue is who would be the potential "losers," possibly requiring direct subsidy, if prices were allowed to find their competitive levels, and how much would direct subsidies cost? In theory, the gain from eliminating cross-subsidization should be more than enough to replace the cross-subsidies with direct subsidies. Three principal groups probably receive cross-subsidies now:

Classes of Mail. Opponents of the postal monopoly often allege that first-class mail is subsidizing the other mail classes.[18] The PRC's administrative law judge noted in rate case Docket R74–1, "the postal service has become a tax-collecting agency, collecting money from first-class mailers to distribute to other favored classes." [19] Repeated attempts by other firms to enter the first-class mail market lend some credence to this, but it is difficult to know whether institutional costs have been allocated properly. It may be that the allegations arise simply from first-class mail's seemingly disproportionate share of institutional costs. It is important to be clear, however, that to the extent that the other mail classes cover their total attributed costs, if attributed costs are really equal to incremental costs, there is technically no cross-subsidization occurring.

If first-class mail is subsidizing second-class mail, then lifting the private express statutes would be likely to increase the rates charged to newspapers, magazines, and periodicals. Some proponents of the mail monopoly have argued that these mailers should be subsidized to encourage the free exchange of ideas. A similar point is made with regard to possible cross-subsidization of third-class nonprofit mail, on which churches and charities depend for fund raising. However, there is no reason why these mailers could not be subsidized directly, or to the extent that they are, that the direct subsidies could not be increased.

Rural Areas. One of the concerns most often voiced about the effects of lifting the private express statutes is that it would lead to greatly reduced mail service to rural areas. Vincent Sombrotto of the NALC noted:

> Privatization would result in either higher taxes from the general public in order to pay the burden of keeping the more costly routes or force cut-backs in delivery, particularly to small towns. Rural areas already

---

year for mail sorters and handlers to memorize complicated sorting schemes, and there are similar specific skills to be learned by mail carriers. The implication of this type of "specific human capital" is that it would take some time for postal workers to be as valuable (and thus command the same wages) in another occupation (or even another postal firm with different routes and sorting schemes) as they are in their current one.

suffer from a similar proposal—airline deregulation. Rural people who lost airline service also are losing prompt mail delivery because the Postal Service can not find flights into their area. [20]*

This concern is based on two assumptions: (1) that it is less costly to deliver mail to more densely populated areas where many more households or businesses can be served in both space and time and (2) that rural post offices are generally not economical due to the small number of people they serve. In other words, the general view is that urban dwellers are subsidizing both delivery and retail service to rural areas.

The evidence suggests that there is more cross-subsidization of rural post offices than there is of rural delivery. Average urban and rural delivery costs appear not to differ significantly.** Based on similar experience with airline deregulation, James C. Miller, III, Director of the Office of Management and Budget, estimates that direct subsidization of rural delivery might cost in the vicinity of $26 million annually—much less than the estimated costs to society of the inefficiency due to monopoly.[21] In any event, proponents of postal privatization argue that evidence from the existing private sector suggests that a competitive postal market might continue to serve rural areas at reasonable cost. In this vein, Douglas Adie testified:

> Both UPS and Federal Express now advertise universal service. Although Federal Express is a high-priced service, UPS serves a diverse clientele, including individuals and very small businesses. There is no reason to expect that firms such as UPS would refuse to serve rural areas, though some companies might specialize in high volume areas.
> It is important to note that critics of telephone deregulation raised the same objections, yet phone service has actually penetrated more households since deregulation.[22]

Nevertheless, there are thousands of small, mainly rural, post offices, which primarily provide retail services, that do not cover their costs. Conversion of these small post offices to "community post offices," which are contracted out to small retail businesses such as grocery stores, would probably largely alleviate the cost problem.

Long-Distance, Low-Volume Mail. As noted earlier, whenever uniform prices exist for products with varying costs, there is the potential for cross-subsidization. It is commonly assumed that distance is a major factor

---

*According to a recent report by economists at the Federal Trade Commission, there is no evidence that airline deregulation has led to reduced service to rural areas. Although there is some evidence that fares to rural areas have increased to reflect actual costs, many small towns have experienced an increased frequency of service since deregulation. See J.D. Ogur, C.L. Wagner, and M.G. Vita, "The Deregulated Airline Industry: A Review of the Evidence" (Bureau of Economics, Federal Trade Commission, January 1988), pp. 12–16.

**A study conducted by the Postal Rate Commission of 1980 data found rural delivery to be about 15 percent more costly than urban delivery, on average: about $80 per household per year versus $71 per household per year.

leading to cost differentials in producing postal services. It is clear that it is relatively more costly to send a letter to places where mail volume is low, but distance per se is not a major cost factor, largely because it is the labor-intensive aspects of mail services that have most effect on cost. As indicated earlier, transportation costs compose only 7 percent of total Postal Service costs; most mail cartage is done by private contractors who do not make the high salaries of postal workers. But mail sorting and distribution make intensive use of highly paid postal workers, and it seems that the major cost differentials have to do with the number of sorts involved. To oversimplify the matter, one could say that mailers sending letters within a Sectional Center Facility (SCF) area, or even within the local post office area, are probably subsidizing those who send letters across SCF areas. In fact, many years ago there used to be a discount for local mail, and there is currently a one-cent discount for bulk mail that stays within a Bulk Mail Center area.

Thus, one possible result of lifting the private express statutes might be differential postage rates for local versus nonlocal mail. This outcome seems less certain than in other cases of cross-subsidization because of the lower transaction costs involved in having a uniform rate.

General Transactions Cost Efficiencies

In light of the experience with the breakup of AT&T, allowing free entry into the provision of postal services seems likely to increase transactions costs for both consumers and providers of postal services. Such things as notifying mail service companies of one's change of address—the Postal Service typically handles 40 million such requests annually—could become more onerous, as would determining the amount of postage necessary if rates were to vary by company, by distance, or both. Similarly, there is potential for difficulty regarding liability for lost mail if it is sent through more than one company, and dealings with foreign postal administrations may become complex. Speaking for the NALC, Vincent Sombrotto noted:

> We also protect the mails—no similar safeguards protect privately carried mail. Statutes provide government enforced legal sanctity for mail, helping to protect the American public from mail fraud, false representation or tragic incidents. . . . Congress provides valuable oversight for the Postal Service and plays an important role in correcting problems. Similarly, the statutes protect international mail and ensure smooth service with over 100 foreign countries.[23]

Clearly, some of these functions could be performed smoothly by the private sector as well. Unfortunately, it is difficult to say, *a priori,* how much any increase in transactions cost is likely to be.

Reliance on Postmarks and Similar Issues

Supporters of the postal monopoly often raise the issue of reliance on postmarks by the Internal Revenue Service and for legal binding of contract bids. However, private posts of the early 19th century used postmarks and there does not appear to be any reason that these matters could not be handled in a competitive market by means of contracts and the courts.

Summary of Benefits of Maintaining the Monopoly

The major costs to society of repealing the private express statutes in their entirety have to do with possible inefficiencies from "cream-skimming," the cost of compensating, relocating, or retraining of postal workers, costs of directly subsidizing those who are currently cross-subsidized (which should be zero or negative on net), and increased transactions costs.

Benefits of Repealing the Private Express Statutes

Quality of Service

As with any monopolist, the U.S. Postal Service faces few incentives to provide high-quality, innovative service. Even in the area of parcel post, where the Postal Service faces competition in the form of UPS, it has failed to compete—instead it has virtually ceded the market to its competitor. The Postal Service admits that first-class delivery today is 10 percent slower than it was in the 1960s. Although the Postal Service is doing fairly well at meeting its internal delivery standards—William Burrus of the American Postal Workers Union testified, "In 1986, 95.5 percent met the overnight delivery standards; 87.6 percent met the 2-day (600 mile) standard, and 88.8 percent met the 3-day (cross-country) standard," [24]—these standards are misleading because they refer to the time taken for a letter to go from the originating post office to the destination post office. Thus, a letter could easily meet the "overnight" standard even when it takes 2 to 3 days to go from sender to receiver, simply by sitting in the mailbox, sitting some more in the originating post office, and sitting again in the destination post office.

Although volume has nearly doubled in the past 12 years and unit costs should decline with volume in a natural monopoly—presumably making it possible to offer better service at the same price or the same service at lower prices—postal service has declined and postal costs have increased. Not only is twice-daily mail service to residences—the norm until the 1950s—a thing of the past, but in 1978, the Postal Service terminated home delivery in favor of cluster boxes for all newly constructed housing developments, apartment buildings, and townhouses.

Efficient Provision of Services

Any discussion of privatization of postal services must address the widespread public perception that, while the current provision of services may not be optimal, USPS performs well enough that any proposed changes are likely to be for the worse. Although major first- and third-class business mailers have increasingly voiced dissatisfaction with the price and quality of current postal services, opinion polls show the public at large is fairly satisfied.[25]

The reason for the discrepancy between "public" perception and the perceptions of the major mailers is crucial: while the consuming public may be relatively satisfied with postal services, it is important to keep in mind that more than 92 percent of all mail either originates from or is destined for business and only 17.5 percent of mail originates from households.[26] The consuming public is a minor customer of the USPS, and postage is usually a minor component of a given household's budget. However, for business mailers, postage can be a fairly high proportion of the budget, and high-quality service can be critical.

Why should the general public be concerned about costs to business mailers? First, because these costs are passed on to the public in the form of higher prices for goods and services, and second, because costs that are unnecessarily high as a result of the inefficient use of resources are real costs to the whole society because the wasted resources could have been put to better use. Estimates of the potential cost savings from lifting the postal monopoly range from $4 billion to $12 billion annually.

These figures are based on two approaches. The first derives from the 21 percent wage premium estimated to be paid to USPS employees applied to the 83 percent of postal costs deriving from labor.[27] The second approach compares USPS price increases with the price decreases of the private mail industry, holding constant profit rates over time and assuming the operations of the USPS to be similar to those of private mail service firms.[28]

Thus, society may be paying a high price for maintaining the Postal Service as a regulated monopoly. Whether that price is worth paying depends on the benefits imparted from maintaining the status quo, and the costs and benefits of alternative market structures.

Comparisons of the rate of increase in postal costs relative to inflation are often used to demonstrate Postal Service inefficiency. In fact, these comparisons are extremely sensitive to the years chosen for comparison (see table 1). For example, between 1970 and 1987, the Consumer Price Index (CPI) increased by 284 percent, whereas first-class postage increased by 367 percent. In other words, postage rates increased about 30 percent faster than inflation. A comparison of 1971 and 1987, however, shows the CPI increasing by 274 percent and first-class postage by 275 percent: virtually identical rates of increase.

TABLE 1.—*Consumer Price Index and First-Class Postage Rates, 1970–1987*

Year	CPI	First-Class Postage
1970	119.1	$0.06
1971	123.1	0 .08
1972	127.3	0 .08
1973	138.5	0 .08
—	—	—
1986	331.1	0 .22
1987	337.7	0 .22

SOURCES: USPS and *CPI Report.*

How Postal Services Might Be Provided in a Free Market

The major stumbling blocks to lifting the private express statutes may well be problems with implementing the transition to a free market, rather than problems with such a market, once achieved. That is, there could well be very high one-time costs to compensating postal employees for forgone benefits or retraining them for other jobs. There may also be significant costs to shifting to a system of direct rather than indirect subsidies for rural customers and certain classes of cross-subsidized mailers.

Transition costs aside, what might such a free market look like? First, one might expect a mix of firms offering universal or near-universal service, with many local companies similar to modern-day courier services. Firms like UPS and Federal Express already deliver to virtually every address and would be well situated to gradually expand mail services. Small firms might deliver mail only within city limits, and medium-size firms might deliver within regions such as the northeast corridor. One would expect subcontracting agreements to be common: that is, because the Postal Service already has a national network in place, Purolator Courier might accept mail bound for anywhere in the country and then contract with the Postal Service to deliver it from the closest major hub to those small towns that Purolator does not serve directly. Similarly, rather than continue its already poor parcel post service, USPS might continue to accept packages, but contract out all handling and delivery to UPS.

Liability for the mail in cases of subcontracting would be handled, as it is in other types of subcontracting of delivery services, by contract and by manifest and logging systems.* Thus, it would always be clear which party was responsible for any lost or damaged mail.

One could easily imagine frequency of delivery being a basis for competition. One could also imagine firms establishing a "basic" delivery schedule, and then a pricing scheme wherein one could pay extra for more frequent delivery.[29] Thus the market would provide not only price competition but also a larger variety of services and service quality.

The postal service market would probably develop principally as competition for mailers, rather than receivers of mail; the individual sending the letter would choose which company to use. The chosen company might subcontract with another company for final delivery, but the flow of contractual arrangements would start with the mailer and flow through the initially chosen company. The recipient would possibly have some options, as mentioned earlier, to purchase extra service from some company or other. But presumably any company that agreed to accept a letter destined for that recipient would still be responsible for getting it there—just as it is possible now to have 6-day delivery service from USPS and occasionally receive something from Federal Express. The recipient, however, would have an incentive to notify the correspondents that the quickest means of communication would be via the company with which special arrangements were made.

In the same vein, it is the mailer, not the receiver who pays the cost of postage. Thus, if the cost of mailing to rural areas goes up, it will only be borne by rural dwellers to the extent that they are sending mail to other rural dwellers. Thus, whereas rural delivery might need direct subsidization in the beginning, it seems quite possible that those firms that want to be national competitors will be induced to serve most rural areas—either directly, or subcontracting with USPS or someone else—as a matter of reputation. If continued subsidies are needed, as already noted, it should still cost society less to provide direct subsidies than it does to maintain the cross-subsidies.

The integrity of mail could still be ensured by law, and enforcement could be provided by a division of the Justice Department, as could the laws against mail fraud. International mail could be negotiated by a trade association of the mail services firms, and changes of address could conceivably be handled by a service similar to that offered by many firms for notifying all one's credit cards in the event of theft or loss.

---

*Mail Boxes Etc., a firm that subcontracts with UPS, USPS, Federal Express, and the like, to collect mail and to receive it, has had no problems in handling this aspect of the transaction.

Summary of Benefits of Lifting the Private Express Statutes

There are many reasons to believe that a competitive market would produce more efficiently than the current monopoly. And, although a competitive market for mail services, left entirely unregulated, might lead to higher prices for some services, such as rural delivery, advocates of lifting the private express statutes believe that the overall cost savings to society from competitive mail service would outweigh the cost of directly subsidizing any "losers," so that everyone would ultimately gain.

Having weighed the costs and benefits of repealing the private express statutes, the Commission believes that society would ultimately be best served by a competitive market for postal services. However, the Commission recognizes that this ultimate goal could not be implemented overnight because of the potential for dislocation of postal workers and the need to put into place safeguards to ensure postal service to those areas that might not be attractive to private entrepreneurs. Thus, in the following sections, the Commission has made a series of recommendations for action as part of a gradual transition to a competitive market. Regarding the private express statutes, the Commission recommends:

Recommendation (1)

The private express statutes should be repealed. The benefits in terms of quality of service, cost-efficiency, and the incentives for innovation clearly outweigh the costs of the transition to a free market. However, there must be a gradual phase-in period with compensation of postal workers and postal management for loss of benefits or earnings.

IMPLEMENTING POSTAL PRIVATIZATION

One general approach to implementing postal privatization, which has varied in its specifics, has been to suggest converting the Postal Service to an employee stock ownership plan (ESOP), both to compensate employees with Postal Service equity ownership, and to increase their incentives to raise productivity. Thomas Gale Moore of the Council of Economic Advisers and Douglas Adie of Ohio University both testified that an ESOP should provide positive incentives for innovation and should be an attractive option for postal workers and management.[30] Representatives of Postal Management were not so sanguine about the ESOP proposals, however. Earl Ogle, President of the National Association of Postmasters of the United States, had this to say:

It does not take long to see through this ploy. After the grace period has expired in this scenario, large private industries will move in to compete. Though the employee-owned post office will own its facilities, most likely it will not have adequate capital reserves because of financial limitations of employee owners. A large corporation could easily eliminate the employee owners by charging below-market rates and absorbing the loss over several years, until the employee-owned companies go bankrupt. Then the employees are left with nothing.[31]

Economists who have studied the Postal Service, however, do not doubt that it would be able to compete once freed from regulatory encumbrances. Indeed, Professor Douglas Adie expressed the opposite concern in his testimony—that the Postal Service might have so much market power as to make competition difficult for others.[32]

The ESOP proposal has been put forth in three major guises:

1. Sell the Postal Service in its entirety as a public stock offering and give postal workers a special option on the stock—then give them 5 years to improve efficiency before lifting the private express statutes. This approach has the advantage of leaving the Postal Service largely intact and allowing it to realize whatever transactions and other economies result from vertical integration. However, as noted above, some people have expressed concern about the ability of private express companies to compete with an intact, efficient Postal Service.

2. Divest the Postal Service into five companies corresponding to the current regional divisions, in order to make the stock offering more manageable and to encourage competition. Then sell it to the employees and repeal the private express statutes. The disadvantage to this alternative is that, given evidence of how Federal Express and UPS operate, there are economies to be gained from vertical and horizontal integration that would be lost in this type of divestiture.

3. Simply allow the postal employees at any given postal facility to buy the facility and contract with the Postal Service to provide the same services as before. Repeal the private express statutes after some adjustment period. This might be more manageable for the employees, since they would only be buying into that aspect of the Postal Service with which they were most familiar. Again, the disadvantage here would be lost economies from disturbing the current vertical integration.

Having reviewed the various proposals for converting the Postal Service to an ESOP, the Commission believes that, although employee ownership should be encouraged, the specifics of how the Postal Service should be turned over to the private sector should be developed as part of the gradual phase-in of privatization, with substantial employee participation. Thus, the Commission recommends:

Recommendation (2)

In exploring the possibilities for private ownership of the Postal Service, priority should be given to employee ownership, either in whole or in part. Employees should be active participants in the decision-making process.

Removing the Private Express Restrictions in a Limited Fashion

Since the transition to a complete repeal of the private express statutes must take place gradually, one means of introducing competition into the Postal Service immediately is to remove the monopoly restrictions in a limited fashion.

Third-Class Mail

Allowing competition in the delivery of addressed third-class mail is an approach being advocated by the Third Class Mail Association. Addressed, third-class mail is currently held by USPS to be covered by private express statutes along with first-class mail; second-class mail (periodicals, magazines, etc.), unaddressed third-class mail, and fourth-class mail are not covered because they are not considered to be "letters." Gene Del Polito of the Third Class Mail Association testified that lifting the private express statutes for third-class mail might be a useful experiment with private mail delivery:

> If private third-class mail delivery proves to be a success, then our nation's policymakers will better know the benefits that can be derived from private sector alternatives. If private delivery proves to be a bust, nothing will be lost. Retention of the letter mail monopoly over first-class mail during the period of experimentation will ensure the preservation of our current universal mail delivery system. . . .[33]

Supporters of the postal monopoly are opposed to any diversion of the mail, out of concern that its economies of scale would be threatened by significant decreases in volume (third-class mail constitutes about 40 percent of the mail stream today). Nevertheless, the Commission found the evidence in favor of removing the private express restrictions on the carriage of third-class mail to be compelling, and recommends:

Recommendation (3)

The private express restrictions on third-class mail should be removed immediately. There is no justification for the monopoly on third-class mail, and allowing private delivery would serve as a useful test of the viability of a competitive postal system.

Rural Areas

Another proposal has been to allow competition in the delivery of mail only for certain well-defined rural routes. The underlying reasoning for this proposal is that there could be no cream-skimming of the more profitable urban routes if only the rural routes were made available to competition. If the Postal Service is providing efficient service *and* heavily cross-subsidizing rural routes, then competing with USPS on these routes should be difficult. If, however, the private sector succeeds in serving the rural routes at prices no greater than under USPS, this strategy could go a long way toward calming the fears of rural America that postal privatization would leave them underserved. If the private sector cannot compete with the Postal Service's ability to cross-subsidize rural delivery, that would be an indicator that some direct subsidization would be needed to maintain universal service. One drawback of this approach is that it is difficult to define what constitutes a rural area.

The Commission believes that private delivery of mail to rural areas could not jeopardize any economies of scale or scope enjoyed by the Postal Service, because, if anything, rural delivery is being cross-subsidized by revenue from other postal operations. The Commission thus recommends:

Recommendation (4)

The private express statutes should be repealed for rural delivery immediately.

The Letter Box Prohibition

A common proposal is to repeal the prohibition on the use of letter boxes for any item that does not bear postage. Opponents argue that allowing access to letter boxes by other than Postal Service personnel would endanger the integrity of the mail. Supporters argue that the letter box rule is an arbitrary prohibition that serves no useful purpose, but only inhibits private delivery of items that are not covered under the other private express statutes. The Commission recommends:

Recommendation (5)

The prohibition on private use of letter boxes should be repealed immediately. The letter box prohibition is an unnecessary barrier to competition and an imposition on the rights of citizens.

Urgent Letters

Another possible stimulus to competition would be to loosen the restrictions on what constitutes an "urgent" letter. In written testimony, James Campbell, legal counsel to the Air Courier Conference of America,* argued in favor of reducing the amount by which the private rate for "urgent" mail is required to exceed that of first-class mail:

> Unfortunately, USPS regulations which delimit the scope of permissible competition effectively require private express companies to charge at least *double* the first class mail rate (in which term, for simplicity, we include the priority mail rate) or more than $3, whichever is higher. 39 CFR 320.6(c) (1987). The purpose of this minimum price requirement is, of course, to protect first-class mail against "cream skimming" private competitors. . . . Without settling this debate, however, it is possible to observe that the "double postage" rule is a case of regulatory overkill.
>
> The current double postage rule gives first-class mail so much protection that it interferes with the pricing of express services.[34]

Here again, the issues have to do with how much it is necessary to protect the Postal Service from losing volume to competition. The greater the price advantage of first-class mail, the less incentive mailers will have to use private express carriers, and the less risk that substantial mail volume might be diverted from the Postal Service. However, proponents of competition argue that any price differential should be adequate to ensure that competition occurs only on the basis of quality of service, and that if the private companies can offer that much better service, consumers should be allowed to benefit from that better service. The Commission believes that the current criteria for qualification as urgent mail are too restrictive, and recommends:

----

*The Air Courier Conference of America is a trade organization of private express couriers, including Federal Express, UPS, and Purolator Courier.

Recommendation (6)

The restrictions on urgent mail should be loosened immediately.

Contracting Out

As observed earlier, the Postal Service already engages in extensive contracting out of certain functions; in fiscal 1987 roughly one-tenth of the Postal Service budget went to contracted services—principally transportation and rural delivery. Because of the high price of unionized postal workers, and, in particular, the union-imposed restrictions on the use of part-time help, replacement of postal workers with contracted workers often leads to cost savings. However, there are several major areas where contracting out may have additional benefits.

Increased contracting out of retail functions is likely to lead not only to cost savings but also to tangible improvements in service. While consumer surveys do show high overall rates of satisfaction with USPS, especially in urban areas there are frequent reports of consumer frustration with both the limited hours of retail services and the frequent long waits necessary to transact business.[35] Franchised postal outlets at retail stores such as Sears and Safeway would provide better hours, more convenient locations, and possibly better service.

The Postal Service currently comprises about 29,000 post offices and 500 SCFs. According to the PRC, roughly 25,000 of the post offices now operating are so small that they effectively serve as mailboxes that also sell stamps and weigh packages. A GAO study, conducted in the early 1980s, estimated that roughly 7,000 post offices could be closed or contracted out as community post offices with no significant deterioration of service.[36] Data from the PRC suggest that these community post offices, wherein postal services are provided by a local merchant, usually in a section of an existing store, are roughly half as costly to run as those run by USPS.

Because of peak loading, the restrictions regarding part-time workers are most inefficient for the mail processing or sorting function (note that UPS makes extensive use of cheap part-time labor for sorting). In a written submission to the Commission, John Crutcher noted studies showing that "access to more part-time labor could have saved $200 million in costs in mail processing in 1989."[37] For this reason, increased contracting out of the mail-processing function could lead to large efficiency gains.

Delivery service is another function that could be contracted out to a greater extent. Currently, about 4,500 rural routes, or about one-tenth of the total, are served by private "star route" carriers. In 1987 delivery made up 29.9 percent of Postal Service costs, or $9.8 billion. If the 21 percent wage premium is correct and could be saved by contracting out, that would yield potential savings of roughly $2 billion annually.

A 1982 GAO study showed significant cost savings to be had from contracting out cleaning functions.[38] This study, comparing the cost of using private contractors for cleaning buildings of less than 10,000 square feet versus using postal employees, found that the cost for cleaning by a private contractor averaged $0.77 per square foot, as opposed to $1.88 for cleaning by postal employees. The estimated savings from only those three (out of five) regions examined were $15 million per year from using private contractors. GAO also estimated that savings of 20 to 30 percent could be realized for buildings in excess of 10,000 square feet, yielding a savings of $45 million to $77 million annually.

In view of the extensive evidence as to the benefits of increased contracting out, the Commission recommends:

Recommendation (7)

The Postal Service should more actively pursue contracting out opportunities in all its functions, and should focus special attention on retail, delivery, and sorting functions. In pursuing contracting out, full consideration should be given to employee interests.

SALE OF POSTAL ASSETS

The Extent of USPS Facilities

The United States Postal Service (USPS) oversees what is probably the largest number of square feet operated by a single civilian entity in the country. The USPS has some 210 million square feet as of 1988. Of that, about half is leased, and the other half owned. The USPS uses this space primarily to provide retail postal services and to sort (or "process") mail.

As of 1988, USPS operated out of roughly 35,000 buildings, about 29,500 of which were leased, and about 5,500 of which were owned.* As a rule of thumb, USPS prefers to own rather than lease any building providing in excess of 5,000 square feet. Thus, although USPS owns only about one-seventh of the buildings it uses, that one-seventh comprises over half the space, or about 120 million square feet. Not surprisingly, these 5,500 owned buildings include virtually all of the Sectional Center Facilities where the major processing of mail occurs.

---

*These numbers do not include "community post offices," which are contracted out to small businesses, such as grocery stores.

Net Book Value of USPS Assets

The most recent figures available on the value of Postal Service assets are shown in table 2. The $5.6 billion figure shown in table 2 for the Net Book Value (NBV) of USPS's "accounting" depreciation. Because of accounting rules and incentives built into the tax code, "accounting" depreciation may be quite different from "economic" depreciation, which can be thought of as the actual decline in productivity of a capital asset. NBV also does not take into account changes in market value over time, whether changes specific to the market for the particular type of asset, or general price inflation. For example, real estate prices have generally increased rapidly in the past 20 years. Part of that increase is due to general economy-wide inflation, and part of it is due to increases in the relative price of real estate as undeveloped land has become scarce. Thus, NBV fails to accurately portray the current value of the property if sold in today's market.

TABLE 2.—*USPS Capital Assets, September 30, 1984*

Property and Equipment	Thousands
Land	$548,352
Buildings	3,969,337
Equipment	2,795,619
Subtotal	7,313,308
Less allowances for depreciation	2,500,644
Subtotal, net book value	4,812,664
Construction in progress	686,965
Leasehold improvements, net of amortization	109,512
Total, net book value	5,609,141

SOURCE: U.S. Postal Service.

Fair Market Value

The fair market value (FMV) is the value of assets in current dollars under prevailing market conditions, and thus best represents the price for which those assets could be sold. The only accurate way to determine FMV is to conduct individual appraisals of each facility. This obviously extremely costly exercise has never been done for Postal Service assets.

In the absence of individual appraisals, the best source for evaluating Postal Service assets is a 1985 study by L.B. Christensen and Associates,

USPS Real Output, Input and Total Factor Productivity, 1963–84. This study uses USPS data to develop an estimate of the fair market value for USPS facilities based on a methodology that attempts to account for economic depreciation or the rate of replacement. The study derives the estimated real capital stock for each asset in 1972 dollars and uses Bureau of Labor Statistics asset-specific price indices to derive an estimate of the 1984 fair market values from the real capital stock. These figures are shown in table 3.

TABLE 3.—*USPS Capital Assets*
Christensen's Estimated Fair Market Value, 1984

[In millions of dollars]

	Real Stock 1972 dollars	Price Index	FMV 1984 dollars
Land	$761.3	4.742	$3,610.085
Buildings	2,303.3	2.379	5,479.551
Equipment:			
Vehicles	186.3	2.026	377.444
Customer Service Equipment	31.7	1.892	59.976
Postal Support Equipment	226.5	1.401	317.327
Mail Processing Equipment	481.3	1.973	949.605
Optical Character Readers	139.5	0.946	131.967
Total Equipment			1,836.319
Total Estimated Fair Market Value			10,925.955

SOURCE: L.B. Christensen and Associates, *USPS Real Output, Input and Total Factor Productivity, 1963–84*, October 1985, p. V–31.

Table 3 shows that Christensen's estimated fair market value of USPS's real capital assets (not including new construction) in 1984 dollars is approximately $10.9 billion—more than twice the net book value. However, the FMV is still likely to be understated because it is based only on average asset-specific price indices, while the Postal Service has quite a few extremely large urban buildings, such as the Grand Central Station Office in Manhattan, whose value has appreciated considerably more than the average for real estate.

Highest and Best Use Program

USPS has an ongoing project to convert obsolete buildings in central business districts to their "highest and best" use. In the past 3 to 5 years USPS has taken about 12 of these downtown facilities and either sold them or entered into joint ventures to develop them. In the latter instances, the developer puts up the money and USPS either sells the land and rents back whatever space is needed for a continued postal "presence," or it continues to own the land and leases it to the developer. The latter is the case in the recent plans for the Grand Central Station Office, where the developer will develop about 1 million square feet and the Postal Service will continue to occupy about 150,000 square feet. According to USPS staff, the present discounted value (PDV) of the stream of earnings to USPS from this arrangement is expected to be in the vicinity of $100 million, and the total PDV of those projects already contracted is about $180 to $200 million, including the Grand Central project. It should be noted, however, that these figures appear low in light of the estimate in the *USPS Comprehensive Statement on Postal Operations, 1985* that the aggregate income from the long-term lease agreement for the San Francisco Rincon Annex property was "anticipated to exceed $3 billion over its 65-year term." Such a flow of earnings would yield a PDV in the vicinity of a half-billion dollars.

In addition to the dozen or so projects already contracted, USPS is looking at another 10 to 12 projects similar to that carried out with the Grand Central Station Office, but not so large. The present discounted value of the total anticipated earnings from these ventures was estimated by USPS staff to be in the area of $250 million.

The Commission believes there is great potential for converting Postal Service assets to their highest and best use. This is particularly important if the Postal Service is to be in a position to compete in the private sector. Conversion to highest and best use should be consistent with preserving the asset value of the Postal Service for conversion to an ESOP, and, to that end, postal employees should be involved in the decisionmaking. The Commission recommends:

Recommendation (8)

The Commission supports the efforts of the Postal Service to ensure, to the maximum extent possible, the highest and best use of its assets.

SUMMARY

The introduction of competition into the market for postal services has already been quite successful in those niches of the market where it has been allowed. Complete repeal of the postal monopoly promises to provide better, more innovative service at competitive prices. At the same time, the Commission recognizes the potential dislocations this action may cause to postal employees and the potential disruption in service to isolated areas. For these reasons, competition must be phased in with consideration and adequate compensation of affected postal employees; direct subsidies should be provided for rural areas as needed.

The Commission has recommended less dramatic steps that can be taken to improve the quality and efficiency of postal services by introducing and encouraging competition in limited areas. Competition in the carriage of third-class mail and in rural delivery as well as increased competition in express mail should stimulate the Postal Service to improve its own efficiency. At the same time, the results of injecting competition in these limited areas should serve as useful guides to policymakers as they move toward a fully competitive postal system.

NOTES FOR CHAPTER 7

1. University of Michigan, *Mailstream Study 1977*, U.S. Postal Service and United Parcel Service.

2. Testimony of Douglas Adie, Ohio University, submitted to the President's Commission on Privatization, Hearings on the Postal Service (hereinafter cited as the Postal Hearings), January 28, 1988.

3. See 39 CFR 320.1, Note 1.

4. For a discussion of Ramsey pricing as it applies to the Postal Service, see Bruce M. Owen and Robert D. Willig, "Economics and Postal Pricing Policy," in Joel L. Fleishman, ed., *The Future of the Postal Service*, Praeger, 1983. For a more technical discussion of the difficulties in determining and allocating postal costs, see Melvyn Fuss, "Cost Allocation: How Can the Costs of Postal Services Be Determined?" and Leonard Merewitz, "Commentary," Chapter 3 in *Perspectives on the Postal Service*, Roger Sherman, ed., American Enterprise Institute for Public Policy Research, Washington, DC, 1980.

5. Testimony of Preston R. Tisch, House Post Office and Civil Service Subcommittee Appropriations Hearings, March 4, 1987. The *USPS Comprehensive Statement on Postal Operations, 1987* gives the figure $4.57 billion, but this includes all standard procurement.

6. USPS, *AP13 Financial and Operating Statement Report 1987.*

7. Jeffrey M. Perloff and Michael L. Wachter, "Wage Comparability in the U.S. Postal Service," *Industrial and Labor Relations Review*, vol. 38, no. 1, October 1984.

This study was done under contract with the U.S. Postal Service during the 1981 labor negotiations.

8. Douglas K. Adie, *An Evaluation of Postal Service Wage Rates* (Washington, DC: American Enterprise Institute for Public Policy Research, 1977).

9. Martin Asher and Joel Popkin, "The Effect of Gender and Race Differentials on Public-Private Wage Comparisons: A Study of Postal Workers," *Industrial and Labor Relations Review* 38(1), October 1984. This study was done under contract to the APWU and the NALC during the 1981 labor negotiations.

10. Sharon P. Smith, "Are Postal Workers Over- or Underpaid?" *Industrial Relations*, vol. 15, no. 2, May 1976.

11. Testimony of Vincent Sombrotto, National Association of Letter Carriers, Postal Hearings, January 28, 1988.

12. W.J. Baumol, J.C. Panzer, and R.D. Willig, *Contestable Markets and the Theory of Industry Structure* (San Diego: Harcourt Brace Jovanovich, Inc., 1982).

13. Rodney E. Stevenson, "Postal Pricing Problems and Production Functions," Ph.D. Dissertation, Michigan State University, 1973.

14. Testimony of Thomas Gale Moore, Council of Economic Advisers, Postal Hearings, January 28, 1988.

15. Testimony of Gene A. Del Polito, Third Class Mail Association, Postal Hearings, January 28, 1988.

16. See G. Faulhaber, "Cross-Subsidization: Pricing in Public Enterprise," *American Economic Review*, vol. 65, December 1975, pp. 966–977, and W.J. Baumol, J.C. Panzer, and R.D. Willig, *Contestable Markets*.

17. Adie testimony.

18. Adie testimony.

19. Initial decision, Docket R74-1, vol. 1, p. 13.

20. Sombrotto testimony.

21. James C. Miller, III, "End the Postal Monopoly," *Cato Journal*, vol. 5, no. 1 (Spring/Summer 1985), p. 155.

22. Adie testimony.

23. Sombrotto testimony.

24. Testimony of William Burrus, American Postal Workers Union, Postal Hearings, January 28, 1988.

25. For public opinion, see *USPS Comprehensive Operating Statement 1985*, p. 31. For the third-class mailer's perspective, note Gene Del Polito's testimony that "the service is bad and it is continuing to deteriorate. And it is not even up to where the Postal Service says the level of standards should be for third-class mail."

26. University of Michigan, *Mailstream Study 1977*.

27. See Perloff and Wachter, "Wage Comparability."

28. See Paul MacAvoy and George McIsaac, "The Record of the United States Federal Government Enterprizes," p. 17. presented at the University of Rochester

"Conference on Privatization in Britain and North America," Washington, DC, November 6–7, 1987.

29. See Owen and Willig, "Economics and Postal Pricing Policy."

30. Moore testimony and Adie testimony.

31. Testimony of Earl Ogle, National Association of Postmasters of the United States, Postal Hearings, January 28, 1988.

32. Adie testimony.

33. Del Polito testimony.

34. Testimony of James Campbell, Air Courier Conference of America, Postal Hearings, January 28, 1988.

35. For example, see "Why Your Mail Is So Slow," *New York Magazine,* November 1987.

36. Comptroller of the United States, "Replacing Post Offices with Alternative Services, a Debated, but Unresolved Issue," September 2, 1982, GAO report GGD–82–89.

37. Testimony of John Crutcher, Postal Rate Commission, Postal Hearings, January 28, 1988.

38. Report by the U.S. GAO, "The Postal Service Can Substantially Reduce Its Cleaning Costs," December 28, 1982, GAO–AMD–82–23, pp. 5, 8.

Chapter 8

Contracting Out:
Military Commissaries; Prisons

Contracting has been one of the government's principal ways of doing business throughout our nation's history. In fiscal 1987, federal departments and agencies used contracts to purchase $197.3 billion worth of goods and services from private firms. Private firms working under contract produce rocket launch vehicles; manage the development of future national airspace system technology; provide automated data processing services; conduct medical and educational research; build the airplanes, tanks, and ships essential to national defense; and provide pencils, paper, and other basic but essential goods and services. The federal government also produces commercially available goods and services on its own. By contracting out these commercial goods and services to the private sector, the government might save $7 billion while improving services. This chapter discusses contracting in general and specifically contracting out military commissaries and prisons.

Although a bipartisan consensus has supported reliance on the private sector for commercially available goods and services since 1955, many government agencies have resisted contracting out. They have also initiated new commercial activities using government employees rather than relying on commercial sources to meet new requirements. The federal government began to formalize procedures for contracting out when the Eisenhower administration issued Bureau of the Budget Bulletin 55–4 in 1955. As mentioned earlier, that bulletin affirmed that the "Federal government will not start or carry on any commercial activity to provide a service or product for its own use if such product or service can be procured from private enterprise through ordinary business channels."[1]

Once the policy favoring private provision was adopted, government managers could contract as they saw necessary, with few systematic guidelines about cost comparison procedures. On March 3, 1966, the Bureau of the Budget issued Circular A–76 to establish formal rules governing cost competitions and defining protections to mitigate any adverse effects on government employees.[2] Although that policy has been reaffirmed by every administration of both political parties since 1955, the principle has not been applied effectively. Instead, each administration renews its commitment to the principle, tinkers with procedures, and ends up accomplishing little to contract commercial functions to the private sector.

In March 1979, the Office of Management and Budget (OMB) revised Circular A-76 through administrative procedures providing for public comment. This revision introduced the concept of encouraging the government to compete with the private sector for work currently being done by government employees. This competition would be based on a performance-oriented statement of the government's work requirements, thus shifting the emphasis from "how the government does business" to "what the government needs done." The shift from "how" to "what" did more than provide an opening for private firms to compete with government operations; it also gave government managers incentives to review their organizations to develop more efficient procedures.

In 1981 OMB again proposed reforms of Circular A-76 procedures and published a comprehensive revision of the document in August 1983. Today, OMB estimates that nearly $20 billion of commercial goods and services are produced by the government.[3] If those activities were competed with the private sector, the government could procure the same level of goods and services at $7 billion lower cost. OMB also estimates that about 750,000 positions—450,000 of them within the Department of Defense—could be competed with the private sector. Nearly half of these positions are accounted for by 28 job categories ranging from pipe fitters and motor vehicle mechanics to librarians and automated data processing specialists.[4] OMB directed federal agencies to give these job categories priority as they conduct Circular A-76 cost competitions.

The Congressional Budget Office has estimated that federal government contracting for commercial services could affect as many as 1.4 million employees, but this estimate includes positions now protected by legislation.[5] If all of these services that could be contracted out are considered, the value of government-operated commercial services could approach $40 billion annually.

The policy of encouraging private firms to compete with government-operated commercial activities to produce goods and services to meet government's responsibilities was supported by most witnesses testifying before the President's Commission on Privatization. The continuing broad support for these goals reflects the many potential benefits from a greater role for the private sector. Therefore, the Commission recommends:

Recommendation (1)

The federal government should rely on the private sector for provision of commercially available goods and services. Because contracting provides a means to procure the same level of service at reduced cost, it is not in the public interest for government to perform functions in competition with the private sector.

Contracting-Out Procedures

Procedures for Federal Commercial Activities

Circular A–76 is predicated in part on the idea that competition will both reduce costs and increase service quality. Rather than seeking to contract out all commercial activities, Circular A–76 permits government agencies currently providing goods and services to compete with private firms for government's work requirements.

Current A–76 procedures require detailed management planning before activities are transferred to the private sector. The circular requires a review of all commercial activities within the federal government to determine whether they are appropriate for contracting out. Functions essential to national defense, related to patient care in government medical facilities, or otherwise excluded by legislation are protected from competition.

The circular and its supporting documents require agencies to identify all commercial activities and schedule them for competition with the private sector.[6] It provides both the policy framework and detailed instructions for agency managers to compare costs of government commercial activities to private sector bids to perform the same function.

If a function is performed by an organization of fewer than 10 employees within a civilian agency and "if fair and reasonable prices can be obtained from qualified commercial sources," the function may be contracted out without competition. Within the Department of Defense, managers have some discretion to contract out using a simplified cost comparison procedure for work performed by units of fewer than 45 employees. For larger activities, a cost competition must be conducted.

Once a function is identified for competition, the agency must develop a performance work statement (PWS) describing the government's needs in terms of measurable performance standards. This PWS becomes the baseline against which competitors will bid. Once the PWS is developed, agency managers whose activity is under review must analyze their operations to develop a most efficient organization (MEO), which then becomes the government's bid. The government manager is encouraged to adopt innovative, flexible management techniques, rather than follow previously established operating procedures. To win an A–76 competition, private competitors must beat the government's bid by 10 percent, a factor added to reflect costs anticipated in any transition. For new commercial functions, the government is not given the chance to bid. The private provider is preferred as long as the government contracting office determines that costs are reasonable.[7]

How A-76 Competitions Produce Savings

A-76 procedures benefit the government even when agencies win competitions with the private sector (as they do about 40 percent of the time).[8] In normal operations, government agencies do not face the same pressures for cost-efficiency as does the private sector. Although few organizations ever achieve the levels of efficiency depicted in economics texts, the analysis required for cost comparisons helps identify inefficiencies in government operations and promotes reforms to address them.

Government managers face obstacles to efficiency rarely encountered in the private sector. Government managers lack a baseline for comparisons, have no imperative to make a profit, and are not challenged by competitors who might capture their business if they fail to deliver in the most efficient manner. Although government managers can be encumbered by legislative and fiscal restrictions that force them to operate inefficiently, competition can identify the managerial changes necessary to effect savings within a government organization, or provide for transfer to more efficient providers in the private sector. Even when functions remain in-house, the Department of Defense (DOD) has reported to Congress, "With competition as a motivator, in-house organizations streamlined their operations 18 percent, on average, and won. . . . Total anticipated annual dollar savings was $21.8 million" for these competitions.[9] To help in-house organizations win cost competitions, DOD commissioned a study "How Winners Win" highlighting organizational changes, methods of eliminating unnecessary work and developing multiskilled workers, and other strategies that strengthen organizations facing competition.[10]

Promise and Performance

A December 1986 report by the General Accounting Office (GAO) reviewed studies of the A-76 process done after 1982 by the Congressional Budget Office, the National Academy of Public Administration, the Office of Management and Budget, the President's Private Sector Survey on Cost Control, and the Heritage Foundation. The GAO found that contracting out could result in the transfer of between 95,000 and 500,000 current government positions to the private sector, at savings of between $0.9 billion and $4.6 billion, depending on the number of positions converted.[11]

Some observers, especially labor organizations representing potentially affected employees, contend that contracting is not so cost-effective as its proponents claim. As Robert E. Edgell, government procurement specialist for the American Federation of Government Employees (AFGE) testified to the Commission, "We have found that . . . forecasts are based on estimate-to-estimate accounting. The hard reality that you must search for in your deliberations is the [comparison of the] estimated cost to the actual payment."[12]

Precise comparisons between the amounts awarded in contracts and the cost of services when they are delivered present several accounting challenges. In a 1986 review of contracting under Circular A-76, OMB reported to the House Committee on Appropriations that costs increased for 95 of the 609 contracts awarded by 10 civilian agencies between 1982 and 1986. All but three of the agencies had at least one contract for which costs increased. Overall, however, actual costs for all 4 years were 0.2 percent less than the amounts awarded in the contracts. OMB maintains that wage determinations by the Department of Labor, required under the Service Contract Act, often force employers to pay higher wages than they had anticipated in their bids. Over time wage increases also would usually increase the government's costs. Moreover, in many contracts, the government requests additional services or modifies work requirements after the contract is awarded, making cost comparisons with the previous work invalid.[13]

The Department of Defense reported to Congress in 1984 and 1986, covering 235 contracts and 181 contracts, respectively. The contracts were written in fiscal years 1982 through 1984, so that DOD analysts had at least a full year's performance on each one as a basis for the report. The analysts discovered that contract costs rose over the 1 to 3 years following the awards by 11.2 percent in the first report and 9.7 percent in the second report. However, government wage increases would have raised the government's cost, so that contract savings were reduced from 24 percent to 22 percent in the first report, and from 36 percent to 33 percent in the second report. The savings are understated in these comparisons because, in calculating costs for postcontract workloads, the government includes only wage increases and does not attempt to estimate the full costs to the government of work requirements added to the original contract.[14]

From 1981 through 1987, agencies studied approximately 72,000 positions for contracting to the private sector using Circular A-76 procedures. Robert F. Bedell, Administrator of the Office of Federal Procurement Policy in OMB, testified that these studies resulted in savings (or shift to higher-priority needs) of 45,737 positions. The cumulative cost reduction for the period totaled $2.8 billion.[15] During 1986 alone, these savings included $86.5 million and 5,506 positions from DOD, $9.2 million and 409 positions from the General Services Administration, and $5.2 million and 869 positions from the Department of Transportation.[16] The evidence clearly indicates that contracting out has resulted in substantial savings. The Commission recommends:

Recommendation (2)

The federal government should pursue aggressively competition through contracting because it has proved generally
to be cost-effective.

Contracting Experience

Private firms of all sizes, state and local governments, and the federal
government itself have had considerable experience in contracting for
commercial activities. Private firms contract for functions such as food
services, automated data processing, legal services, architectural and
design services, and secretarial and word processing services. They do so
because they need help to handle intermittent excessive workloads or because contracting costs less than providing the service in-house. State and
local governments' interest in contracting has been heightened by a growing demand for services, overloaded public delivery capability, and increasingly constrained budgets.

The Commission is impressed by the range of opportunities identified
for transferring commercial activities to the private sector. It believes that
more aggressive leadership could achieve more substantial savings. The
Commission recommends:

Recommendation (3)

Current OMB Circular A–76 management within the federal
government has not proved effective. Aggressive promotion
is needed throughout the Executive Branch. Management
incentives and penalties, including decentralization, should
be strengthened to improve program performance throughout the federal government.

Implementation of guidelines requiring agencies to designate some portion of their activities for cost competition with the private sector has
been a problem for every administration. OMB establishes categories for
positions that might be considered commercial, then penalizes agencies by
withdrawing the estimated savings from their budgets. If the agency does
not meet its study quota, the quota will be carried over to the next year,
along with additional requirements for competitions. In discussion with
Commission staff, OMB officials claimed that unless the cost comparison
goals are directed centrally, through budget pressure, they will not be

achieved. Agency managers allegedly prefer to have implementation instructions imposed rather than to deal directly with employees who might be adversely affected.

At the same time, agency managers believe that directions from OMB do not coincide with their priorities, their perception of the Administration's position, commitments required by authorizing and appropriations committees of the Congress, or effective management strategies.

Recent Changes in Federal Efforts

The level of resistance to centralized management of contracting studies indicates the need for a better system of penalties and incentives related to contracting if performance is to improve. OMB procedures used to require all government-operated commercial activities that remained in-house to be reviewed and cost-competed on a 5-year cycle. The goal was not met at the scheduled end of the first cycle in September 1987. Executive Order No. 12615, signed by the President on November 19, 1987, articulated a new policy requiring federal agencies to meet specific annual study goals. These were established by *Management of the United States Government, Fiscal Year 1988*. Beginning in fiscal 1989, agencies are to conduct annual A–76 cost comparisons at a rate of not less than 3 percent of each agency's total civilian personnel.[17]

No one testifying before the Commission believes that the fiscal 1988 quotas will be met, even though OMB indicated an intention to propose several administrative modifications to Circular A–76 in its fiscal 1988 management guidelines. These included requiring (rather than permitting) commercial activities with 10 full-time-equivalent (FTE) positions to be contracted out without competition, extending the 45 FTE discretionary range now used by DOD throughout the government, and allowing OMB to direct agencies to contract services performed by organizations with more than 500 FTE positions when similar organizations had been studied over time and agencies had lost more than 75 percent of competitions.[18] More than a year later, OMB had not implemented these proposals.

OMB projects that 47,000 positions, including 25,000 DOD positions, should be competed under A–76 in fiscal 1988. In 1986, fewer than 11,000 positions were competed, approximately 80 percent by DOD. In 1987, 12,068 positions were competed, 78 percent of them from DOD.[19] Between 1981 and 1987, federal departments and agencies studied only 72,068 of the 757,000 positions that OMB estimated possible for cost competition with the private sector.[20]

A great deal remains to be done, even within DOD, if the President's management improvement goals are to be achieved. Executive Order No. 12615 and the guidance already published by OMB make contracting for current commercial services established policy and provide ample instructions to government agencies for implementing that policy. The issue is one of executing, rather than establishing, policy.

The Commission supports the principle that competition is one of the most effective means of identifying more effective methods and of allocating resources. At the same time, current employees have experience in their positions and familiarity with their responsibilities. Current employees, after all, win nearly 40 percent of all cost competitions, so their skills are a resource on which program officials should be able to rely. Direct contracting without allowing current federal employees to compete for their positions would be unfair to them and would deny the government the benefits that can be achieved by defining an MEO and reorganizing internally. Therefore, the Commission recommends:

Recommendation (4)

Commercial activities should not be contracted without appropriate in-house competition.

Resistance to Contracting

Witnesses at the Commission's hearings on contracting identified three sources of resistance to effective competition for providing commercial goods and services to the federal government: government managers, government employees and their unions, and members of Congress who have large constituencies of federal workers.

The resistance of government managers stems from three concerns. First, they fear that contracting out will to some degree erode their managerial control, causing performance to suffer and diminishing their effectiveness. Second, managers are concerned that jobs lost through contracting could lead to reductions of their grade levels, because the number of employees supervised is often a factor in job classification. Finally, managers want to protect their employees from adverse actions.

Managers opposed to contracting can obstruct implementation. Even when a government agency's MEO wins a competition, the agency sometimes retains its original organization rather than completing managerial reforms identified in the MEO. According to Gene L. Dodaro, Associate Director, General Accounting Office (GAO), an Army Audit Agency analysis of 25 commercial activities that had remained in-house found that the MEO was not implemented properly or promptly in 8 cases.[21] When government managers believe their functions might be contracted out, they tend to use their discretion to drag out the competition with the private sector. GAO's review of DOD contracting between October 1978 and December 1986 revealed that approximately 40 percent of A-76 studies required more than 2 years to complete and some took as long as 8 years. Dodaro observed that these lengthy studies can result in lowered morale and reduced productivity.[22]

Failure to conduct Circular A-76 studies is clearly one of the biggest obstacles to transferring additional commercial functions to the private sector. During fiscal years 1984 through 1987, 22 federal departments and agencies competed only 5.1 percent of the positions eligible for contracting under Circular A-76.[23] The Veterans Administration, for example, has delayed for more than 2 years A-76 studies for services such as food preparation, laundry services, and grounds maintenance at VA hospitals, using the exemption for services "incident to direct patient care."[24]

Eight of the 22 largest agencies and departments within the government have not studied contracting any of the commercial activities within their organizations. Some of these agencies have few positions identified for competition (for example, the United States Information Agency had goals of competing only 184 positions, and the Federal Emergency Management Agency was assigned to compete only 107 positions during fiscal years 1984 through 1987). The Department of Justice failed to compete any of the 1,547 identified positions in this period. Only five agencies (the Departments of Commerce, Defense, Energy, Transportation, and the General Services Administration) achieved more than 10 percent of their goals, and no agency surpassed half of its goals.[25]

Government managers have legitimate concerns about A-76 procedures. Staff devoted to planning, conducting, and deciding cost evaluations related to competitions are diverted from other activities. Robert A. Stone, Deputy Assistant Secretary of Defense for Installations, testified that DOD has 1,700 people devoted full-time to its A-76 program—at a cost of between $150 million and $300 million a year.[26] These cost figures, however, include staff support for DOD management that are part of general DOD administrative expenditures.

Management resistance can be minimized when managers perceive limits to their mission performance as a result of resource shortages and when savings generated by A-76 competition are retained by the agency. For example, DOD's top management supported contracting when it concluded that competition would enable shifting personnel and funds to higher priority requirements. As a result, DOD leads all agencies in implementing A-76 programs.

Management resistance to A-76 competition might be reduced if agencies had better incentives to promote contracting. Until 1981, all savings resulting from A-76 competitions were required to be returned to the Treasury. Managers contended that they lost both the positions and the funds involved in competition. In 1981, the Department of Defense was allowed to retain all A-76 cost reductions and to reallocate them among other budget categories. Under this procedure, savings gained by contracting can be used to achieve other agency priorities. The Commission recommends:

Recommendation (5)

Competition and contracting may reduce budget demands, but they are primarily means to improve the efficiency and effectiveness of government services. Savings generated by this program should be eligible to be used as incentives to pursue competition and contracting.

Unless managers are induced to support contracting, it is unlikely that needed improvements in efficiency will be achieved. OMB has recognized the need for stronger incentives in administration of the A–76 program, and Executive Order No. 12615 contains a provision allowing agencies to plan on the basis of funds that reflect "retention of expected first year savings . . . for use as incentive compensation to reward employees covered by the studies for their productivity efforts, or for use in other productivity enhancement projects."[27] That program change was issued too recently for the Commission to assess its effects, but it is consistent with the Commission's recommendations.

It is also consistent with the policy favoring private sector provision of commercially available goods and services. Indeed, opponents of contracting have proposed legislation requiring that funds saved through contracting be returned to the Treasury.[28] Although the Commission recognizes the complex challenges involved in developing incentives within the budgetary process, such incentives are a precondition to making contracting out work in the public interest.

Effects on Employees

Successful implementation of this report's recommendations depends on the support of the people involved, especially employees of affected federal agencies. Congress and the executive branch both recognize the importance of safeguarding the employment protections of those who serve the public through government. Contracting out by government agencies is already regulated by procedures safeguarding the rights of federal employees within the executive branch, and wage protections enacted under the Service Contract Act of 1965.

The Commission does not intend to abrogate any of the rights and privileges of any federal employees who might be affected by transferring some functions to the private sector. This consideration applies not only to the concept of contracting out but also to the Commission's recommendations related to the air traffic control system, Amtrak, the Postal Service, the management of loan portfolios, and other specific policies discussed in other portions of the report.

The Commission recognizes that employees will resist, rightfully, any suggestion of transferring their work without proper consideration of their rights and needs. Wherever possible, the Commission supports proposals that encourage federal employees to become partners in improving service to the public through the private sector. The Commission recommends:

Recommendation (6)

The federal work force should be assured that normally any staff reduction should be achieved through attrition.

The Commission's overriding goal is improved service to the American people. As citizens, federal employees will share in the improved services and reduced costs that will result from implementation of these recommendations.

Government employees and their unions often consider cost competition a direct threat, either from a diminution of benefits and seniority, or, in the worst case, from loss of jobs. People who choose government careers for security, stability, and patriotic reasons tend to see their commitment as devalued by a forced move to the private sector. Federal employees' unions have lobbied vigorously against contracting out and have opposed competition for existing functions and for new government requirements. Books and pamphlets, such as *Passing the Bucks* by the American Federation of State, County, and Municipal Employees (AFSCME), contend that contracting out threatens the American way, fails to provide good-quality service, and saves less money than proponents claim.[29]

Lobbying by employees and unions has resulted in some restrictions on contracting for commercial services at the federal, state, and local levels. At the federal level, many of the congressionally imposed restrictions on contracting for commercial activities are, in part, responses to concerns expressed by federal employees. OMB submitted a list of 28 legislative restrictions—nine of them affecting DOD—that not only prohibit contracting out for designated services, but at times retain small-scale personnel limitations that inhibit managerial improvements within agencies.

The Army, for example, is required to maintain civilian personnel strength at Army depots performing communications-electronic depot maintenance above the strength on September 30, 1985. The Army Corps of Engineers is prohibited from conducting A-76 studies at any reservoir in Mississippi. The Department of Housing and Urban Development's public and Indian housing programs must maintain a minimum average staffing level of 1,270, regardless of need. Although automated cargo examining and processing are reducing the need for staff, the Customs Service was required to maintain an average of 14,891 employees in 1987. The VA is required by law to maintain medical care employment at an average of 194,140 FTE, regardless of improvements in services and savings that might be achieved at lower levels. The Federal Aviation Administration (FAA) is prohibited even from pilot testing the contracting of maintenance for national airspace systems facilities, even though the systems maintenance work force is short of trained personnel.[30]

In 1987, Congress placed a new provision in the DOD authorization bill permitting base commanders to establish their own policies regarding OMB Circular A-76 and presidential contracting policy. Although service headquarters opposed such a measure, fearing that it would bring A-76 competitions to a halt, some base commanders indicated that, given such discretion, they would use it for activities different from those promoted by headquarters.[31] DOD managers expect the amendment to decrease the Pentagon's A-76 output substantially. With this legislative mandate, achieving the executive order's requirement of competing 25,000 DOD positions in fiscal 1988 will require aggressive management by DOD.

This array of administrative and legislative restrictions demonstrates that even policies with clear general statements can be resisted in many particular applications. The Commission considered recommending a broader legislative mandate to the A-76 program, proposing simplified administrative procedures, or suggesting elimination of the 10 percent cost differential that now gives agencies an advantage over private competitors. These changes, however, are administrative, not policy, changes. They could be made easily, once Congress and the executive branch concur on applications of a long-established, bipartisan policy.

Employee Protections

Current Provisions

People are any organization's greatest resource, and the government's programs for contracting out through competition pay considerable attention to the people who might be adversely affected by contracting decisions. They are entitled to "right of first refusal" privileges to go to work for the contractor if the agency's bid loses. (N 48 C.F.R. 7.305[c]. See also 48 C.F.R. 52.207-3.) If they go to work for the contractor, employees must be paid at a comparable wage, as provided under the Service Contract Act. Employees who chose to remain with the federal agency after a contract award receive priority for transfer to positions within the agency and cannot lose their grade for a 2-year period. Their salary will never be reduced, but they could lose cost-of-living increases until the wages of the lower grade exceed their pay at the higher grade.

If placement within the government is not immediately possible, adversely affected employees receive priority consideration for new positions within their agencies and are eligible for out-placement assistance, including reasonable costs for training and relocation. In large cities with substantial federal employment, OMB and the Office of Personnel Management (OPM) are considering experimental programs to improve the placement of adversely affected employees within the government.

The Commission is concerned about appropriate assurances for people who might be adversely affected by changes resulting from contracting. Therefore, the Commission recommends:

Recommendation (7)

Competition through contracting of services should be accelerated to generate increased savings. Adequate safeguards against employee displacement should be maintained.

This recommendation should be understood in light of Recommendation (6), above. The Commission intends for no layoffs to occur but recognizes that an acceleration of competition for government-operated commercial services could result in changed requirements in affected agencies. OMB, OPM, and other agencies should intensify efforts to improve opportunities to identify appropriate vacancies and to place people so as to make effective use of their talents.

Additional Opportunities

Opportunities available to federal employees to retain their jobs could be strengthened. OPM Director Constance Horner testified in support of a modified employee stock ownership plan (ESOP) that would provide opportunities for federal employees to join corporations that bid for government-operated commercial activities, or to become owners of any company that won a contract. Known as the Federal Employee Direct Corporate Ownership Plan (Fed CO-OP), the plan contains procedures for current federal employees to buy firms that win contracts to perform their work.

Under current laws governing ESOPs, Fed CO-OP would apply to organizations with a minimum of 50 full-time employees that provide commercial services.[32] Once a function is designated for contracting by the agency, current employees could form a corporation and bid on the function; or an outside firm could bid, with a requirement to hire all the government employees who did not obtain other government jobs and to provide them with equity in the firm. The government would take half of the money saved by contracting out and award it to the former government employees in the form of stock. The stock would accumulate in each employee's account until the employee leaves the Fed CO-OP, when it would be collected as an additional employee benefit.

Fed CO-OP contains an extensive range of safeguards for current employees. No employee could be discharged from a Fed CO-OP during the first 180 days of the contract. If the Fed CO-OP had to separate employees involuntarily after the 180-day interval, employees would retain all the benefits to employees under federal reduction-in-force procedures, including full payment for placement assistance.

As OPM Director Horner testified, this proposal is intended to change employees' perspective on contracting. She observed, "The same federal employees who, in the past, feared losing their jobs because of contracting out will now retain their jobs and have a strong interest in the success of the contract and the company." [33] This changed perspective results from developing a stake in the success of one's work, and it offers genuine opportunities to improve the lot of workers involved in transferring commercial activities to the private sector. Fed CO-OP is only one application of the ESOP approach, a method that has successfully assisted privatization efforts in other nations. The Commission recommends:

Recommendation (8)

Employee stock ownership plans (ESOPs) can be excellent devices for furthering competition and contracting. Although Fed CO-OP is still a demonstration program, it, and other ESOP options, should be pursued by the federal government.

Effective organizations are as attentive as possible to the human needs of their people. The recommendations addressing the effects of contracting out on government employees are a major step to enhance these employees' personal security while improving government operations.

Applications

The principle of contracting for government's commercial needs so that agencies do not compete directly with the private sector is long-established, bipartisan, and efficient. The Commission shares these commitments and the concern of those who believe that many needs could be met more efficiently if the principle were more frequently applied in practice. The Commission has not compiled a comprehensive list of functions that might benefit from contracting. The Commission considered contracting issues related to national airspace system operations, the management of the government's loan portfolios, Postal Service operations, and several other areas of government operations. Those recommendations are addressed in other sections of the report. It received public comment related to opportunities to use contracts for the commercial development of space, to conduct research presently done through the National Institutes of Health, to manage some of the government's solid and hazardous waste facilities, and for several other areas. The Commission decided to make no recommendations on those issues, because of their technical complexity and the limited time for completion of this report. The Administration should consider the full range of government organizations with commercial counterparts for contracting at appropriate times. In this chapter we offer two areas—military commissaries and prisons—as examples where contracting appears likely to enable the private sector to improve government's performance.

MILITARY COMMISSARIES

Created in 1825 to serve military personnel at remote posts where provisions were unavailable or very expensive, the military commissary system today operates 428 grocery stores—240 in the continental United States and 188 overseas. Both Congress and the Department of Defense regard commissary privileges as an indirect benefit within the military compensation package. The benefit—which totals approximately $1.8 billion annually—comes from price advantages and savings resulting from the nonprofit, tax-exempt status of the commissaries. It is made possible in part by funds appropriated for DOD—$735 million in fiscal year 1987 and $760 million in fiscal year 1988. According to the last independent survey conducted for DOD, members of the military, retirees, and their dependents save an average of 25 percent on their grocery bills by shopping at commissaries.[34]

In many continental U.S. markets, commissaries compete with local merchants. Retailers contend that, if they managed the commissaries, they could provide the same 25 percent discount to military customers at less cost to DOD.[35] Although the cost-effectiveness of the commissary benefit has been questioned, the Commission examined only competition between commissaries and commercial groceries, seeking more effective means of securing that benefit. The Commission has no intention of recommending its elimination.

The Privatization Task Force of the President's Private Sector Survey on Cost Control (the Grace Commission) explored the possibilities of privatizing the commissary system to improve the stores and reduce the need for appropriated funds. It estimated that total privatization through the sale of commissaries could save approximately $2.4 billion over 3 years. In a review of these findings, the GAO concluded that the analysis had been insufficient to support selling the commissaries. It estimated that the projected savings were overstated and that $1 billion was a more realistic projection. GAO recognized that military personnel have come to regard commissary privileges as an important component of compensation. Hence, GAO recommended that Congress should redefine the criteria justifying support of commissaries to recognize their role in military compensation; their effects on recruitment, retention, and motivation; and the cost-effectiveness of alternative methods of achieving these recruitment, retention, and morale benefits.[36]

Among armed forces personnel, commissary privileges consistently rank among the top three benefits of military service, particularly among married personnel (51 percent of those surveyed).[37] DOD believes in-house management of commissaries is very important, and doubts that private industry could improve the efficiency of commissary operations. Lieutenant General Anthony Lukeman, of the Marine Corps, serving as Deputy Assistant Secretary of Defense for Military Manpower and Personnel Policy, testified that commissaries' costs, which include shipping provisions to overseas commissaries, are at least as efficient as commercial retailers' costs on a percentage-of-sales basis.[38]

DOD concerns about private sector operation of commissaries include fears (1) that a loss of direct control might make it difficult to retain the compensation benefit at the 25 percent level over the long term; (2) that, over time, contractors would cut corners or raise prices to increase profits; and (3) that, if the private contractors proved unsatisfactory, DOD would be unable to generate the political support needed to regain control of the commissary system.[39]

The food marketing industry maintains that the military commissary system within the continental United States is especially suited for privatization because the private sector has ample capacity to perform the task. The industry contends that employees managed by a private company could operate commissaries more efficiently. The systemwide contracting of shelf-stocking has already yielded a 40 percent savings for that function. Although one contracting test in Yuma, Arizona, yielded no savings, the President has called for further testing of contracting in commissaries.

The President's fiscal 1988 budget called for a test to assess the private sector's ability to manage commissaries. The private sector manager must continue to offer a 25 percent savings to military shoppers, maintain or improve service, and accomplish both goals with fewer appropriated funds than currently required by military managers. OMB wants the test to start in July 1988. The food marketing industry has asked to participate actively in designing the test.[40]

The Commission concluded that, given the abundance of commercial retail grocery stores in the United States, contracting could be an appropriate method to involve the private sector in strengthening the military commissary system. The Commission recommends:

Recommendation (9)

Private sector operations can offer greater efficiencies as a result of competitive stimulus. Therefore, private sector businesses should participate in managing and operating military commissaries in the United States.

Commissaries provide an example of opportunities to use contracts to achieve greater private sector participation in an area where there is substantial private sector experience. Although many people would argue that incarceration, as an integral part of law enforcement, is an inherently governmental function, officials at the local, state, and federal levels are exploring methods of using contractors to improve current conditions.

PRISONS

The nation's prisons and jails are under increasing strain. From 1979 to 1986, state and federal prison populations increased by approximately 74 percent, to a total of about 550,000 persons.[41] Local jails in mid-1986 held another 274,444 inmates.[42] Total capacity has not kept pace with the increase in prisoners, however, and confinement facilities are seriously overcrowded. Taking into account different methods of reporting, the Bureau of Justice Statistics, an arm of the Department of Justice, reports figures under both "highest" and "lowest" measures of capacity. State prisons, as a group, operated in 1986 at 106 percent of their highest capacity and at 124 percent of their lowest capacity. Federal prisons operated at 127 percent and 159 percent of their highest and lowest capacities, respectively.[43] Crowding in federal institutions has intensified in the wake of relocations required by facility destruction by Cuban inmates at two federal prisons in Georgia and Louisiana.

Many prisons are out-of-date as well as overcrowded. The average prison cell is 40 years old, and 10 percent of convicts are placed in prisons built before 1875.[44] As a result of these conditions, 41 states and the District of Columbia were either under court order to improve conditions or subject to litigation challenging their operations as of 1983.[45]

Some states have invoked emergency provisions, allowing the premature release of prisoners to relieve pressure. In 1983, 15 states reported the early release of 21,420 prisoners.[46] These actions may diminish deterrence. However, crowding is not diminishing either, and judicial pressure to do something about it is increasing. Judicial solutions—closing institutions, limiting their population, and fining jurisdictions that do not respond to court orders—tend to increase population pressures at other institutions and financial pressures on governments. Although crime rates have declined slightly in recent years, many citizens still support incarceration as a necessary part of law enforcement. They do not believe that early release is an appropriate response to crowding. At the same time, however, the public often rejects prison construction bond issues at election time.

Recently, federal, state, and local governments have begun to contract with private firms to design, construct, and operate confinement facilities. These firms involve private ownership, at least of the management company, and sometimes of the buildings and grounds. Contracting gives public officials a method to meet their responsibilities to provide facilities to accommodate prisoners while avoiding some of the constraints imposed by spending limitations and local resistance to prison siting decisions.

Authority to enter contracts for the construction and operation of federal prisons has been derived from statutes. Federal law (18 U.S.C. Section 4082) commits convicted federal offenders "to the custody of the Attorney General of the United States," who "shall designate the place of confinement where the sentence shall be served." (18 U.S.C. 4082[a].) The Attorney General may "designate as a place of confinement any available, suitable and appropriate institution or facility whether maintained by the federal government or otherwise. . . ." (18 U.S.C. 4082[b]). The General Counsel to the Federal Bureau of Prisons, drawing on the legislative history of Public Law 89–176, which amends Section 4082, has concluded that "there is authority to contract with private facilities, both halfway houses and traditional prisons and detention facilities. . . ."[47]

Contract prison operations can add another layer of accountability when current prison authorities are found deficient by the courts. A private contractor who operates the prison in violation of the law or fails to comply with contractual provisions can be brought into court to enforce the contract or be subjected to fines or civil penalties. If private contractors fail, government agencies can take over responsibility for the facility. Severely mismanaged government prisons can also be placed under the control of a court, but that sanction has not proved very effective, precisely because the court will probably have to rely upon the very agencies being found in violation for continued operations of the facilities.

Overview of Current Contracts

Contracting for services and nonsecure facilities is a common practice in the field of corrections. Virtually all the individual components of corrections (such as food services, medical services and counseling, educational and vocational training, recreation, maintenance, transportation, security, and industrial programs) have been provided by private contractors. Private, low-security facilities have served the juvenile justice system in America throughout this century. In 1983, nearly two-thirds of the 3,000 juvenile detention and correctional institutions in the United States were private facilities.[48] A recent survey found nonsecure, community-based adult facilities (such as group homes, halfway houses, and community treatment centers) under contract in 32 states.[49] The federal Bureau of Prisons (BOP) contracts out its 330 Community Treatment Centers, 234 of them to private agencies.[50] Most current contracts involve relatively low security facilities. Contracted jails, however, do include maximum security wings or cells, because they must accommodate pretrial suspects, including some violent offenders.

Private operation of at least minimally secure confinement institutions, however, is more recent, less familiar, and more controversial. These newer contracts are for places of true incarceration, such as prisons, reformatories, jails, and detention centers. As of early 1988, private companies were running confinement institutions (totaling more than 3,000 beds) in at least nine states. These include secure juvenile facilities, minimum security state facilities for preparole cases and for return-to-custody parole violators, jails, county prisons, and federal detention centers for the Immigration and Naturalization Service (INS).[51]

These facilities are managed under contract to government agencies. Facilities are owned by the government and leased to the management company, or vice versa, through a variety of leasing arrangements. In either case, government bears all current costs of ownership, including amortization payments on construction and financing. Savings occur because facilities can be more quickly constructed, better designed, and more efficiently operated under contractual arrangements.

Prison contracts include contingency plans to deal with emergencies or disruptions, such as strikes, riots, or bankruptcy. It is unclear whether contracted prison guards have the right to strike, but the absence of such a right has not prevented public guards from engaging in strikes, sickouts, and other job actions. Provisions could be written for state police and National Guard units to be the ultimate recourse in the event of a strike by private guards, as they are now for public prison employees. Because a strike or other disruption would allow the government to terminate a contract, however, unemployment as the result of a strike may be a more credible threat to private than to public guards. Moreover, private contractors can be required to post a performance bond to defray the government's cost if it has to take control of a contracted facility.

Current contract periods range in length from 1 year to 32 years. All contracts have provisions for termination, and the longer contracts can include provisions for periodic renewal and renegotiation of terms. Some contracts allow the operator to fill unused space with prisoners from other jurisdictions, thus reducing requirements for additional facilities.[52] Interjurisdictional prisons and jails have been long and widely advocated. Where cooperation between governments has been difficult to achieve, private contracting might help to overcome some political, fiscal, and administrative obstacles to establishing such facilities.[53]

Opposition to Correctional Contracting

Opposition to contracted prisons comes from several sources. Some critics believe that only government employees may legitimately carry out a coercive sanction such as imprisonment, because they consider law enforcement inherently a government function. Private wardens might directly or indirectly influence the allocation of "good time" credits, thus affecting the application of the punitive powers of the law.[54] Current prison officials sometimes view contracting as a challenge to their control, and they usually oppose transferring these functions to private contractors.

Political dimensions of the operation and management of prisons inevitably enter into discussions of imprisonment. Even among segments of the population that strongly support the idea of imprisonment as appropriate punishment, nearly every specific proposal for establishing or constructing a facility encounters opposition from the community surrounding the potential site.

There may be some indirect legal obstacles to prison contracting, although no state has enacted legislation specifically prohibiting privately operated correctional facilities.[55] Most state statutes are silent on the matter, but a few states have passed specific legislation authorizing contractual prison operations.

Recommendations for Correctional Contracting

Contracting appears to be an effective method for the management and operation of prisons and jails at any level of government. Contracting cannot properly extend to the policymaking, legislative, or judicial functions. By contracting, the government delegates some of its executive or administrative responsibilities. It does not relinquish its authority or abdicate its ultimate responsibility. Prisons remain subject to the supervision and regulation of the government—and, most important, subject to the rule of law—whether they are run by government employees or by a private agency.

The Commission recommends:

Recommendation (10)

Contracting should be regarded as an effective and appropriate form for the administration of prisons and jails at the federal, state, and local levels.

The Commission believes that contracting for the operation of entire facilities—and not just particular programs within them—is an appropriate option for government. It therefore recommends:

Recommendation (11)

Proposals to contract for the administration of entire facilities at the federal, state, or local level ought to be seriously considered.

The Commission noted there are legitimate concerns about accountability and liability in the private operation of prisons. Although these questions cannot be conclusively resolved at this time, they have not proved to be insurmountable obstacles in jurisdictions where contractual operations have been established.

Accountability

Critics charge that contractors will be insulated from the public and not subject to the same political controls as government officials. Proponents respond that properly written contracts require private facilities to adhere to government standards, thus ensuring control by public officials. In addition, some operators are contractually bound to the standards of the American Correctional Association (ACA), the field's primary professional association.[56] Several facilities have been accredited by the Commission on Accreditation for Corrections, a private organization that applies ACA standards in a voluntary program of accreditation. (Most government correctional facilities, outside the federal Bureau of Prisons, however, are not accredited.) Accreditation offers several advantages to prison operators, including lower liability insurance premiums as a result of sound operations. Moreover, all contracts include provisions for government monitoring. Competition thus supplements, rather than supplants, political and legal mechanisms of control.

Liability

All witnesses testifying before the Commission agreed that government should retain ultimate legal liability for the operations of its prisons, including those under contract. This premise is supported, at least at the federal level, by the statutory authority that allows "places of confinement" to be maintained by groups other than the government but specifically commits "the custody" of the prisoners to the Attorney General. (18 U.S.C. Sec. 4082.)

Government liability for the private operation of prisons might arise directly against a government for violating the constitutionally protected rights of prisoners [57] or under traditional theories of tort law.[58] In certain instances, governmental liability might arise through the acts of its con-

tractors.[59] The degree of government liability and its apportionment between a government and its prison contractor could be influenced by a
number of factors, including state tort laws, specific contract provisions,
the degree of government control and supervision of day-to-day contract
activities, and other factors. These issues and others [60] will be subjects of
future litigation. The Commission notes that the American Bar Association, with the support of the National Institute of Justice, is currently
working to develop model prison contract provisions to guide resolution
of issues related to future prison contracts.[61]

Despite the many unresolved liability issues surrounding prison contracting, these issues have not prevented the establishment of current
lower security contract facilities and should not be seen as insurmountable
obstacles to further prison contracting initiatives.

The Commission recommends:

Recommendation (12)

Problems of liability and accountability should not be seen
as posing insurmountable obstacles to contracting for the
operation of confinement facilities. Constitutional and legal
requirements apply, and contracted facilities may also be required to meet American Correctional Association
standards.

Quality and Cost Control

Because experience has been limited, there is little foundation for comparing the quality and costs of government-managed facilities with contractually managed ones. In a national survey of 52 correctional agencies
having contracting experience with the private sector,[62] responding administrators cited more benefits than liabilities. Although 31 listed "better
quality of service" as a benefit, 21 listed "poor quality of service" as a
liability. Three-quarters of the agencies reported some savings. Although
some agencies also reported losses, some contracts were initiated in response to court orders to improve conditions and thus not intended primarily to save money. Moreover, even agencies not reporting savings
"concluded that the operational benefits more than outweighed the cost
factor." [63]

A review of recent total-management contracts, conducted by the Council of State Governments and the Urban Institute, concluded that these facilities "are perceived by government agency oversight officials as being
quite satisfactory. We have seen no indication to date that a government

agency has been dissatisfied to any significant extent with the quality of the service provided." [64]

Most available figures on costs of government prison operations are incomplete. If taken from budgets that include only direct operating costs, they may not include items such as design, construction, depreciation, debt servicing, rent or its equivalent, taxes paid or forgone, pensions, benefits, staff training costs, other general personnel costs, legal services and insurance and other liability costs, some maintenance and transportation costs, administrative overhead, external oversight, and other interagency or indirect costs. In contrast, a contractor's fee tends to capture more of the costs of running a prison and to clarify which costs remain with the government. In general, it would seem reasonable that contracting for many of the functions involved in operating a prison would be subject to the same cost advantages as the other government operations discussed earlier in this chapter.

Federal agencies could rectify the lack of information about total government costs in corrections by developing and publishing accurate and thorough cost information. Therefore, the Commission recommends:

Recommendation (13)

The Bureau of Prisons should be asked to prepare an analysis of total government costs for an existing federal correctional institution, following guidelines similar to those of OMB Circular A–76, Part IV (Cost Comparison Handbook), Chapter 2 (Developing the Cost of Government Performance). The General Accounting Office, the Office of Management and Budget, and/or the National Institute of Justice should be asked to cooperate with the Immigration and Naturalization Service (INS) in preparing cost studies that compare currently contracted detention facilities with those run directly by the INS.

Further Experiments

The foregoing recommendations emphasize evaluating current activities of the Bureau of Prisons and the INS. The Commission believes, however, that the case for contracting is strong enough to justify further experimentation to learn more about the feasibility of contracting.

The INS has reported considerable satisfaction with its current contracts for operations of prisons at about a half-dozen of its detention facilities.[65] The Commission recommends:

Recommendation (14)

The INS should be encouraged to continue to experiment and to evaluate the cost and effectiveness of contracting its detention facilities.

The Bureau of Prisons has not contracted any of its higher security facilities but has contracted all its community-based facilities and some facilities for youth offenders. The Bureau of Prisons appreciates the potential contribution of contracting to the speed and flexibility of needed expansion.[66] It has proposed contracting a new, 500-bed, minimum-security facility for convicted immigration offenders, and it has explored contracting for low-population or special-needs prisoners, such as juveniles, women, protective custody cases, or medical patients. The Bureau of Prisons has been cautious, however, about contracting any facilities for its "mainstream" population—those confined in U.S. prisons.

The Bureau of Prisons has a reputation for excellent management of its facilities. Although the Bureau of Prisons is not under court order and most of its facilities are accredited, it is already interested in private construction, financing, and at least some private management.

If the Bureau of Prisons were to contract even one representative new facility, it would be valuable as a test for prison contracting. The Bureau of Prisons should participate in the design and execution of the evaluation.

Therefore, the Commission recommends:

Recommendation (15)

The Bureau of Prisons, in cooperation with the National Institute of Justice and the National Institute of Corrections, should commission a study of the feasibility of contracting for the private operation of a Federal Correctional Institution or U.S. Penitentiary. As part of this study, the Bureau, as an experiment, should contract for the private operation of one new facility comparable to at least one government-run facility, and cooperate with outside researchers in an evaluation of the results.

New Construction and Lease-Purchasing

Private contractors can effect savings in financing and constructing, as well as in operating, new prisons. Private companies are more likely to design for efficient operation; they can build faster, at better prices, and can usually pay off debt more quickly than governments can. The flexibility offered by the private sector can help the government adjust the size of its prison system more rapidly and at less cost. Under lease-purchase arrangements, private companies design, finance, and construct new prisons, which they own and the government leases or lease-purchases. The Bureau of Prisons has expressed interest in lease-purchasing for new facilities, but its authority to do so is still under discussion in the executive branch.[67]

Many people, however, do not want the prison system to expand. Other opponents of lease-purchase arrangements are concerned that besides avoiding debt limitations and capital budget restrictions—which are advertised as advantages of lease-purchasing—this approach may bypass the will of voters, who frequently defeat referenda on the issuance of new bonds to finance prison construction.[68] These objections, of course, would apply to state, rather than federal, institutions, because federal prison siting decisions are not subject to control by local governments. Nor are federal prisons financed through bonds that are subject to referenda.

The Commission recommends:

Recommendation (16)

The Bureau of Prisons and the Immigration and Naturalization Service should be encouraged and authorized to pursue lease-purchase arrangements for the addition of new facilities.

Research

The greatest potential in contracting for prison management is at the state and local levels, where the role of the federal government is mainly that of an adviser, facilitator, and clearinghouse of information. The Department of Justice has played this role effectively since the emergence of modern private prisons in the early 1980s. Through the National Institute of Justice (NIJ) and the National Institute of Corrections (NIC), the Department of Justice has sponsored research on privatization of police, court, and correctional services; of prison industries; and of financing and construction, as well as operations of prisons. NIJ also sponsors a project by the American Bar Association to develop model statutes and contracts for private prisons. NIJ's National Criminal Justice Reference Service and

NIC's Information Center provide reports, publications, national conferences, training and demonstration projects, briefing books, and videos.

Continued research will be needed to help governments at all levels identify what administrative reforms and conditions are best for the administration of prisons. Therefore, the Commission recommends:

Recommendation (17)

The Department of Justice should continue to give high priority to research on private sector involvement in corrections.

SUMMARY

Contracting is a technique for transferring some activities from government agencies to the private sector. Where similar functions are readily available in the private sector, and where services show genuine likelihood of being improved by private providers, long-standing, bipartisan national policy supports transferring the functions to the private sector. The Commission has reaffirmed that policy and has considered contracting as a means of achieving privatization goals under the topics reviewed. The decisions that will transform long-standing policy into effective practice rest with the managers who are responsible for the administration of government programs. They, too, will benefit as citizens from every improvement in performance that results from drawing on the experience of the private sector in providing services to the public.

NOTES FOR CHAPTER 8

1. The historical discussion summarized here was attached to the testimony of Robert P. Bedell, Office of Management and Budget, submitted to the President's Commission on Privatization, Hearings on Contracting Out (hereinafter cited as Hearings on Contracting Out), January 7, 1988. See attachment 1, Joseph R. Wright, Jr., "Let's Get the Feds to Use the Private Sector," *Privatization Review* (Winter 1987). His account was corroborated by the testimony of William D. Russell, Contract Services Association, Hearings on Contracting Out, January 8, 1988.

2. Russell testimony.

3. Bedell testimony.

4. See Attachment 3 of Bedell testimony.

5. Bedell testimony.

6. Supplement, OMB Circular A–76 (Revised), U.S. Office of Management and Budget, "Performance of Commercial Activities," August 1983, Part I, pp. 11–15. See also Executive Order No. 12615 of November 19, 1987, *Federal Register*, vol. 52, no. 225 (November 23, 1987), p. 44853.

7. Ibid.

8. Bedell testimony.

9. U.S. Department of Defense, "Report to Congress: The Department of Defense Commercial Activities Program," April 1986, p. 6.

10. John B. Handy and Dennis J. O'Connor, "How Winners Win: Lessons Learned from Contract Competitions in Base Operations Support" (Bethesda, MD: Logistics Management Institute, September 1984).

11. U.S. General Accounting Office, *Federal Productivity: Potential Savings from Private Sector Cost Comparisons* (GAO/GGD–87–30), December 1986, appendix II; see the table, p. 11.

12. Testimony of Robert E. Edgell, Hearings on Contracting Out, January 7, 1988.

13. Letter dated April 9, 1986, from Carole J. Dineen, Office of Management and Budget, to the Honorable Edward R. Roybal, Subcommittee on Treasury-Postal Service and General Government, Committee on Appropriations, U.S. House of Representatives. These findings are supported by a General Accounting Office review of DOD contracting. See U.S. General Accounting Office, "DOD Functions Contracted Out under OMB Circular A–76: Contract Cost Increases and the Effects on Federal Employees," GAO/NSIAD–85–49 (April 15, 1985).

14. U.S. Department of Defense, "Report to Congress on the Commercial Activities Program," submitted March 12, 1984, and U.S. Department of Defense, "Report to Congress: The Department of Defense Commercial Activities Program," submitted April 15, 1986.

15. Bedell testimony.

16. U.S. Office of Management and Budget, *Management of the United States Government, Fiscal Year 1988*, p. 73.

17. Executive Order No. 12615, 52 *Federal Register* 44853, November 23, 1987.

18. U.S. Office of Management and Budget, *Management of the United States Government, Fiscal Year 1988*, pp. 72–73.

19. Ibid., p. 149.

20. Bedell testimony.

21. Testimony of Gene L. Dodaro, January 7, 1988.

22. Dodaro testimony.

23. Bedell testimony.

24. Testimony of Frank S. Swain, Small Business Administration, Hearings on Contracting Out, January 8, 1988.

25. Bedell testimony.

26. Testimony of Robert A. Stone, Department of Defense, submitted to the Hearings on Contracting Out, January 7, 1988.

27. Executive Order No. 12615, 52 *Federal Register* 44853, November 23, 1987.

28. Letter from Kenneth Blaylock, President of AFGE, to Chairman David Linowes, President's Commission on Privatization, January 20, 1988. See S. 909, sent as an attachment to the letter.

29. American Federation of State, County, and Municipal Employees, *Passing the Bucks: The Contracting Out of Public Services*, 1983.

30. Bedell testimony.

31. Stone testimony.

32. This discussion is based on U.S. Office of Personnel Management, "Federal Employee Direct Corporate Ownership Opportunity Plan: Fed CO-OP, Blueprint for Implementation," November 1987.

33. Testimony of Constance Horner, Office of Personnel Management, Hearings on Contracting Out, January 7, 1988.

34. Testimony of Lieut. Gen. Anthony Lukeman, U.S. Marine Corps, Hearings on Contracting Out, December 22, 1987.

35. Testimony of Michael C. Bourgoine, Food Marketing Institute, Hearings on Contracting Out, December 22, 1987.

36. U.S. General Accounting Office, "Compendium of GAO's Views on the Cost Savings Proposals of the Grace Commission," GAO/OCG 85-1, February 19, 1985.

37. Lukeman testimony.

38. Ibid.

39. Testimony of L. Wayne Arny, III, Hearings on Contracting Out, December 22, 1987.

40. Bourgoine testimony.

41. Testimony of James K. Stewart, National Institute of Justice, before the President's Commission on Privatization, Hearings on Prisons (hereinafter cited as Hearings on Prisons), December 22, 1987.

42. U.S. Department of Justice, *Jail Inmates in 1986. Bulletin* (Washington, DC: Bureau of Justice Statistics, October 1987).

43. U.S. Department of Justice, *Prisoners in 1986. Bulletin* (Washington, DC: Bureau of Justice Statistics, 1987).

44. Stewart testimony.

45. U.S. Department of Justice, *Prisoners in 1983. Bulletin* (Washington, DC: Bureau of Justice Statistics, 1984).

46. Ibid.

47. U.S. House of Representatives Committee on the Judiciary, "Authority to Contract with Private Institutions for Placement of Federal Prisoners," memo of June 10, 1983 from Claire A. Cripe, General Counsel, to Norman A. Carlson, Director, Bureau of Prisons entered into the record, *Privatization of Corrections, Hearings before the Subcommittee on Courts, Civil Liberties, and the Administration of Justice*, November 13, 1985, and March 18, 1986, Serial No. 40, 1986, p. 150.

48. U.S. Department of Justice, *Children in Custody: 1982/83 Census of Juvenile Detention and Correctional Facilities* (Washington, DC: Bureau of Justice Statistics, September 1986).

49. Joan Mullen, Kent Chabotar, and Deborah Carrow, *The Privatization of Corrections*, Abt Associates report to the National Institute of Justice (Washington, DC: U.S. Department of Justice, February 1985), pp. 56–68.

50. U.S. Congress, House of Representatives, Committee on the Judiciary, "Privatization in Federal Corrections," a Bureau of Prisons staff report entered into the record, *Privatization of Corrections. Hearings before the Subcommittee on Courts, Civil Liberties, and the Administration of Justice,* November 13, 1985, and March 18, 1986, Serial No. 40, 1986, p. 168.

51. Historical examples of private prisons, along with the private leasing of convict labor, have little relevance to corrections today, because of the revolution in prisoners' rights since the 1960s.

52. Testimony of Thomas W. Beasley, Corrections Corporation of America, Hearings on Prisons, December 22, 1987.

53. William L. Megathlin, Dennis D. Murphy, and Robert E. Magnus, *Feasibility of the Establishment of Regional Prisons* (Washington, DC: U.S. Department of Justice, National Institute of Corrections, May 1984), pp. 45–50.

54. Testimony of Ira P. Robbins, American University, representing the American Bar Association, Hearings on Prisons, December 22, 1987.

55. *Report of the Private Prison Task Force* (Harrisburg, PA: General Assembly of the Commonwealth of Pennsylvania, Joint State Government Commission, March 1987), p. 13. Pennsylvania legislated a 1-year moratorium on new contracts for the operation of private prisons while a task force studied the matter.

56. Beasley testimony.

57. For example, state and local governments can be found liable for violating a prisoner's civil rights under 42 U.S.C. 1983. See also the Eighth and Fourteenth Amendments to the U.S. Constitution.

58. The federal government may be found liable under the Federal Tort Claims Act for the acts or omissions of its employees. See 28 U.S.C. 1346 (b). The federal government has expressly excluded tort liability for the acts or omissions of its contractors' employees. See 18 U.S.C. Sec. 4002, and 28 U.S.C. 1346 (b), 2671. Also see *Logue* v. *United States*, 412 U.S. 521 (1973).

59. Government liability might arise for the actions of its contractors under some theory of respondent superior, that is, when a court finds that the government exercises such control or supervision over the activities of the contract employee that the employee is essentially acting on behalf of the government and therefore is a government employee.

60. For instance, courts have found that public officials can be sued and found liable in their individual capacities for the arbitrary deprivation of an individual's constitutional rights, a so-called constitutional tort. See *Bivens* v. *Six Unknown Narcotics Agents*, 403 U.S. 388 (1970).

61. Stewart testimony.

62. Camille G. Camp and George M. Camp, *Private Sector Involvement in Prison Services and Operations* (Washington, DC: National Institute of Corrections, 1984).

63. The Council of State Governments and the Urban Institute, *Issues in Contracting for the Private Operation of Prisons and Jails* (Washington, DC: Department of Justice, National Institute of Justice, 1987), p. 122.

64. Camp and Camp.

65. Stewart testimony.

66. J. Michael Quinlan, Federal Bureau of Prisons, Hearings on Contracting Prison Management, December 12, 1987.

67. Ibid.

68. Robbins testimony.

Chapter 9

Federal Asset Sales:
Amtrak; Naval Petroleum Reserves

To many people, the term "privatization" is synonymous with the sale of government assets. Sale of government assets is not only the most visible form of privatization but also the most controversial.

In the United States, pressure to reduce the federal deficit has led many policymakers to view asset sales as a convenient means of raising revenues. As a result, the benefits of asset sales other than the short-term infusion of cash into the federal Treasury have often been overlooked, and privatization has been transformed from a resource management issue into a budget issue.

The President's Commission on Privatization firmly believes that asset sales merit serious attention regardless of the state of the public finances. The question that must ultimately be addressed is whether various capital assets now owned by the federal government could better serve the American people if owned and managed privately. Answering that question requires careful consideration of the nature of public and private ownership, the benefits claimed by privatization's proponents, and the drawbacks asserted by its critics.

Pros and Cons of Asset Sales

Preservation of Service

Although a major goal of asset sales is to improve the quality of service to the public, fears about selling government assets are often rooted in the suspicion that these sales could erode or eliminate the services that government currently provides. In many instances, this fear is unfounded, for a principal goal of asset sales is to encourage the private sector to perform the same or improved services more effectively.

Private ownership of assets can lead to more responsive management, because private owners have financial incentives to employ those assets so as to best serve their customers. A businessman who fails to produce an attractive product at an appropriate price may lose business to the competition, lose his job, or even go bankrupt. Consumers can thus have a direct influence over business decisions through their buying decisions. Lawrence Hunter, Deputy Chief Economist of the U.S. Chamber of Commerce, argues as follows:

> Markets are perceived as a necessary evil—as ruthless—the price we must pay for efficiency. This conjures up the specter of markets achieving efficiency through extermination. In fact, it is the *threat* of termination and the *adaptation* it produces that permit markets to meet needs and satisfy preferences better than any other institution known to man. Markets are not destructive. They are creative.[1]

Citizens can influence public decisions, however, only through voting and expensive lobbying campaigns. Because of this lack of public input, managers of public resources do not always know whether they are in fact carrying out the will of the public. Even if public officials could unerringly determine the will of the public, their monopoly status means that they have few direct incentives to do so.

Even the most conscientious public servants, devoted to managing federal resources wisely for the benefit of all Americans, must face the reality that organized interest groups often exercise more influence over government decisions than the average citizen. Consequently, the managers of federal resources often find that they are ultimately accountable not to the public as a whole, but to some segment of the public. Privatization gives those consumers who benefit most from wise management of public assets a much greater opportunity to make their preferences known.

In cases where government ownership and management of an asset is actually a vehicle for subsidization of some users of the service, the sale of some assets could threaten continuation of a service. Even in these cases, society need not forgo the benefits of private ownership and management. Covenants, for example, let the government ensure that the owners of a newly privatized asset continue to provide specific services. Several witnesses testified about the example of the Conrail sale, in which the private sector buyers agreed to maintain certain types of service.

The Commission realizes that such covenants should be imposed only after careful evaluation, for they often reduce the value of the asset to the private buyer. Regulation of the newly privatized enterprise is another possibility, but regulation also attenuates the benefits of privatization. In the context of Amtrak, the Commission also discussed the possibility of transferring ownership to the private sector in order to enhance efficiency while temporarily continuing subsidies to preserve service.[2] In short, people who depend on federal services need not view asset sales as a threat to the continuation of those services.

In addition to providing services more effectively, privatization through asset sales can offer benefits that continued government ownership never could. Many asset sale plans have been structured to achieve the social goal of widespread ownership by small investors and employees. In the United States, the federal government's 85 percent of Conrail was sold in

March 1987 for more than $1.6 billion; it was the largest initial public offering in U.S. history.[3] A portion of the shares for domestic offering was allocated to brokerage firms for sale to small investors. Another block of shares was given to a "special bracket of minority-owned firms" for sale to small investors, and the balance was allocated for institutional sales.[4]

Well-planned asset sales can also help achieve other public goals. Privatization of public housing can improve the quality of living environments for families by turning tenants into homeowners. The sale of public housing units under a pilot program administered by the Department of Housing and Urban Development (HUD) is designed to explore ways of making property owners out of tenants. In announcing the program, HUD Secretary Samuel Pierce said, "HUD's demonstration program will allow public housing residents to share in the dream of homeownership." Under the British housing privatization program, new homeowners improved their homes and gardens, cleaned up common areas, and tackled such social problems as vandalism.

The British government has tried to encourage widespread ownership of privatized enterprises. Since 1979, Britain has seen a massive shift of resources from the state to the people; one in five British adults now owns stock, up from only 6 percent before 1979. Such are the additional public benefits that asset sales can bring.

Budget Objections

Another set of objections to asset sales focuses on their budgetary effects. Asset sales have been labeled "smoke and mirrors" because they are alleged to reduce the federal deficit only through bookkeeping tricks. This objection is an unfortunate result of the fact that asset sale proposals have become entwined in the budget debate.

It is true that the federal government operates on a cash rather than an accrual system of accounting. Asset sales, therefore, can reduce the deficit in the current year but increase it in future years, because the government does not collect the revenues that the assets would otherwise generate in future years.

The claim that asset sales are simply a "bookkeeping gimmick" is not really an argument against asset sales; it is an argument against counting the proceeds from asset sales as deficit reduction for the purpose of meeting legislated deficit reduction goals. The Gramm-Rudman-Hollings Deficit Reduction Act already restricts the government's ability to count asset sales as deficit reduction, and the Commission recognizes the importance of preventing the government from using the proceeds from asset sales as a substitute for other actions to reduce the deficit.

Regardless of how asset sale proceeds are treated for deficit reduction purposes, the relevant question is whether the government sacrifices *more* revenue in the future than it receives from sale of the asset. Witnesses testified before the Commission that the private sector generally is more efficient at delivering services than the government. Accordingly, they argued that although the government might forgo a future stream of income by selling, a private buyer would anticipate a *higher* future income stream because it expects to employ the asset more efficiently. The price this private buyer would be willing to pay for the asset would reflect the present value of the higher anticipated income. Therefore, the price the government could get for the asset could be higher than the government value of the income the government could anticipate if it kept the asset.

A final budgetary objection to asset sales is that private buyers might acquire assets for less than they are "worth." This objection arises when the original cost of the asset to the government, or "book value," is used as the measure of its worth. However, an asset's true value should be measured by the income it is capable of producing in the future, not by the original cost of producing or constructing the asset. Book value, which is the "face value" in the case of loan assets, says nothing about an asset's true value today. Many federal loan portfolios, for example, are worth only a fraction of their face value because many debtors will default on their payments. Neither the government nor the private sector is likely to or expects to collect the full face value of the portfolio. In some instances, selling the loan portfolios could give the government more revenue because of the greater efficiency of private collection agencies.

Asset Sales Policy

In comparison with Britain and many other countries that have a wide array of nationalized industries and commercial operations, the United States has a more limited number of candidates for asset sales. The Federal Communications Commission has proposed auctioning off portions of the radio frequency spectrum. Proposals have also been made to privatize all or parts of the National Institutes of Health.

Proposals to privatize the Power Marketing Administrations (PMAs), uranium enrichment facilities, and others have encountered strong congressional opposition, leading to laws that prohibit government officials and agencies from studying various plans. The Commission received a list of 27 statutory impediments to privatization in 12 agencies. Included among them were:

- The administration is prohibited from studying or proposing any initiative to privatize the uranium enrichment programs unless the General Services Administration is used to dispose of the enterprise as surplus property (P.L. 100–202).

- The executive branch is prohibited from using any federal funds to study or propose PMA divestiture, with the exception of the Alaska PMA (P.L. 99–349).

- The Department of Energy is prohibited from using federal funds to privatize the Naval Petroleum Reserves (P.L. 99–500 and P.L. 99–591).
- The Department of Transportation is prohibited from using federal funds for a commission to study the privatization of Amtrak (P.L. 100–71).

These impediments generally were enacted not because Congress decided that enough information had been gathered on the issues, but because influential interest groups who feel threatened by privatization proposals had successfully lobbied key legislators. The Commission is concerned about the effects of congressional bans on study of privatization proposals, and therefore concludes:

Recommendation (1)

Statutory prohibitions on studying divestiture of federal assets cannot be justified. Current statutory prohibitions should be repealed and future attempts at legislating such prohibitions should be strongly resisted. Without adequate study, there is insufficient evidence to determine whether or not federal assets would be more effectively used by private owners. There is also insufficient evidence that federal ownership is necessary to achieve stated public policy goals.

Recommendation (2)

The federal government should forcefully pursue the divestiture of capital assets. Although assets are generally more efficiently managed by private owners, constituencies, particularly affected employees, should first be developed for divestiture before it can be successful. U.S. sales should proceed, and successful sales should be widely publicized in order to build support for divestiture in other areas.

Those involved in offering public assets for sale should be and have been sensitive to the interests of the affected employees. Employee ownership is one means of sharing the benefits of privatization. The Urban Mass Transportation Administration reports that investment banks have expressed interest in privatizing local commuter rail systems. Employee ownership programs have been introduced by the Office of Personnel Management to form new companies to take over some government operations. Although similar proposals have been discussed for federal asset sales, no formal proposals have been presented. The Commission believes that exploration of such options should be pursued.

Some observers fear that sale of federal assets means that the public purposes for which those assets were acquired would no longer be served. Amtrak was created in 1970 to preserve intercity rail passenger service. The Naval Petroleum Reserves were established to ensure that the U.S. Navy's fleet would have adequate supplies of fuel in wartime. Public housing was constructed to provide needy families and individuals with shelter. Obviously, it is important to assess both the validity of the policy goals that public ownership is intended to achieve and the extent to which government ownership is the most effective method of achieving them.

In some instances there are disagreements about the nature and validity of the policy goals claimed as reasons for government ownership. Some groups argue that Amtrak's subsidy should be eliminated even if it means the disappearance of rail passenger service. Other forms of transportation, they say, could easily absorb Amtrak's ridership. Rail passenger groups strongly disagree. Byron Nordberg, Vice President of the United Rail Passenger Alliance, testified that "a strong rail passenger service is vital to this nation. It is inconceivable that the United States would have no such service, especially after the lessons of reduced energy supplies are considered." [5] Ross Capon, Executive Director of the National Association of Railroad Passengers, stated that railroads are more energy-efficient and less damaging to the environment than other modes of transportation.[6] Such differences over public policy objectives themselves emphasize the need for careful definition of those objectives.

Even when government originally acquired an asset to accomplish a public purpose, government ownership of that asset may no longer be the best way of accomplishing the policy objective. One example is the Naval Petroleum Reserves. Jeffrey Jones, Director of Energy Policy for the Department of Defense, pointed out that the major U.S. military need for oil is for jet fuel, not fuel for ships, and implied that the naval reserves would not be very useful in supplying oil to airbases thousands of miles away. "From a strictly defense viewpoint," Jones testified, "the need for oil once presented in the Naval Petroleum Reserves can be met far better by the establishment of a smaller, but more flexible, Defense Petroleum Inventory" in conjunction with the Strategic Petroleum Reserve.[7]

Some federal assets clearly represent parts of the national heritage that should not be sold. These would include national historic sites, national parks, and national monuments set aside for preservation. Nonetheless, environmentalists have pointed out that federal management of some public lands may fail to protect the environment adequately in some cases. The U.S. Forest Service has been attacked for damaging ecologically fragile areas by building roads and cutting down trees, which no private firm would find it profitable to do. The Bureau of Land Management has been criticized for permitting environmentally destructive overgrazing on public lands for the past 100 years. In contrast, private groups like the Audubon Society and the Nature Conservancy own and operate wildlife sanctuaries that protect the environment while permitting carefully monitored activities like tourism, grazing, and even oil drilling.[8]

Divestiture of a government asset does not mean that a government policy objective would not be fulfilled.

The Commission recommends:

Recommendation (3)

The transfer of assets from government ownership to private ownership need not adversely affect the implementation of public policy goals. In considering asset transfers, government managers should reanalyze the current applicability of public policy goals. Further, they should assess whether private ownership, in combination with covenants, regulations, or other protections, could better achieve those goals.

The Commission has explored two government assets that have been proposed for sale—Amtrak and Naval Petroleum Reserves. The analysis and recommendations follow.

AMTRAK

In 1970, Congress created the National Rail Passenger Corporation, or Amtrak, as a for-profit company. The railroad was conceived as a 2-year, federally assisted experiment that would become profitable on its own thereafter.[9] After 17 years, however, Amtrak remains dependent on federal subsidies.

Amtrak officials' original goals were to increase ridership, to offer good-quality service and well-maintained equipment, and to issue accurate information to passengers.[10]

In its first year of operation, Amtrak's budget and staff were much smaller than today, and it had to contract with other companies for most of its services. The railroad had only 1,500 employees and operated 26.3 million train miles over a 23,376-mile system. Amtrak owned no railroad tracks, stations, terminals, or repair facilities, and it leased or was given the locomotives it operated.[11]

In 1976, Amtrak acquired the 621 route-miles of the Northeast Corridor (NEC) from the Consolidated Rail Corporation (Conrail) for $86 million. In addition, Amtrak owns 83 miles of track in the Midwest and several stations and repair facilities. The company continues to lease most of its track and stations from freight railroads.[12]

The Federal Role

Although its enacting legislation specified that Amtrak is not a federal agency, the U.S. government does in fact own the railroad. The Department of Transportation owns almost all voting shares of Amtrak stock, and Amtrak's directors are all federal appointees. Moreover, since 1978, Amtrak has been required by law to follow the same budget procedures as federal agencies. Amtrak's budget is evaluated annually within the context of all federal spending for transportation.

Amtrak is funded by earned revenues and federal grants. In fiscal 1971, it began with $40 million in federal funds. Since then, Amtrak has received over $13 billion from the U.S. government, including approximately $9.6 billion for operating subsidies and $2.3 billion for the Northeast Corridor Improvement Plan. The government relieved Amtrak of responsibility for another $1.1 billion in federal loan guarantees in 1983. Federal subsidies are projected to total $3.1 billion over the next 5 years and $7 billion over the next decade.[13] Total Amtrak staff numbered almost 19,000 in 1987.

The Carter administration attempted to slow the growth of Amtrak subsidies, proposing to cut the railroad's route mileage by 43 percent in 1979. Then-Secretary of Transportation Brock Adams summed up the

Administration's delemma: "We can no longer afford to provide disproportionately large and continually increasing amounts of federal funds for a passenger transportation system that is used by less than one-half of 1 percent of the intercity traveling public."[14]

In 1981, cost and subsidy reductions were enunciated as corporate objectives, and Amtrak's financial performance has improved substantially: whereas Amtrak covered only 48.5 percent of its expenses from revenue in 1981, the revenue-to-expense ratio improved to 62 percent in 1986, with further improvements forecast.[15]

Meanwhile, federal subsidies to Amtrak fell from a high of $881 million in 1981 to $581 million in 1988, a real decline of 66 percent.[16] Amtrak operates approximately the same number of route miles today as in 1981, and service in several areas has increased.

Amtrak's improved financial performance is primarily the result not of revenue increases but of cost reductions. Annual maintenance costs on equipment and roadbed have been reduced by effective capital investments, some yielding an average return exceeding 20 percent.[17] The modernization of maintenance facilities and the replacement of antiquated cars in the long-distance fleet have been the most significant factors in reducing costs. The Federal Railroad Administration (FRA) estimates that the Superliner fleet purchased in 1981 has reduced unit maintenance costs by 50 percent and that Amtrak's new maintenance facilities have cut costs more than $151 million annually.[18]

Other areas of Amtrak cost reduction include the following:

• The Department of Transportation's (DOT) forgiveness of Amtrak's $1.1 billion debt to the government in 1983, which saved the railroad $74 million annually in interest payments.[19]

• New labor agreements, which resulted in savings of $20 million in 1983. Savings are expected to increase to $50 million when the agreements are fully implemented in 1988.[20]

• The transformation of manned stations in some western states to unmanned stations and the negotiation of new agreements to share facilities.

Amtrak ridership, including ridership along the popular NEC, has remained almost constant since 1981. Passenger revenues have gone up 6 percent, largely attributable to the Metroliner service.[21]

Nonoperating revenues have grown considerably in the 1980s. Sources of such revenues include fiber optics right-of-way leases along the NEC, contract work at maintenance facilities, commuter rail service operations, real estate development, and mail delivery contracts. In particular, joint ventures with developers for commercial activities at stations (as at

Washington, D.C.'s Union Station and Philadelphia's 30th Street Station, currently) offer potential for future revenue enhancement.

Amtrak Privatization

Some analysts have proposed the sale of Amtrak as a way to free the railroad from political controversy, preserve passenger rail service, and relieve taxpayers of the burden of federal subsidies. In hearings before the President's Commission on Privatization, several witnesses favoring such privatization suggested that the government should first strive to make Amtrak more profitable.

Three related privatization initiatives suggest some potential components of a credible Amtrak privatization plan:

Conrail. In 1976, after the failure of seven northeastern railroads, Conrail was formed as a federal corporation to provide freight rail service in the Northeast. As with Amtrak, Congress provided Conrail with substantial funding for operations, capital improvements, and labor protection, and it was hoped that the railroad could be profitable soon after its creation. By 1980, however, Conrail had total operating losses of $1.6 billion.[22]

In 1981, Congress enacted the Northeast Rail Service Act, aimed at providing "an orderly return of Conrail freight service to the private sector." [23] This legislation helped Conrail become profitable by granting relief from state taxes and labor protection requirements, and allowing Conrail to expedite the abandonment of unprofitable lines. Under the plan, if Conrail was found to be profitable by 1983, DOT was to solicit competitive bids to buy the government's 85 percent ownership interest. The remaining 15 percent was to be held by the employees in a stock ownership plan.

Conrail's operating performance soon began a dramatic turnaround. The railroad received its last federal operating subsidy in June 1981 and posted its first operating profit of $39 million in 1981. Profits continued: $174 million in 1982; $313 million in 1983; $500 million in 1984; $442 million in 1985; and $431 million in 1986. While DOT attributes the profits for 1981 and 1982 to the sale of tax benefits and special statutory provisions, Conrail improved its own service by eliminating excess track, halting its commuter passenger service, and reducing its number of employees from approximately 89,000 to 38,000.[24]

In October 1986, Congress approved a plan to sell Conrail through a public stock offering. The transfer of the railroad to the private sector was achieved early in 1987, when Conrail was sold for over $1.6 billion, the largest public stock offering in U.S. history.

In testimony before the Commission, Amtrak President Graham Claytor expressed doubt that a Conrail-type plan would work for Amtrak. Unlike

Conrail, he said, Amtrak has no "profitable core" and was unlikely to develop one in the foreseeable future. In contrast, FRA Administrator John Riley testified that it should be possible to structure a similar plan. Riley also claimed that "Amtrak's chance of surviving beyond the near-term depends on our ability to move it into the private sector." [25]

Britain's National Freight Corporation. In 1982, Britain's largest trucking company, a perennial money-loser, was sold for 53 million pounds (approximately $80 million). Current and retired employees received more than 80 percent of the stock. Following the sale, labor productivity rose by 30 percent and the value of the workers' stock rose 20-fold. The corporation is now profitable.

Although union leaders opposed privatization in this case, the company's 40,000 workers supported it as a more promising road to job security than government ownership of the company. Management similarly supported the sale because it felt the company would be more stable and profitable under private ownership.

One proposal to privatize Amtrak, based on this model, would first separate Amtrak into two companies—one in charge of Amtrak's long-distance routes, the other to operate in the NEC. This would separate the issue of preserving long-distance service from the issue of maintaining the rail infrastructure in the NEC. Eighty percent of the NEC company's stock could be sold at a discount to workers and management. The rest could be distributed to NEC riders through a bonus system similar to airlines' "frequent flyer" programs. Essential to this plan would be a federal government pledge to protect employees who could not find jobs in either company. To ease fears that privatization would cause service to decline, the newly privatized company would be required to retain at least 80 percent of the passenger-miles Amtrak currently travels in the NEC for 20 years. It has been estimated that such a proposal could relieve U.S. tax payers of about $250 million of the Amtrak subsidy.

Japanese National Railways. In 1987, the Japanese government began to implement a plan designed to turn the entity that owned and operated the nation's intercity rail lines over to the private sector. Of the railroad's 265 passenger lines, the railroad had previously made profits on only 9. In 1982 and 1985, government-appointed reform commissions had recommended that the railroad be broken up into several companies and privatized.

Of the 12 companies created in 1987, 3 regional companies and the high-speed "bullet" train lines on the main island of Honshu are expected to be profitable immediately, and they are expected to retire about $94 billion of the railroad's debt. According to one study, Japanese taxpayers "picked up about $105 billion of the outstanding debt." [26]

Passenger groups such as the National Association of Railroad Passengers (NARP) and the United Rail Passenger Alliance (URPA) told the

Commission that they will not accept any reforms that would substantially reduce service. This point was emphasized during the Commission's hearings by both Ross Capon of NARP, who opposes privatization, and Byron Nordberg of URPA, who favors a multi-year plan that would privatize Amtrak after it achieves profitability.[27]

Taxpayer and business organizations seek primarily to eliminate Amtrak's subsidy. A plan acceptable to them cannot involve massive new subsidies as a prelude to privatization. Lawrence Hunter, an economist at the U.S. Chamber of Commerce, testified that "the federal government should cease to subsidize Amtrak regardless of whether or not private enterprise moves in to provide rail passenger service." [28]

Given the complex issues involved, structuring an economically and politically successful Amtrak sale will require careful planning. Both economic theory and practical experience, however, suggest that it is possible to transform unprofitable government-owned assets into profitable private enterprises. Therefore, the Commission recommends:

Recommendation (4)

The federal government should adopt a multi-year plan to move Amtrak or major portions of its operations to the private sector. Such a plan should include incrementally reduced subsidies, a full review of legislative restrictions, and a deadline at which the Department of Transportation must ascertain whether Amtrak or portions of its activities should be continued. The plan should also take into consideration the interests of labor, management, taxpayers and riders.

All the witnesses before the Commission agreed that, despite impressive progress in the 1980s, there is still room for improvement in the railroad's financial performance. Suggestions for improvement included revenue enhancement proposals, greater private sector involvement, and relief from federal laws and regulations. The Commission believes that a multi-year reform program exploring all these options offers the best opportunity for ultimately turning Amtrak over to the private sector.

The Commission heard several proposals for enhancing passenger revenues, including a reconfiguration of existing routes. In addition, a number of specific opportunities for further cost savings were proposed. Amtrak's food and beverage service, for example, generates losses of $42 million annually. Although Graham Claytor testified that in-house provision of food services by Amtrak was actually less expensive than contracting it out, FRA estimates that contracting out food service might save at least $15 million annually.[29] This disagreement points up the need for further study of the possibilities for contracting out of Amtrak services. The

Commission believes that the possibilities for contracting out of many Amtrak services should be explored and therefore recommends:

Recommendation (5)

Amtrak and FRA should undertake a comprehensive study of all contracting out opportunities, including food service and station operation. Amtrak should contract out operations where service can be performed at an equal or improved level and cost savings will result. Such contracting out should take into consideration the interests of employees.

Amtrak could also reduce its costs on local train operations. The railroad loses money on local trains ("403b trains") that run at the request of state governments. Amtrak is required by law to run these trains if the state wishes, but states cover only 65 percent of the costs. Charging states the full cost of the local trains they request could generate millions of dollars.[30] In addition, commuter agencies in the Northeast do not pay the full costs for the use of Amtrak track and facilities. Allowing Amtrak to charge a market price for use of its track and facilities could bring in an additional $25 million.[31] FRA Administrator John Riley testified before the Commission that Amtrak essentially subsidizes state and local trains through these lower rates.[32] For this reason, and as another step to improve Amtrak's profitability, the Commission recommends:

Recommendation (6)

Amtrak should charge states and other users the full costs associated with providing rail service and trackage rights.

Many Commission witnesses testified that Amtrak forgoes substantial revenues because it needs more sleeper cars to meet peak-period demand on western routes. An FRA study notes that Amtrak currently forgoes "millions, and perhaps tens of millions of dollars in revenue for want of equipment to service peak season demand."[33] Purchase of new cars to replace the nearly 40-year-old fleet east of the Mississippi could also reduce maintenance expenditures, as was the case when Amtrak replaced its western fleet of cars in the early 1980s. According to FRA, it is possible to finance new cars in a manner that requires no commitment of tax dollars. Such a plan could use Amtrak's revenue enhancement and real estate investments as collateral.[34] Another possibility is financing by the car manufacturers much as aircraft manufacturers finance aircraft purchases.

Byron Nordberg testified that passenger car manufacturers are prepared to enter into discussions regarding such agreements.[35]

Private investment in Amtrak could help improve the performance of the system while reducing federal subsidies. Therefore, the Commission recommends:

Recommendation (7)

To cut maintenance costs and further reduce dependence on federal subsidies, Amtrak may need new capital acquisitions, including new equipment. Amtrak, FRA and the Treasury should find ways to fund capital needs if the purchases can be justified as a reduction of the federal subsidy and the transfer of Amtrak to the private sector. Such purchases should not entail any new commitment of federal funds, including government loan guarantees.

The Commission believes that operating cost reduction should not be used to justify the commitment of federal funds for capital acquisition. Such an arrangement would probably reduce Amtrak's operating subsidy, but it is not likely to advance the goal of reducing Amtrak's dependence on the federal government for financial support. Maximizing the private sector's involvement in meeting Amtrak's capital needs helps accomplish both goals.

Amtrak's legal monopoly on passenger rail service prohibits private rail carriers from competing with it in the passenger market without Amtrak's consent. In the Rail Passenger Service Act of 1972, Congress gave Amtrak monopoly privileges in order to keep private firms from taking the lucrative routes and leaving Amtrak only with the unprofitable ones. However, as John Riley testified, all Amtrak routes currently lose money, so if the private sector is willing to assume responsibility for any route, it can reduce Amtrak's losses.[36] According to Riley, "Repeal of this provision will strongly signal DOT's intention to push private initiatives, rather than the expansion of government initiatives, in the intercity rail business."[37] In an effort to encourage private carriers to reduce Amtrak's losses while preserving passenger service, the Commission recommends:

Recommendation (8)

Congress should repeal the statutory provision granting Amtrak exclusive rights to provide intercity passenger rail service. Private sector initiatives should be encouraged. Any legislatively established monopoly prohibitions of potential private sector investment impair competition.

Although Amtrak can grant other railroads permission to compete with it, the Commission is uncertain about whether Amtrak would in fact ever do so. Such initiative on Amtrak's part would certainly be a positive step, but the best way to ensure that private operators can enter the market is to repeal the monopoly privilege outright.

The Commission believes that the federal government should enact such reforms to help make Amtrak profitable. This approach could ultimately allow the railroad to operate without subsidies and make it more attractive to potential private owners. Eliminating the need for subsidies through better business management would also help defuse the opposition to privatization that is rooted in the conviction that Amtrak will fail if turned over to the private sector.

NAVAL PETROLEUM RESERVES

At the turn of the century when the Navy was shifting from coal to oil as fuel for its fleet, President Theodore Roosevelt became concerned about assuring a secure source of oil. He directed the U.S. Geological Survey (USGS) to identify public lands that contained oil. This study was completed early in the Taft administration, and President Taft signed an executive order on September 27, 1909, withdrawing large areas of California and Wyoming from settlement under the public land laws then in effect. Because the legal authority of the President to do this was questioned, the Congress authorized this action with the Pickett Act in 1910, and President Taft confirmed the withdrawal by executive order on July 2, 1910.

Naval Petroleum Reserve No. 1 (Elk Hills)

In 1912, the Secretary of the Navy asked for sufficient oil-bearing lands in California to assure a supply of 500 million barrels of oil. The USGS recommended 38,073 acres in Kern County, California, of which about 12,100 acres were privately owned, and President Taft, by executive order, set aside the area, known as Elk Hills, as Naval Petroleum Reserve No. 1 (NPR-1).[38] Subsequent additions over the years have brought the size of the reserve to a total of 47,985 acres.

Although the reserves had been established, the Navy had no authority to operate them until 1920, when legislation placed them under the authority of the Secretary of the Navy and directed him to develop or conserve them at his discretion.[39] A year later, this authority was transferred by executive order to the Secretary of the Interior.[40] Portions were leased noncompetitively between 1921 and 1927, but most of these leases were canceled in 1927 following a congressional investigation. The reserves were transferred back to Navy control in that year.[41]

In November 1942, a unit plan contract was executed with the only remaining private owner of NPR-1 lands, Standard Oil Company of California (SOCAL, now Chevron), which had bought out the other private owners. This contract allowed for the cooperative exploration, development, and operation of all lands within NPR-1.

In June 1944, when wartime shortages of petroleum were becoming critical, the NPR legislation was amended to allow the Secretary of the Navy to produce petroleum for national defense when needed. A new unit plan contract was signed by the Navy and SOCAL on June 19, 1944, which is still in effect.[42]

From the end of World War II until the 1970s, little activity took place at NPR-1. Production beyond what was needed for "protection, conservation, maintenance, and testing" of the reserves was earmarked for defense needs and had to be approved by the President and authorized by a joint resolution of Congress.

Naval Petroleum Reserve No. 3 (Teapot Dome)*

President Woodrow Wilson established Naval Petroleum Reserve No. 3 (NPR-3) by executive order in April 1915. The original reserve, which covered 9,321 acres, was enlarged to the present 9,481 acres by executive order in 1932. The Navy took control of the reserve in June 1920, and President Warren Harding transferred responsibility to the Department of Interior in May 1921.

NPR-3 was leased to the Mammoth Oil Company, which began operations in 1922. Drilling began on the first well in July, and production began in November. The leases were questioned when the Secretary of the Interior was found to have profited from the deal, and Mammoth operations were placed in receivership in March 1924. Production continued until December 1927, when the Supreme Court ruled that the leases were void and the field was placed in a shut-in status (i.e., production reduced to the minimum feasible level). At that time, 84 wells had been drilled and about 3.6 million barrels of oil produced. Although the Navy resumed control in 1928, the field remained inactive until 1951.[43]

From 1951 to 1976, some exploration was conducted, along with protective drilling to prevent reservoir damage. Production became necessary in 1965 to avoid drainage of the field and flood damage due to private operations outside the NPR boundaries, and another 4.2 million barrels of oil were produced by 1976.[44]

Post-embargo Exploration and Production at the NPRs

As a result of the 1973 Arab oil embargo, Congress directed a 5-year Development and Exploration Program for the NPRs to begin in 1974. In April 1976, President Ford signed the Naval Petroleum Reserves Production Act,[45] which required oil production at the reserves at the maximum efficient rate (MER)** for a period of 6 years. The act also provided that production could be extended in 3-year increments if the President made a finding that such production was in the national interest. This has been

---

*NPR-2 is a small reserve (less than 3,000 barrels per day) located near Elk Hills at Buena Vista, California. Divestiture proposals have generally not included NPR-2 because all productive lands are leased to private producers.

**MER is defined as "the maximum sustainable daily rate from a reservoir which will permit economic development and depletion of that reservoir without detriment to the ultimate recovery."

done three times, in 1981, 1984, and 1987, and both reserves are now authorized to continue production through April 5, 1991.

For NPR-1, production prior to the 1976 act had totaled about 148 million barrels of oil. Following the NPR Production Act, the rate of production increased to a peak of 181,000 barrels per day (bpd) in July 1981 before beginning a steady decline. The current rate of production is about 110,000 bpd; the government's share is about 90,000 bpd. This field is projected to decline at an annual rate of about 5 percent until the field ends its productive life or until tertiary recovery operations are employed.[46] Total production from the field through 1987 approached 877 million barrels of oil.[47]

NPR-3 is much smaller than NPR-1, both in production and size of reserves. Following the NPR Production Act in 1976, NPR-3 production started slow and peaked at about 4,400 bpd in fiscal 1980. Production at NPR-3 through fiscal 1987 totaled about 17 million barrels; the current rate of production is about 3,000 bpd.[48]

Administration of the Reserves

The Secretary of the Navy continued to manage the reserves until October 1, 1977. At that time, the Office of Naval Petroleum and Oil Shale Reserves was transferred to the newly created Department of Energy (DOE).[49] Although the reserves are managed by onsite government personnel, the day-to-day operations are conducted by contractors, currently Bechtel Petroleum Operations, Inc., at NPR-1 and Lawrence-Allison & Associates West Inc. at NPR-3.

Several approaches have been tried to dispose of NPR oil, such as competitive exchange for Strategic Petroleum Reserve oil, swaps for products needed by the military, and pipeline transport to the strategic reserve. Currently, all NPR oil is sold through competitive bidding to commercial firms. All contracts do, however, have a 10-day cancellation clause.

The Strategic Role of the NPRs

The world has changed dramatically since the Great White Fleet took to the seas, and the military's fuel needs have changed along with it. When President Theodore Roosevelt set aside the NPRs, the need was for an assured supply of oil for Navy ships. Today, the military needs lighter petroleum products such as jet fuel. In a wartime environment, that demand could be in almost any part of the world.

The volume required by the military also needs to be placed in perspective. In peacetime, the military uses less than 500,000 bpd, which is not quite 3 percent of total annual U.S. domestic consumption.[50] This demand may double or triple in wartime, but the amount is still a small portion of normal U.S. consumption, which averages more than 16 million bpd.

Military needs share priority in an energy emergency with agriculture, vital industrial uses, and essential civilian services (police, fire, medical care). Normally, military fuels are bought competitively; and to the extent possible, competitive contracts are sought in emergency conditions.

To ensure that the national security need for oil can be met in an emergency, the U.S. maintains the world's largest inventory of crude oil, the Strategic Petroleum Reserve. The strategic reserve is located in the heart of the large U.S. refinery center along the Gulf Coast, and it currently contains more than 540 million barrels of assorted crudes.[51] In its current configuration, the strategic reserve can be pumped at a rate exceeding 3 million bpd, about 35 times the government's share of NPR production. As more caverns are leached and filled, the pumping capacity will grow to more than 4 million bpd.

Government Operation of the NPRs

Management of the engineering and production operations of a major oil field is a complex and time-sensitive undertaking. Any activity of the federal government operates under a wide variety of constraints not found in the private sector, and many of these constraints can cause operations in a competitive market to be inefficient at best.

Testimony presented to the Commission suggested that private ownership could lead to reductions in operating costs by several million dollars per year. Specifically, testimony suggested that government policies and procedures lead to significant overstaffing. In addition, the government was reported to lack the infrastructure common to oil companies and other commercial enterprises that would substantially reduce the cost to operate a commercial oil field; the government was also said to be ill-equipped to make reservoir management decisions, including determining the MER.

The more volatile the market conditions, the less effective the government operations will be in maximizing the value of taxpayer resources. A quick look at the application of federal budget and procurement processes to NPR operations makes this point clear.

The Federal Budget. At any one time, there are three budgets being addressed—one being executed (fiscal 1988 currently), one moving through Congress (fiscal 1989), and one being planned for submission to Office of Management and Budget (OMB) (fiscal 1990). This means that decisions on any further exploration, developmental drilling, and levels of production are being made *now* for 1990, and these decisions will be fixed at least 18 months in advance of their execution in order to move through the budget process. Once the budget is passed, it provides a relatively rigid plan for how these operations will be carried out.

Another destabilizing factor is the inability to plan for the long term because of the unpredictability of the year-to-year budget. A capital investment program that extends beyond 1 year may not be funded at expected levels in successive years. This can be a function of factors that are unrelated to the program, such as a major budget reduction that must be absorbed.

Federal Sales Procedures. On the marketing side, government procedures are equally lengthy, cumbersome, and inflexible. A case in point is the DOE experience in oil sales for the period from April 1 through September 30, 1986. Because of the sales procedures in place at the time, some DOE oil was sold for as little as $3.91 per barrel, which represented a discount of $6.98 over prices posted by major oil companies in the area.[52] All the production for that period was sold at below market value. In response to this situation, DOE has made changes in the sales procedures, but the government still must sell to the highest qualified bidder and its flexibility is limited.

Political Constraints. In addition to the institutional constraints described earlier, the reserves, as federal properties, are subject to a wide range of political pressures. Political factors make multi-year planning for NPR production extremely difficult and can affect revenues from the field. Testimony presented to the Commission stressed that private owners would not face the constant threat that production might be curtailed because of political or strategic concerns. Furthermore, private owners could commence long-term projects without being concerned that the reserves could be shut in at the next 3-year decision point required by the NPR Production Act.

Department of Defense (DOD) Concerns

The Defense Department's recent concern with losing dedicated access to petroleum supplies from the NPRs is based on experience with shortages during the disruption of the oil supply caused by the revolution in Iran in 1979. DOD has consistently emphasized its requirements for a dedicated supply of oil directly under DOD control. Defense officials believe that if the NPRs are to be sold, those supplies must be replaced by another source that is under equally direct control.[53]

Although all NPR oil is now being sold into the open market, every sales contract contains a 10-day cancellation clause that can be invoked by DOD, and the NPR oil can be transferred directly to DOD control, where most likely it would be swapped for other products. Jeffrey Jones, Director of Energy Policy for the Department of Defense, made clear in his testimony before the Commission that NPR oil must be in continuous production if quick access to this supply is to be assured.[54]

Jones candidly addressed the shortcomings of using a producing oil field as a source of emergency supplies. He discussed the problems of depletion, the inland location, and the trading of oil away from one sector of demand to supply another.[55] Furthermore, the NPRs have no capability for a rapid production increase (surge capacity) to meet an emergency, and demand in the initial stages of a military action would most likely have to be met in part from sources outside the United States. Despite these problems, DOD's master mobilization plan attaches substantial importance to the NPRs.

Pending legislation on NPR sales addresses DOD's concerns by creating a Defense Petroleum Inventory of 10 million barrels, to be held at the Strategic Petroleum Reserve storage sites and drawn down at the direction of the Secretary of Defense.[56] Such an inventory would offer DOD substantially improved access to oil compared with that provided by the NPR. Jeffrey Jones expressed DOD's support for this plan in his testimony before the Commission, stating:

> This Inventory addresses all the relevant shortcomings of the Naval Petroleum Reserves today. . . . From a strictly Defense viewpoint, therefore, the need for oil once represented in the Naval Petroleum Reserves can be met far better by the establishment of a smaller, but more flexible Defense Petroleum Inventory.[57]

Economic Considerations Concerning NPR Privatization Proposals

Fair Market Value

One major issue that has been raised by the Congress and many others is whether the government would be able to ensure that it would get a fair price for the NPRs if they were sold. The principal concern relates to the volatility of the oil market, and how the government would deal with the potential for lost revenues if there were a sharp rise in prices. One school of thought leans toward retaining ownership of the reserves if the sell-hold analysis is close.

Both the American Independent Refiners Association and the California Independent Producers Association take issue with the timing of the sale and the arguments that buyers will value the reserves based on expected future prices for oil. W. Scott Lovejoy, Executive Director of the West Coast Division, American Independent Refiners Association (AIRA), told the Commission:

> A sale at this time would result in bids based upon oil prices, which, on an inflation-adjusted basis, are near their historical lows, and at that

level would deprive the government of a fair price for this valuable asset.[58]

In his testimony before the Commission, Thomas R. Hunt, Executive Vice President, California Independent Producers Association (CIPA), provided statistics showing that the light Elk Hills crude sells today at $9.35 below its selling price of 2 years ago. Hunt said, "Simple math . . . demonstrates that now is not the opportune time to maximize [this] transaction's value." [59]

Congress authorized DOE to study the divestiture of NPR–1 and NPR–3 (placing a cost ceiling of $500,000 on the study). In February 1987, DOE awarded a contract to Shearson Lehman Brothers, directing that firm to develop a marketing plan for the sale of the reserves. The contractor's "Marketing Plan for Naval Petroleum Reserves 1 and 3," delivered to the DOE in May 1987, recognized the concern about timing of the sale. It included an optional phased approach for the sale of NPR–1; this approach would begin the privatization process by selling a minority interest in the reserve to create a new private sector operator, but the government would withhold a major share of the property. This remaining interest would be structured into a government-chartered corporation to provide maximum flexibility for eventual sale. These retained shares in the field would be sold at some point in the future when the market appeared to become more favorable. Although this phased approach would gain a few of the advantages of a sale while waiting for prices to rise, it still places the government in the difficult position of determining when, over the life of the reserves, to sell and get the best price. In addition, it could make operation of NPR–1 more difficult by adding a third party to the existing ownership and management structure.

Transaction Costs

In addition to the issue of fair market value, some concern has been expressed about whether the transaction costs might outweigh the potential gains from selling the reserves, given that those costs are somewhat higher than normally would be the case for private sector assets. There will be costs to the government for unit plan contract (UPC) renegotiations and sales fees. In addition, the cost of the Defense Petroleum Inventory must be considered as part of the overall legislative package. Highest among these costs will be filling the inventory, which is specified as 10 million barrels *in addition to* the oil set aside for the Strategic Petroleum Reserve. If the price of oil, for example, averages $20 per barrel over the period of fill, the cost will be $200 million.

Under certain circumstances, sales fees could be significant. Fees would probably be $4 million to $6 million for the first two phases of the Shearson plan; but typical fees for royalty trust offerings, if they are included in

the third phase, are 6 percent of the offering.[60] Costs of UPC renegotiations are more difficult to estimate. This contract agreement allows the
field to be operated as a single unit under the ultimate control of the government. Although Chevron owns only about 22 percent of the Elk Hills
reserves, the UPC gives them certain benefits, such as equal representa-
tion on the Operating Committee and the Engineering Committee. The
former sets the number, depth, and location of all wells and approves all
facility expenditures; and the latter is responsible for redetermining ownership percentages as the field is developed and produced.[61] It is uncommon for a minority owner in a private unit to have such a voice. The
compensation required by Chevron to give up these benefits in preparation for selling the NPRs will have to be determined by new contract negotiations.

Revenue Transfers from Federal to State Treasuries

If the reserves are sold, prospective purchasers will develop offers
based on an analysis of after-tax cash flows, operating under the assumption that they would be paying federal, state, and local taxes. These offers
will include a buyer's discount attributable to the $78 million per year in
state and local taxes for which the federal government will receive no
direct compensation. These revenue streams will, in effect, be transferred
from the federal government to state and local governments. This "structural" difference, according to the DOE report, could amount to as much
as a half-billion dollars in the proceeds from the sale.[62]

Discount Rate Assumptions

The discount rate used by a prospective purchaser reflects the annual
rate of return that a bidder requires to invest in a certain project. All
other things remaining equal, the lower the rate, the more the project—in
this case the reserves—is worth to the bidder now and the higher the bid
will be. However, a question has arisen as to whether the discount rate
the government should use to determine the worth of continuing to hold
the reserves rather than selling them should be different from the rate a
typical private sector purchaser would use to determine how much to bid.

DOE takes the position that private sector rates should be used on both
sides of the analysis. In his testimony before the Commission, Richard D.
Furiga, Deputy Assistant Secretary for Petroleum Reserves, stated that
DOE has

> . . . adopted the concept that business risk is associated with the charac-
> teristics of the asset rather than the characteristics of the owner. If the
> Government used [U.S.] Treasury borrowing rates to evaluate its
> business-type assets, asset divestiture would rarely look like a wise busi-
> ness decision.[63]

The General Accounting Office (GAO) takes issue with this rate, stating that it prefers to use the average yield of long-term government securities as the basis for evaluating the present value of government assets. Flora H. Milans, GAO Associate Director for Fossil Energy, stated in her testimony before the Commission:

> We use this basis because we believe decisions concerning government investments or divestitures must be viewed economically from a government-wide perspective. . . . Because most government funding requirements are met by the Treasury, the government's estimated borrowing cost is a reasonable basis for establishing the interest rate to be used in a present value analysis.[64]

Discussions with congressional staff revealed points of view similar to those expressed by the GAO. A prevailing congressional viewpoint seems to be that the sell analysis is fine, and a market-oriented discount rate is appropriate for getting a good estimate of the market value of the reserves. However, the hold analysis should be done using the Treasury rate with some small increment for risk, but not the same risk increment that a prospective buyer would apply in the private sector.

Sell-Hold Analysis

Shearson developed the sell-hold analysis for NPR–1 using a 12 percent nominal discount rate, showing the government's share of the Elk Hills field to be worth $3.6 billion if sold but only $3.4 billion if held. This analysis was based on reserve estimates made by the firm of Babson and Sheppard. The same analysis, using reserve estimates from the DOE Long-Range Plan, gave similar results: $4.3 billion if sold and $4.0 billion if held. In order for the comparison of sell-hold values to be accurate, the figures for the "hold" analysis exclude implicit taxes that are calculated as if the federal owner paid taxes.[65]

In summary, the Commission finds:

- The reserves no longer play a key role in DOD planning for an energy emergency. The strategic role for which they were set aside is an anachronism. The more recent DOD need, an immediate oil supply under direct DOD control, is satisfied much more effectively with the proposed legislation for a Defense Petroleum Inventory.

- Government operation of an oil field is inherently inefficient. The government does not have the cost-saving infrastructure of a commercial oil company; and federal budget and procurement practices simply do not allow production strategies that can achieve maximum efficiency and revenue.

- Although revenue transfers to the states and potential questions about the appropriate discount rate must be considered, the Shearson analysis shows a net benefit to the government in selling the NPRs, using a relatively conservative valuation of potential improvements under private sector management.

The Commission recommends:

Recommendation (9)

The federal government should begin immediately to divest both NPR-1 and NPR-3.

Impacts on California Petroleum Markets

Small and Independent Refiners

Seven of the eight major refiners in California are also major crude producers. These eight supply 76 percent of California's refinery market. The independents are particularly concerned about access to crude oil supplies in this environment. Over the past 6 years, small and independent refiners have purchased more than half of the NPR-1 production sold by the government. The NPR Production Act provides that small refiners always will be able to get at least 25 percent of NPR production, and prohibits sale of more than 20 percent of production to any one buyer. Although small refiners make up only 4 to 5 percent of the state's refining capacity (the remainder is made up of large, independent refiners), the refiners have a disproportionate effect on competition because California's market for refined products is so highly concentrated.[66]

Four refiners in particular are likely to be affected by the sale of NRP-1 and might be forced to close if they lost access to that source of crude. They are small inland operations with total refining capacity of about 72,000 barrels per day and little access to other sources of crude: Beacon Oil Company, which suspended operations last fall; Kern Oil & Refining Co.; Sunland Refining Corp.; and Newhall Refining Company Inc. A November 1987 GAO analysis of their operations shows that when these firms did not win NPR-1 production contracts, they either purchased oil from traders who did win, to keep their operations going, or reduced operations.[67]

Scott Lovejoy of AIRA gave the Commission a detailed picture of the problems of refiners in the San Joaquin Valley of California. The major problem is their inland location, which limits their access to light crudes other than that from Elk Hills, even though such crudes are in abundant supply along the coast. There are no inbound pipelines from the coast, and supplies would have to be trucked in, a situation that is not economically feasible.[68]

Most of these refiners report they would have difficulty surviving without access to light crude oil, because most cannot afford to upgrade their refineries to handle more of the very heavy Kern County crude oil. If the Elk Hills field is bought and operated by a major oil company, these refiners believe that they would have no protection in the event that company decided to use the oil for its own purposes and not sell it on the open market.

Pipelines and Independent Producers

Thomas Hunt of CIPA told the Commission that availability of NPR light crude to facilitate pipeline transportation is critical for CIPA's members. Production from NPR-1 is primarily a light crude, whereas most of the other oil production in Kern County is very heavy crude, some almost solid, which needs to be heated or blended with light crude to flow through pipelines. If NPR oil were not sold into the open market, independent heavy oil producers would be limited in the amount of oil they could transport through pipelines. Currently, the Four Corners Pipeline Company is the only common carrier transporting crude out of the San Joaquin Valley. It can transport about one barrel of heavy crude for every two barrels of NPR-1 light crude. Heated pipeline capacity, which will preclude the need for blending, will be available in the area when the All American Pipeline is completed in 1989.

Hunt pointed out that if Elk Hills crude were not available to blend with the heavy crudes, the only alternative for transporting much of the heavy crudes would be by truck.[69] The GAO reported that, in June 1986, when the government reduced production by 20,000 barrels per day, the pipeline company reduced its volume by 30,000 barrels per day. A third of this reduction fell on independent heavy oil producers, which were forced to cut production by the amount that the pipelines could no longer carry.

When Lovejoy and Hunt were questioned by the Commission as to whether some form of assured access to light crude for small and independent refiners and producers would remove their opposition to selling the reserves, both said yes. When John Cameron, from Chevron, was asked the same question, he agreed that Chevron could accommodate such a provision, depending on its scope, but that any such provision would reduce the attractiveness of the reserves to a potential buyer.[70] Cameron further explained that Chevron had had the opportunity to buy much more Elk Hills crude but had not found it to be in the company's economic interest to do so. He thought that the market would work in the favor of the independents whether there was an assured access provision or not.[71]

The Commission recommends:

Recommendation (10)

The issues of access to light Elk Hills crude oil for small refiners, as well as structuring the sale to maximize the number of potential bidders, should be considered when the Reserves are sold.

Summary

The Naval Petroleum Reserves no longer play a key role in DOD planning for an energy emergency. The strategic role for which they were set aside is an anachronism. The more recent DOD need, an immediate oil supply under direct DOD control, is satisfied much more effectively with the proposed legislation for a Defense Petroleum Inventory.

Government operation of an oil field is inherently inefficient. The government does not have the cost-saving infrastructure of a commercial oil company, and federal budget and procurement practices simply do not allow production strategies that can achieve maximum efficiency and revenue.

Although revenue transfers to the states and potential questions about the appropriate discount rate must be considered, the Shearson analysis shows a net benefit to the government in selling the NPRs, using a relatively conservative valuation of potential improvements under private sector management. Therefore, the Commission believes that selling the reserves is the appropriate course of action for the government to take.

In selling the reserves, however, the government needs to consider the issue of access to light NPR crude for small refiners. Several small refiners in the San Joaquin Valley are dependent on the NPR as the source of the type of crude oil that they are configured to refine, and most cannot afford to upgrade their refineries to accept heavier crudes. Their access to other sources of light crude is restricted by a one-way (outgoing) pipeline system. Furthermore, independent producers in the region depend on the ability to blend light NPR crude with their heavier crudes in order to ship their oil through the pipeline. Loss of access to this supply of light crude would probably result in shutdown of small refineries and cutbacks in heavy crude production.

NOTES FOR CHAPTER 9

1. Lawrence Hunter, "Statement of the Chamber of Commerce of the United States on the Privatization of Amtrak" before the President's Commission on Privatization, Hearings on Asset Sales (hereinafter cited as Hearings on Asset Sales), January 29, 1988.

2. President's Commission on Privatization, Hearings on Asset Sales, January 29, 1988.

3. Beth Selby, "Inside the Conrail Deal," *Institutional Investor* (April 1987), p. 95.

4. U.S. Department of Transportation, *Privatization of Conrail: The Public Offering* (1988), p. 5.

5. Testimony of Byron Nordberg, United Rail Passenger Alliance, Hearings on Asset Sales.

6. Testimony of Ross Capon, National Association of Railway Passengers, Hearings on Asset Sales, January 29, 1988.

7. Testimony of Jeffrey Jones, Department of Defense, Hearings on Asset Sales, January 29, 1988.

8. John Baden, "Destroying the Environment: Government Mismanagement of Our Natural Resources," paper presented at the *Privatization and Public Policy* Seminar sponsored by the Political Economy Research Center, September 1986, pp. 80 and 84.

9. National Railroad Passenger Corporation (Amtrak), "Background on Amtrak," fact sheet, June 1977, p. 5.

10. Ibid., p. 6.

11. Department of Transportation, "Final Report to Congress on the Amtrak Route System," January 1979, p. 22.

12. National Railroad Passenger Corporation, "Background on Amtrak," p. 17. This does not include 56 miles of track from the Connecticut state line to New Haven, owned by the State of Connecticut, and 37 miles from the Massachusetts State line to the Boston Square Station, owned by the Massachusetts Bay Transit Authority.

13. Office of Management and Budget, *Major Policy Initiatives 1987*, p. 45; and Congressional Budget Office, *An Analysis of the President's Budgetary Proposals for Fiscal Year 1987*, February 1986, p. 74.

14. Jeffrey Shedd, "Amtrak: Congress' Toy Trains," *Reason*, May 1981, p. 2.

15. Federal Railroad Administration (FRA), "The Economics of Amtrak," November 24, 1986, p. 2.

16. Ibid.

17. Ibid., p. 3.

18. Ibid., p. 16.

19. Ibid., p. 17.

20. Ibid.

21. Ibid., pp. 2, 15.

22. FRA, *The Sale of Conrail—From Public to Private Sector*, November 1985.

23. Northeast Rail Service Act (NERSA) as amended through 1982 (P.L. 97-36).

24. FRA, *The Sale of Conrail*.

25. Testimony of John Riley, Federal Railroad Administration, Hearings on Asset Sales, January 29, 1988.

26. Joint Center for Urban Mobility Research, "Japanese National Railways," report prepared for the Urban Mass Transportation Administration, June 1987, p. 12.

27. Testimony of Byron Nordberg, United Rail Passenger Alliance, Hearings on Asset Sales, January 27, 1988.

28. Ibid.

29. FRA, "The Economics of Amtrak," p. 28.

30. Ibid., p. 27.

31. Ibid., p. 29.

32. John Riley, Federal Railroad Administration, Hearings on Asset Sales, January 27, 1988.

33. FRA, "The Economics of Amtrak," p. 33.

34. Ibid.

35. Nordberg testimony.

36. Ibid.

37. FRA, "The Economics of Amtrak," p. 26.

38. U.S. Department of Energy, "Divestiture of the Naval Petroleum Reserves," DOE/FE-0089, p. A-2.

39. 41 Stat. 813, June 4, 1920.

40. President Harding, Executive Order No. 3473, May 31, 1921.

41. President Coolidge, Executive Order No. 4614, March 17, 1927; confirmed by Congressional action, 45 Stat. 148, February 25, 1928.

42. U.S. Department of Energy, "Divestiture."

43. Ibid., pp. A-3, A-4.

44. Ibid.

45. Naval Petroleum Reserves Production Act of 1976, P.L. No. 94-258, April 5, 1976.

46. Supplementary information, Clifford Gardner, Resources, Community, and Economic Development Division, U.S. General Accounting Office.

47. U.S. Department of Energy, "Divestiture," p. A-4.

48. Ibid.

49. Department of Energy Organization Act, P.L. No. 95-91, August 4, 1977.

50. Testimony of Jeffery A. Jones, Department of Defense, Hearings on Asset Sales, January 29, 1988.

51. *Department of Energy News Bulletin*, "Big Hill Strategic Reserve Site Named One of Six Top U.S. Engineering Achievements," January 28, 1988.

52. U.S. General Accounting Office Fact Sheet, "Naval Petroleum Reserves: Oil Sales Procedures and Prices at Elk Hills, April Through December 1986," GAO/RCED-87-75FS, January 1987, p. 4.

53. Letter from Secretary of Defense Caspar W. Weinberger to Secretary of Energy, John S. Herrington, September 21, 1987.

54. Jones testimony.

55. Ibid.

56. Letter from Secretary of Energy John S. Herrington to Honorable George Bush, President of the Senate, transmitting draft legislation titled "Naval Petroleum Reserves Divestiture and Energy Security Enhancement Act," December 10, 1988.

57. Jones testimony.

58. Testimony of W. Scott Lovejoy, American Independent Refiners Association, Hearings on Asset Sales, January 29, 1988.

59. Testimony of Thomas R. Hunt, California Independent Producers Association, Hearings on Asset Sales, January 29, 1988.

60. Supplementary information, Robert Bidwell, Office of Petroleum Reserves, U.S. Department of Energy.

61. U.S. Department of Energy, "Divestiture," pp. 23, A-3.

62. Ibid., pp. 9-10.

63. Testimony of Richard D. Furiga, U.S. Department of Energy, prepared statement, Hearings on Asset Sales, January 29, 1988.

64. Testimony of Flora H. Milans, U.S. General Accounting Office, prepared statement, Hearings on Asset Sales, January 29, 1988.

65. Shearson Lehman Brothers, "Marketing Plan for Naval Petroleum Reserves 1 and 3," May 1987, pp. 76-78.

66. U.S. General Accounting Office Fact Sheet, "Naval Petroleum Reserve-1: Government and Industry Comments on Selling the Reserve," GAO/RCED-88-43FS, pp. 13-17.

67. Ibid.

68. Lovejoy testimony.

69. Ibid.

70. Ibid.

71. Ibid.

Chapter 10

Other Programs:
Medicare; International Development Programs; Urban Mass Transit

The Commission examined three disparate areas, Medicare, funding for international development, and urban mass transit, in which privatization efforts have already been initiated by their federal agencies: the Health Care Financing Administration (HCFA), the Agency for International Development (AID), and the Urban Mass Transportation Administration (UMTA).

In the Medicare and urban mass transit programs, the impetus for privatization has come primarily from the pressing need to introduce cost-containment incentives into the provision of services. In the case of international development, privatization initiatives have been motivated less by concern about the funds expended than by a desire to use resources more effectively.

Of the three areas, Medicare is the largest in a number of dimensions. First, the 1987 total Medicare budget was roughly $70 billion. Second, the Medicare program directly touches the lives of the entire United States population, as everyone is either a current or future beneficiary, and most members of the working population contribute to the Medicare system through income and social security taxes. Third, the issues involved in privatization of Medicare are probably the most involved and the most difficult, since the service in question is the health care coverage for our nation's elderly.

The Medicare program faces serious financial crisis, with the Hospital Insurance fund projected to run out before the turn of the century. The basic challenge has been to introduce cost-containment incentives into the financing and provision of health care for the elderly without compromising the quality of that care. HCFA has begun a program designed to meet that challenge by introducing competition into health care financing through the use of vouchers or "capitation" payments.

AID assists developing countries through grants, loans, technical assistance, and food relief. Until 1986, most AID monies went to governments that channeled them to state-owned enterprises, often with limited results in terms of economic development. Increasing frustration with the general inefficiency and unresponsiveness of these state-owned enterprises was the impetus for AID's privatization program. Many leaders of developing nations also began to promote privatization because of the growing subsidies needed to run state-owned enterprises. Under its Private Enterprise Initiative, AID emphasizes direct assistance to private business ventures, involvement of the private sector in the delivery of traditional foreign assistance programs such as family planning and health care, and the provision of both technical and financial support for privatization of state-owned enterprises in host countries.

The urban mass transit program affects millions of Americans. Although annual expenditures have increased threefold in the last 10 years to $3.2 billion in 1987, ridership has fallen from 13 to 9 percent of urban commuters over the same period. Here, a concern about steadily increasing costs is accompanied by concern about the apparent decrease in the attractiveness of urban mass transit as an option for commuters. UMTA has responded by creating an Office of Private Sector Initiatives in 1985 to help UMTA grant recipients develop routine processes for involving the private sector in the provision of urban mass transit.

In all three areas, Medicare, international development, and urban transit, increased private sector involvement has demonstrated the potential for increased efficiency and quality of service.

MEDICARE

Medicare Financing

The Medicare program was initiated in the latter part of the 1960s as part of the Johnson administration's agenda for the Great Society. Like Social Security, Medicare was conceived not as a form of public assistance, but as a form of forced savings, to be returned in the form of a benefit in later years.

The Medicare program as currently operated faces a fiscal crisis. Because of increased consumption and the use of more elaborate technology, medical costs have been increasing at a much faster rate than inflation. Even holding consumption constant, the average annual percentage increase in the price of medical care has been approximately 8 percent per year since Medicare's inception, compared with an average rate of inflation for all goods of about 6.1 percent.[1] In addition, the elderly population has been increasing rapidly relative to the working-age population. Thus, there are more and more people drawing benefits from the system relative to those who are contributing to it.

Perhaps the major cause of accelerating health care costs is the lack of cost-containment incentives. Because consumers do not directly pay the major cost of medical care, their decisions about whether to consume medical care involve virtually no consideration of that cost. An estimated 70 percent of the elderly avoid any copayment by virtue of either Medicaid or private supplemental health insurance, although they must pay any amount billed above Medicare's customary, prevailing, and reasonable (CPR) rate.* Health care providers therefore have little incentive to compete on a price basis. Although there may well be benefits to consumers from the nonprice competition that presumably results, much of health care quality is difficult for consumers to gauge, and it is unclear how much real quality competition exists.

Health Care Financing Today

Under the current Medicare program, HCFA acts as the health insurer for approximately 28 million elderly people, 3 million disabled people, and approximately 102,000 people afflicted with end-stage renal disease. Eligibility for the elderly begins at age 65. Health care is provided to this population through a mixture of private and public sector services. Under "traditional" Medicare, which still covers some 97 percent of Medicare

---

*The copayments covered by supplemental insurance policies generally are only the difference between the 80 percent of CPR that Medicare pays and the CPR. Supplemental insurance does not cover any amount billed above the CPR.

recipients, outpatient health care is provided by private physicians on a fee-for-service basis, and a major percentage of the fee is paid by HCFA. Hospital care is provided by private hospitals, which are reimbursed under HCFA's Prospective Payment System. All claims processing is contracted out to nine major private insurers and a number of Blue Cross/Blue Shield plans.

Medicare coverage consists of two parts: hospital coverage and physician services coverage, referred to as Part A and Part B, respectively. Under Part B, Medicare recipients pay a monthly premium, just as with private health insurance, of $24.80 per month for coverage of physician care.* For all those qualifying for Social Security there is no premium charge for Medicare's Hospital Insurance.**

Medicare covers 100 percent of a beneficiary's liability for inpatient hospital care for the first 60 days of a stay, after a 1-day deductible of $540, and 80 percent of the (HCFA determined) customary, prevailing, and reasonable fee for physicians, with a $75 deductible. For the 61st through the 90th day, beneficiaries must pay coinsurance of $135 per day, which is equal to 25 percent of the deductible. After 90 days, if the beneficiary remains in the hospital, there are 60 nonrenewable lifetime reserve days for which there is a copayment of $270 per day. If, during the initial 150 days, the beneficiary leaves the hospital and remains out of the hospital or any skilled nursing facility for at least 60 days, and is later readmitted to the hospital, the benefit cycle starts all over again, with 60 fully paid days less the deductible.***

Physicians may charge beneficiaries more than the HCFA-allowed CPR, in which case the beneficiaries must make up the difference. Physicians who agree not to charge more than the CPR are said to "accept assignment." Hospitals are not allowed to charge Medicare patients any additional amounts for covered services.

------

* The figures given in this section are for fiscal 1988, although, as of this writing, the new reconciliation bill may cause the figures for the Part A copayments to change slightly.

** Most people are covered by Social Security. For those that are not, Hospital Insurance coverage can be purchased for $226 per month. Approximately 23,000 people took advantage of this option in 1986.

*** Both the House and Senate recently passed legislation to provide catastrophic health coverage to Medicare beneficiaries. It now seems likely that some version will be signed into law. The catastrophic coverage legislation will limit the out-of-pocket expenditures for Medicare recipients and do away with the limit on number of hospital days. This expanded coverage will be financed by a combination of increased premiums and income tax surcharges for the relatively well-off elderly. Hence, this legislation is expected to benefit the low- to middle-income elderly the most. The poorest elderly will be less affected because they would already qualify for Medicaid—although the extent of Medicaid coverage varies by state.

For the elderly who are especially needy, state-administered Medicaid programs generally pay the premiums, deductibles, and copayments required by Medicare. Also, many Medicare beneficiaries supplement their Medicare coverage with private "Medigap" insurance. Medigap policies typically pay the deductibles and the copayments up to the Medicare CPR rates. They usually do not cover any amount billed above the CPR rate.

The hospital and physician entitlements are funded by separate trust funds. The Hospital Insurance (HI) Fund receives revenue primarily from the Social Security wage tax, with a small contribution from premiums paid by those beneficiaries not covered by Social Security. This fund is not entitled to draw on general revenues. Conversely, approximately 72 percent of the funding for physician services, Supplementary Medical Insurance (SMI), comes from general revenues, although income from premiums accounts for about 22 percent. Interest and "other income" make up the balance.

The HI Fund is projected to run out of money between 1996 and 2000 and to engender billions of dollars of deficits soon thereafter. In fiscal 1986, $18 billion of general revenues went to the SMI fund. Because payouts are growing at about 16 percent annually—much faster than revenues—the SMI program's share of the budget is constantly increasing. Thus, its rapidly growing need for general revenues is contributing to the budget deficit. Total Medicare payments for both programs in fiscal 1986 somewhat exceeded $75 billion.

Approaches to Health Care Financing Reform

The basic issue facing health care policymakers is how to introduce cost-containment incentives into the payment for and provision of health care without jeopardizing incentives to provide an adequate level of care. The standard means of introducing incentives in the private health insurance sector is the use of deductibles and copayment plans to pass on incentives to consumers. There is little latitude, however, for solving the Medicare problem solely by increasing the copayments, because it would thwart the original purpose of Medicare and because most Medicare recipients avoid these payments by purchasing supplementary insurance.*

---

*There are recurring suggestions, specifically a proposal by the American Medical Association (AMA), to "means-test" Medicare payments by increasing the copayments for relatively wealthy recipients. Many people object to this approach on equity grounds. In any event, the amount of savings to be realized in this manner is also not likely to solve the incentive problems intrinsic in fee-for-service reimbursement plans.

HCFA's Current Efforts

Current approaches to health care financing reform have sought to structure payment schemes so as to provide incentives to providers or insurers to contain costs. This is generally accomplished by some type of prospective payment or voucher system, whereby the provider bears some of the risk that the beneficiary's health needs will be more or less costly than the voucher amount received. This risk bearing provides the incentives to keep costs down, because the provider profits if costs are below the voucher amount and suffers losses if they are above it.

For example, in 1983, HCFA initiated the Prospective Payment System (PPS) for hospitalization of Medicare recipients. Under the PPS, the hospital is paid a fixed amount based on the average consumption of services for the beneficiary's particular Diagnosis Related Group (DRG). This payment scheme, which is similar in concept to a risk-weighted voucher, gives hospitals an incentive to limit the length of hospital stays. Critics of the DRG system, however, argue that the hospital's incentive to limit stays may be so strong in some instances as to encourage inadequate health care. Presumably, liability laws should mitigate this problem, but the high cost of bringing suit and the difficulty in gauging health care quality imply that the liability laws, by themselves, are unlikely to be a complete solution.

A similar approach to the PPS is being pursued under HCFA's "Private Health Plan Option." [2] This approach was initially authorized by the 1982 Tax Equity and Fiscal Responsibility Act (TEFRA) and subsequent HCFA regulations promulgated in 1985.

Under TEFRA, HCFA is authorized only to contract with health maintenance organizations (HMOs) and competitive medical plans (CMPs), which are insurer/providers, to provide health care (both physician and hospital services) to Medicare beneficiaries in return for a capitation fee—essentially a voucher. This fee is equal to 95 percent of the adjusted average per capita cost for a Medicare enrollee of the same age, sex, county, public assistance, and institutional status.

The Administration would like to expand the current capitation program under the Private Health Plan Option (PHPO) to allow capitated payments to be made to large employers or other groups that agree to sponsor and administer health insurance plans to cover Medicare beneficiaries. Separate legislation would have to be approved by Congress to accomplish this. Under such a program, a large employer might contract with either an HMO or a fee-for-service insurer to cover retirees, and the employer would receive capitated payments from HCFA for each retiree covered. (The term "insurer" is used generically throughout to refer both to HMOs, which are really insurer/providers, and to fee-for-service insurers.)

Every witness before the President's Commission on Privatization, and others who commented for the record, expressed cautious optimism about the current program. As discussed later, they also pointed out shortcomings in both the current program and the PHPO, chiefly concerning inadequate monitoring and risk-weighting of vouchers, and suggested possible remedies.

There are now about 1 million Medicare recipients enrolled in capitated plans. A crucial aspect of these plans is that HMOs and CMPs act both as insurers and as providers—internalizing incentives to reduce cost—unlike traditional fee-for-service insurance plans. These providers generally offer beneficiaries an attractive package that often precludes the need for supplemental "Medigap" insurance. For this type of package, the beneficiary may pay premiums that are less than the sum of Medicare plus supplemental premiums, but still more than Medicare premiums alone.

The PHPO would have an additional benefit, beyond those of current capitation plans, of easing administrative costs to employers who currently provide supplemental insurance to retirees and must expend valuable resources determining which claims should be paid by Medicare and which should be paid by them. Under the PHPO, employers could consolidate health care financing into one package.

Medicare Voucher Systems

Various proposals have been put forth by the AMA and others to increase cost-containment incentives in Medicare by means of a voucher system.[3] As in the existing capitation program, under a voucher system HCFA would not act as a fee-for-service insurer but would give consumers vouchers to purchase private health insurance coverage for both physician and hospital care from a fee-for-service insurer or from an HMO. The potential benefits to society are twofold. First, the provision and administration of health insurance would be moved to the private sector, where there may be more incentives to carry out these tasks efficiently. Second, the introduction of competition could be expected to reduce costs further and to stimulate innovation. In addition, a voucher system would ease the burden on the taxpayers by shifting some risk to the private sector. This last effect would benefit taxpayers, but would not necessarily be either a gain or a loss to society as a whole.

Unfortunately, because both beneficiaries and insurers can sort on the basis of risk and because the current Medicare system is characterized by market power on the buyer's side (that is, HCFA), the social welfare implications of moving to a voucher system are unclear. A voucher system creates the possibility of adverse selection by beneficiaries and presents private insurers with incentives to sort out high-risk people. This may result in inadequate provision of health care for some elderly people, or increased rather than decreased costs to the government, or both.

Adverse Selection

Adverse selection is a well-studied form of market failure that leads different risk groups to separate due to an asymmetry in the information available to buyers and sellers. For instance, in the market for health care financing, beneficiaries would sort themselves into insurance plans (or HMOs) that cover only similarly healthy people. That is, adverse selection leads to sorting of healthy people into one set of plans and sick people into another.

Adverse selection can be described as follows: first, a comprehensive health plan offering high benefits will require a correspondingly high premium, say, $200 per month. Only people who expect to spend more than $200 per month on health care in the absence of insurance will subscribe to this plan.* Because everyone subscribing is a high user, there are no "average" or "low" users among whom to spread the risk. Thus the insurer must raise the premiums to cover increasing costs. As the premiums increase, the least risky—people who need the high coverage the least—will switch to a lower-option plan, leaving the insurer with an even more self-selected group of high users. Once again, the insurer will be forced to raise premiums because of the higher rate of use, and this in turn will lead to more self-selection. In the extreme, if all risks are known, this pattern continues until the insurer is forced to raise premiums and cut benefits to such an extent that no one wants that plan anymore.

The Federal Employee Health Benefit Program (FEHBP), in which employees are able to choose among a multitude of both traditional fee-for-service insurers and HMOs, is illustrative. The most comprehensive fee-for-service plan, Blue Cross high option, is now 75 percent retirees and was forced to increase its already-high premiums by 42 percent in 1988.[4] In the extreme case, the premiums will come to equal the health care costs that the beneficiaries would have paid out of their own pockets in the absence of insurance—making the insurance worthless.

The selection problem is exacerbated in health care financing because firms as well as consumers have incentives that tend to segment the market, and therefore erode the benefits of competition. Experts in the field of health care financing note that both insurers and insurer/providers have a powerful incentive, and devote many resources, to try to capture only those consumers who are low risk. This effort, known as "risk selection," is typically accomplished by tailoring the benefit plan to attract certain types, by skillful marketing, and by "screens" such as requiring application in person and then locating the office on the fifth floor of a building with no elevator. According to testimony submitted to the Commission, firms have even gone so far as to entice prospective members to

---

*A rational consumer would never pay an insurance premium that exceeded the expected direct cost of purchasing health care from a provider.

dances in order to evaluate their health status.[5] Again, the major concern would be the quality of care provided to those people who are perceived to be undesirable risks. Another serious concern is that the natural "sorting" likely to occur in a voucher system could also lead to increased rather than decreased costs to the government. This is because of the "incentive compatibility" of healthy beneficiaries and private insurers: both groups will act in ways that will tend to sort people who expect to have lower health care costs into the private sector and leave people who expect to have higher health care costs in traditional Medicare. As this occurs, both the amounts paid out by HCFA as fee-for-service *and* the voucher amounts will increase, because the voucher amounts are pegged to the average payment for a traditional Medicare beneficiary.

The social welfare problem here is one of *ex post* versus *ex ante* states of the world. *Ex ante*, when everyone is young and has a similar probability of needing health care in his or her elderly years, everyone benefits from contributing to a common insurance pool to spread the risk. *Ex post*, once people are elderly and their individual probabilities of needing health care are better known, risk pooling essentially becomes cross-subsidization from low-risk people to high-risk people. Thus, a competitive market will lead to sorting if it is imposed *ex post*. The economics literature on insurance markets suggests that under these circumstances it is often optimal to make decisions based on maximizing welfare in the *ex ante* situation.[6] In this case that would mean that people may often be better off making long-term contracts that pool the risk and disallow sorting into risk groups as risks become known. This is how traditional Medicare functions and how the private insurance market functions for nonretirees. But switching to a Medicare voucher system would give people who effectively contracted to pool the risk when they contributed to the system an *ex post* opportunity to sort. And there will be an incentive to sort because once people are elderly, they are already in an *ex post* world where relative risk is fairly predictable. Thus, part of the problem is transitional in that the rules are being changed in midstream. Subsequent generations could avoid the adverse and risk selection problems to a great extent by means of long-term contracts.

The problems of adverse selection and risk selection are not unique to the financing of health care for the elderly, but are common to all insurance markets. The sorting incentives are merely exacerbated in the case of the elderly because individual risks are better known for them. In the existing private market for health insurance for nonretirees, adverse selection and risk selection are minimized by a combination of risk pooling and long-term contracts *ex ante*. The risk pooling occurs in the form of employers' contracting with a single health insurer to cover all their employees. Although occasionally a worker may choose a particular job primarily because of the health insurance package it offers, there are clearly so many other factors involved in job choice that systematic selection on this basis is minimal. The employer, in turn, cannot be an agent for risk selection because of long-term contracting.

Thus, part of the difficulty with shifting to a Medicare voucher system could be alleviated over time if large employers offered retirement health benefits packages for which the contracts were made *ex ante*. One issue is how large the employer would need to be in order to pool the risk across retirees adequately.

Supporters of Medicare vouchers or capitated plans believe that it is possible, and necessary, to mitigate the adverse and risk selection problems by risk-weighting the capitation amounts, that is, by varying the payments by risk categories, as for Diagnosis Related Groups. Risk-weighting reduces the incentives for insurers (both HMOs and fee-for-service insurers) to sort, because they would be directly compensated for differences in relative riskiness among beneficiaries.* John Rother, Director of Legislation, Research, and Public Policy for the American Association of Retired Persons, warned

> The greatest barrier in the development of a Medicare voucher system lies in the inability to match the voucher amount to expected risk. . . . The health status of the individual would have to be taken into account in the calculation of voucher amounts if beneficiaries are to obtain coverage related to their actual needs.[7]

Risk-weighting vouchers is not costless, however; such a program could be cumbersome to monitor and administer. Careful calculation of risk weights is necessary, both because there is a danger of misclassifying people and because, if vouchers are weighted simplistically (for example, according to prior utilization), beneficiaries may develop perverse incentives to overuse health care in order to qualify for higher voucher amounts.

Competition versus Monopsony

Another important issue is whether the cost-containment incentives of competition would be able to compensate for the loss of market power, relative to providers, that would occur if Medicare were effectively "broken up" into many small competing entities. Whenever competition

---

*If such risk-weighting is to work properly, however, some experts feel it crucial that no form of open enrollment be imposed on the market. Even though some of the benefits of competition are lost without periodic open seasons, the benefit of allowing long-term contracts that would prevent "plan hopping" may very likely outweigh this cost. If open seasons are imposed, those who expect to have extensive hospitalization one year may temporarily switch into a high-option plan, switching back to a cheaper plan as soon as they are well. Clearly, this prevents the insurer from spreading risk over time. In the extreme, each insurer finds that everyone subscribing needs the worst-case coverage all the time.

is introduced, it would be expected to provide an incentive to reduce costs in order to compete on the basis of price. In addition, the elimination of market power would be expected to increase the quantity or quality of the product provided, in this case, health care. It is not obvious, however, that competition among health insurers in a voucher system would significantly lower health care expenditures, because it would not address the root of the problem, namely, increased costs of health care provision.

Although, for a given quantity or quality of service, competition should provide the lowest possible price of any market structure, the current Medicare structure may very well provide health insurance at a lower price by reason of monopsony power. That is, HCFA, because it represents 31 million beneficiaries, may be able to extract lower prices from health care providers than could be obtained by smaller competitive firms, albeit at the likely expense of reduced quality of care.* The Commission heard testimony that Medicare receives about a 15- to 20-percent reduction over private payers for physician services.[8] ** It is estimated that Medicare commands a modest 2- to 3-percent discount on hospital charges. This may be a benefit to the taxpayers, and, to the extent that third-party payment (i.e., health insurance) encourages the consumption of a higher quality of care than is socially desirable, the preservation of the monopsony power may be beneficial. However, market power causes distortions in the allocation of resources. In the case of health care, the expected long-run result of monopsony power (and thus, below-market fees) would be to discourage people from entering the health care field. Ultimately, a shortage of physicians would result.

Costs to Taxpayers

Voucher proponents argue that the costs to taxpayers of administering Medicare can be saved by turning the financing of health care over to the private sector. Although turning a costly enterprise over to the private sector would save the government those costs, there is no guarantee that

---

*The classic monopsony model predicts below-competitive prices at the expense of reduced quantity or quality of service.

** It is difficult to assess exactly the extent of the monopsony power, but about 30 percent of physicians in 1987 (159,091 out of 519,635) agreed to accept assignment in all Medicare cases treated. A significant portion of the remainder accepted assignment for some of their patients, but not for others. Thus, an estimate of the total percentage of Medicare recipients who are charged only the CPR would be in the range of 30 to 50 percent. According to private insurers, the HCFA-mandated CPRs are about 25 percent below average market rates. Multiplying the 25-percent discount by 30 to 50 percent would give an average discount due to monopsony power in the range of 7.5 to 12.5 percent, not considering other factors such as regional price variation and quality of care.

the private sector can administer the program more cheaply. Thus, even if the costs could be passed on to the private sector, the federal budget might show an improvement, but the total quantity of resources spent by society might increase under privatization.

In a recent study, the General Accounting Office (GAO) compared HCFA's administrative costs relative to claims payments with the costs of major employers.[9] HCFA contracts out claims processing, so it has a relationship with the major insurers similar to that of a large employer that contracts with insurers. GAO found that HCFA paid insurers about 1.5 percent of claims to cover administrative costs, whereas major employers paid from 5 to 20 percent. HCFA's additional administrative costs are less than 1 percent of claims.* The Health Insurance Association of America expressed doubt that private plans can match the government's administrative costs because of Medicare's monopsony power and the huge economies of scale in Medicare's computerized claims-processing system and standardized benefits.

A related issue is whether a voucher system might actually be more costly than traditional Medicare simply because of the increased monitoring involved. In particular, the Commission heard considerable concern expressed that expansion of a voluntary voucher system, such as the Private Health Plan Option, would require expanded oversight and monitoring of quality by HCFA. James Doherty, President of the Group Health Association of America, noted

> A credible quality of care review system for outpatient settings has not yet been fully developed in spite of HCFA's concentrated efforts. . . . It would be absurd, and perhaps cruel, to proceed with vouchers until the quality assurance system is in place.

Doherty went on to state:

> I suppose that in other areas considered for privatization by this Commission, the imposition of penalties and other sanctions might suffice to minimize fraud and other criminal activity. But here we are talking about the health of the elderly and the enormous consequences of shoddy, inappropriate, or inadequate treatment. Intelligent policing systems carefully administered must remain in place whether in a federal or state setting. Again, HCFA, the state health departments, and the state insurance commissioners are making efforts in this regard. However, we are far short of the necessary sophistication for a sound government-private sector regulatory scheme.[10]

---

* According to the Labor, Health and Human Services, and Education House Appropriations subcommittee staff, for the past fiscal year, HCFA's total administrative costs (including research) were $1.471 billion, of which $1.179 billion was contracted out. Total claims paid out were roughly $70 billion.

"Voluntary" versus "Mandatory" Vouchers

Under a "voluntary" voucher plan, Medicare recipients would have the choice of staying in the traditional Medicare program or of taking a voucher and getting private health insurance. In a "mandatory" or "pure" voucher plan, traditional Medicare would no longer exist, and all beneficiaries would receive vouchers for private health insurance. In essence, HCFA's current capitation program is a voluntary voucher plan on a small scale. Similarly, HCFA's proposed Private Health Plan Option would be a voluntary voucher plan.

Material submitted to the Commission suggests that, in a voluntary voucher system, adverse selection and risk selection by firms might well lead to increased government expenditures.[11] Due to HCFA's monopsony power, it may be difficult for fee-for-service insurers to offer comprehensive plans competitively with Medicare—unless, of course, they are more efficient. Beneficiaries who want comprehensive coverage and do not want to be limited in their choice of provider (as they would be with an HMO) will choose traditional Medicare, and private insurers (including HMOs) would have a strong incentive to steer risky patients back to traditional Medicare. There is already some evidence that it is the lower-than-average risks who are selecting HMOs. Capitation amounts may therefore be too high.[12]

If HCFA pays an average capitation rate, the government could easily end up spending more than it currently does, because it would be paying average rates for people with below-average costs, and it would be paying actual costs for the people with above-average risk. Although experience would lead HCFA to adjust the capitation rates for the following period, conceivably there would always be some loss in the initial period. It is easy to imagine an iterative process in which HCFA is always one step behind in getting the adjustment right. Private insurers are naturally interested in a voluntary voucher plan because, unlike a pure voucher plan, they might well insure only the "cream" of the Medicare population.

HCFA could probably avoid this problem by taking a conservative approach to voucher pricing. If, instead of offering a capitation amount close to the average cost for Medicare beneficiaries (as in the 95 percent of average cost offered now), HCFA offered a much lower fee to start (say, 70 percent of average), it could essentially iterate in the other direction. That is, if few insurers accepted the 70 percent voucher, HCFA could raise it gradually until it became worthwhile for insurers to participate. Obviously, this approach requires some guesswork and would be subject to the reproach from the private sector that voucher amounts were unreasonably low. It also fails to address the problem that as long as voucher amounts are pegged to the average health costs for a recipient of traditional Medicare, any risk-selection that increases the average riskiness of those remaining in traditional Medicare will not only raise the average cost of providing traditional Medicare, but will also increase the voucher amounts. This has the perverse effect that, the better the HMOs are at attracting the least costly beneficiaries, the more they will be reimbursed for them—which increases the incentive for the HMOs to sort in the first place.

One benefit of a voluntary voucher system is that it would provide a safety net in that the government would be the insurer of last resort, insuring only the people with very high risk. Additionally, many believe that because the HMO type of alternative delivery system combines insurer with provider, the prospects for cost containment by encouraging the use of these alternative forms of health care financing (and provision) are good.

Alternatively, the AMA has put forth a proposal to manage the Medicare funding crisis by implementing a mandatory voucher system. Under a pure voucher system, every Medicare recipient would receive a voucher for a capitated amount and be free to take it to whatever health insurer offers the most for the money, with no restrictions on entry into the market or on the type of coverage to be funded. Unfortunately, even strong supporters of the basic voucher concept warn that the problems inherent in a pure voucher system may be virtually impossible to overcome. Alain Enthoven, a health economist from Stanford University, who supports a "managed" voucher system, notes

> Many proponents and critics of the competition idea share the misconception that "competition" means a market made up of health care financing and delivery plans on the supply side and individual consumers on the demand side, without a carefully drawn set of rules designed to mitigate the effects of the market failures endemic to health care financing and delivery, and without mediation by some form of collective action on the demand side. Such a market does not work. It cannot produce efficiency and equity. Health insurance and health care markets are not naturally competitive. Health insurance markets are vulnerable to many failures that result from attempts by insurers to select risks, segment markets, and protect themselves from "free riders."[13]

In particular, the adverse selection or sorting problem may become severe in a freely competitive, pure voucher system. Insurers will have a strong incentive to attract low-risk people and discourage high-risk people. They can do so by offering very little coverage at very low rates. And, in a pure voucher system, traditional Medicare would no longer exist as the insurer of last resort.

Advocates of a mandatory voucher system note that such a system would eliminate the "implicit subsidy" of Medigap insurance. This implicit subsidy occurs because beneficiaries whose Medigap insurance covers their copayments have partially removed a disincentive to use more health care; when they use more health care, Medicare pays 80 percent of it. Medigap insurance has been estimated to result in about a $3 billion annual increase in Medicare costs (about 5 percent) over what they would be in the absence of supplemental insurance.[14] Potentially, this is a large cost saving, but it is likely to be overstated to the extent that some of the increased spending presumably reflects an adjustment for the gap between inadequate Medicare payments and actual health costs.

There is general agreement that some structuring of the market would be necessary for a number of reasons. First, some limitation of participating firms will cut down on monitoring costs. Second, some minimum standard of coverage would have to be required in order to avoid situations in which people find themselves inadequately insured. Third, limitations on the types of coverage that can be offered would encourage price competition and discourage risk selection. Enthoven goes so far as to recommend standardized benefit packages across HMOs and to structure the deductibles and premiums of fee-for-service plans to "make [them] attractive to about the same risk mix as that attracted by the HMO's."[15] Fourth, limiting the number of fee-for-service insurers might preserve some of the monopsony power of Medicare that would otherwise be lost.* The trade-off between competitive pressure and the cost-reducing benefits of dealing with health care providers from a position of market power need not be made if the small number of fee-for-service insurers are competing with a large number of HMOs. Last, there is a general view in the health care field that the resources that would be devoted to marketing and administering individual health policies in a completely free voucher system would constitute a net loss to society, because those resources are not currently expended. For this reason, and because of fears regarding the potential for deceptive advertising, policy analysts advise against permitting this type of marketing in favor of requiring HCFA to oversee the dissemination of information about different plans However, marketing costs would only constitute a net loss to society to the extent that the information imparted to consumers has no value. In an area such as health care where technology is changing rapidly and insurance coverage needs to respond appropriately, advertising is likely to act as a stimulus to innovation as well as a means of informing the public. Although dissemination of all information by HCFA would largely mitigate the possibility of deceptive advertising, it would also dampen competition and innovation.

---

*It is still an open question as to whether preserving the monopsony power is in the public interest. It may reduce costs to taxpayers and counteract quality inflation and monopoly power on the part of providers, to the extent that they exist, but monopsony power in this market is also likely to reduce the quality of health care provided and reduce the supply of health care provision in the long run.

Increasing Private Sector Involvement in Health Care Financing

Although the Commission heard testimony that it is possible to mitigate the two major problems of adverse selection and loss of monopsony power, some concerned parties believe that doing so may be difficult and costly for several reasons, especially in the context of a mandatory voucher system. On the basis of current information, it is difficult to determine whether the gains from competition would offset the increased costs of risk-weighting, monitoring, and loss of monopsony power. Perhaps most important is whether the gains from increased competition would justify the increased risk that some of the poorest and sickest Medicare beneficiaries would receive inadequate health care. Because of the sorting incentives, this risk is likely to increase with a capitated system, even if the average quality of care rises.

Alternatively, the Commission was impressed by the extent to which all parties seem to agree, with only minor caveats, that HCFA's capitation program with HMOs is very promising and that the results of already funded demonstration projects should provide guidance on the extent of problems and means of solving them. Potential adverse selection problems remain, but there appear to be strategies for alleviating them, and, as long as traditional Medicare remains an option, the chance that someone will "fall through the cracks" is minimized.

Because of the impending fiscal crisis in Medicare financing and the complexity of the issues involved, more creative solutions are essential. The Commission recommends the following:

Recommendation (1)

The government should act to increase competition and to introduce cost-containment incentives in the Medicare program by encouraging the use of vouchers or capitated payments to purchase private health care financing.

Incentives for the Private Sector

Most witnesses agreed that the relationship between the government and the private sector needs improvement in several areas. Private health insurers are concerned that the government may be seeking to shift the risk to the private sector without adequate compensation, at least in the long run. Geza Kadar, Assistant Washington Counsel for the Health Insurance Association of America, told the Commission, "First and foremost in our minds is the fear that . . . the government contribution to a voucher plan would be subject to the politics of the federal budget." [16]

James Doherty agreed, saying that "the government is not a reliable partner or a reliable purchaser. Actuarial estimates and values are changed retroactively and wreak havoc with the HMOs' ability to budget and set reasonably consistent rates." [17]

One proposal to ease the risk to private insurers of covering catastrophic expenses for someone for whom they were paid an "average" voucher amount, and to reduce the incentive for private insurers to screen out "risky" beneficiaries, is to use "risk corridors." With a risk corridor, the insurer agrees to cover all expenses in return for a capitated amount, within certain limits. If the capitated amount proves too generous, the private insurer is allowed to keep a certain percentage of the total as profits, which provides the incentive to economize. But, if the capitation amount proves insufficient, the private insurer would bear the extra cost only up to a certain percentage of the total. As long as the actual costs fall within the risk corridor around the capitation amount, the private insurer would either pay the costs or receive the profits. If actual costs fall outside the risk corridor, the government either pays the additional cost or is reimbursed for the profit.

One other refinement could be added to the risk corridor concept. In order to keep the private insurer from being indifferent to whether the costs are 1 percent or 100 percent above the risk corridor, there should be some type of copayment agreement. That is, the risk borne by the insurer should not simply fall abruptly to zero above the risk corridor, but rather should decline gradually from 100 percent, say, down to 70 percent, then down to 50 percent, and so on, as the cost increases.

Recommendation (2)

The government should act to increase private sector incentives for participating in health care financing for the Medicare population. The private sector is naturally reluctant to assume greater risk without compensating benefits. Some risk-sharing plan, such as the use of risk corridors, should be considered in the implementation of any voucher system.

Summary

The costs of financing health care in general, but especially for the elderly, are increasing at an unmanageable rate, largely because of the disassociation of the consumer from the payment in any individual transaction. Because the consumer has little incentive to shop for lower cost health care, health care providers compete almost exclusively on a quality, rather than price, basis. The current fiscal crisis in the financing of Medicare is rapidly coming to a head; the Hospital Insurance Fund could be depleted in 9 to 13 years, and the Supplemental Medical Insurance Fund is already a drain on the federal deficit: more than $18 billion was spent from general revenues in fiscal 1986. Thus, it is imperative to increase cost-containment incentives in the health care industry.

Increased private sector provision of health care financing in the form of capitation, or voucher, programs may offer a partial solution to the cost-containment incentive problem. The Commission believes, however, that it is critical to ensure that health care coverage of adequate quality is not sacrificed in the name of cost efficiency.

INTERNATIONAL DEVELOPMENT PROGRAMS

State-owned enterprises have played a dominant role in the economies of most developing countries during the past three decades. In these countries, the number of public enterprises has mushroomed, as has their portion of production and service activities. In Mexico, for example, there were 150 state-owned enterprises at the beginning of the 1960s; in 1986 there were at least 400.[18] However, this situation is changing.

Privatization in many developing countries is now viewed as a way to raise cash for reducing government debt, to curb public spending, to increase output, to improve the quality of goods and services, or to broaden the base of ownership and participation in the economy. In short, many less developed countries now consider private entrepreneurs and market economies, rather than centralized planning and state-owned enterprises, as the most appropriate mechanisms for encouraging economic growth and improving the standard of living.

As of 1986, in many less developed countries, state-owned enterprises accounted for 10 to 20 percent of gross national product (GNP). They often dominate the service, industrial, and agricultural sectors of the economy and are the major recipients of capital investment. State-owned enterprises are responsible for between 20 to 60 percent of total investment spending in developing nations.[19] This trend cuts across all ideologies and economic systems.

The growth of the state-owned sector in the former colonial nations of Africa, Asia, and Latin America that began around 1960 can be attributed to a number of factors. The leaders of the newly independent nations often inherited state domination of the economy. Socialist ideas encouraged leaders to perceive state ownership as the most effective way to achieve economic independence from "neocolonialism." In some instances, government came into ownership when private sector firms, seen as important to development, failed because of mismanagement, a lack of capital, or insufficient technical skills. Finally, political exigencies required governments in developing nations to find employment for their supporters and the growing populations of their urban centers.[20] By the early 1980s, many of these governments were living with the failures of centrally planned economies, and they began to explore alternative methods of development by relying on the private sector.

The Problem Defined

After World War II, United States foreign assistance to developing nations was directed to governments that frequently channeled it into various state-owned enterprises. Both donor and host governments believed that the public sector could best provide the resources necessary to plan and implement many critical development activities, such as providing transportation, water, and health services; marketing crops; and even producing basic consumer goods.

The billions of dollars channeled through state-owned enterprises for development projects often had limited results. In many cases, the capital was ill-managed and the state-owned enterprise proved unable to perform its intended tasks effectively. As a result, these state corporations came to rely on government subsidies, and drained resources rather than spurred development.

The subsidization of unprofitable state-owned enterprises placed a staggering burden on many developing nations. In Niger, for example, the cumulative deficit of 23 state-owned enterprises exceeded 4 percent of Niger's gross domestic product for a single year.[21] In many other countries the figures are even higher: 10 percent for Zimbabwe and 11 percent for Sri Lanka.[22] According to the World Bank, large state-owned enterprises owe at least 60 percent of the external debt of Latin American countries.[23]

While accumulating these debts, state-owned enterprises in less developed countries have failed to meet popular expectations in the production and delivery of goods and services. Manufactured goods are often poorly produced and in short supply. Services are irregular and, in many instances, the state agency responsible can barely function. Throughout the Third World, state-owned enterprises have failed to provide badly needed services such as health care, trash removal, or road maintenance services. In particular, state corporations—known as national marketing boards— often are the sole legal buyers and marketers of agricultural products. Their policies have distorted prices and resulted in decreased production of necessary food and export crops.[24]

The experience of over two decades of financially draining, inefficient, and politically, rather than economically, responsive state-owned enterprises encouraged the leaders of many less developed countries to consider privatization as a means to stimulate economic development.[25] In Bangladesh, more than 400 public sector assets have been divested, including newspapers, a fishing fleet, chemical and food-processing plants, and 8 percent of the government-owned steel and engineering corporations.[26] In Senegal, the government's large-scale agricultural enterprise ONCAD was liquidated, and discussions exploring the possibility of privatizing some of the government-owned banks are under way.[27] In Costa Rica, dozens of state industrial, agricultural, and service enterprises held by the state holding company CODESA have been, or are, in the process of sale or liquidation.[28]

Although there is a growing consensus among experts regarding the need for more reliance on the private sector and individual initiative to fuel economic growth in the less developed countries, some analysts still believe state-owned enterprises are necessary in these countries.[29] Expertise and resources required to provide essential services may not be available from the private sectors of some less developed countries. State-owned enterprises also service the more remote areas of the country, which private firms might neglect because they appear unprofitable. Moreover, state-owned enterprises provide the sole source of employment for many sectors of the population. Finally, some experts believe that the privatization of certain basic industries and services will result in the escalation of prices of essential goods to levels beyond the means of the poor.

AID Policy and Approach

In recent years, the Agency for International Development (AID) has changed its approach to promote development through free-market institutions and private enterprise. Its Private Enterprise Initiative [30] emphasizes not only direct assistance to private business ventures but also the use of the private sector (including profit-making private enterprises and nonprofit private voluntary organizations) to deliver traditional assistance programs in areas such as health care.

A major component of the initiative involves supporting the transfer of state-owned enterprises in less developed countries to the private sector. In 1986, each AID Mission was directed to engage in privatization activities or projects with its host government. Approximately 70 major activities are now under way worldwide, and about a dozen have been completed successfully.

To encourage overseas missions to make privatization an important aspect of their work, specific policies have been instituted. Agency guidelines now stipulate that "AID assistance to or through a parastatal (state-owned enterprise) should be given in the context of exposing the parastatal to market forces and scheduled divestiture of the government interest." [31] In short, government-owned enterprises should be moving toward market-based operations and divestiture to qualify for AID assistance. Thus, the use of AID funds should be accompanied by clearly articulated divestiture planning. They should not be used solely to improve the ability of state-owned corporations to respond to market forces.

AID has several resources to help host governments implement their privatization programs. These include technical experts to help plan strategies, evaluate financial records, prepare legal documents for change of ownership, and locate suitable buyers. If the government is incapable of discharging the state-owned company's debt or labor obligations before divestiture, the local AID Mission may be requested to provide small loans or grants. [32]

As more governments in the Third World have viewed public sector activities as "targets of opportunity" for privatization, AID Missions have assisted in the divestiture of industrial firms, agricultural enterprises, and public services. For instance, in Jamaica, AID recently assisted in the privatization of the National Commercial Bank. In Guatemala, AID is working with the government to open the air routes to private carriers. Previously, AID activities included the promotion of retail fertilizer distribution by the private sector in Bangladesh and the sale of government-owned banana plantations to private growers in Belize.[33] These efforts have strengthened the economies of these countries.

The Commission recommends:

Recommendation (3)

The Agency for International Development should increase its support of privatization in developing countries by directing its funds to the private sector. It should facilitate, where possible, the privatization of those state-owned enterprises that are recipients of U.S. foreign assistance.

Employment and Ownership Concerns

A number of critical concerns are associated with the privatization of state-owned enterprises in developing nations. Besides broad issues of economics, privatization raises issues of the financial strategies best suited to accomplish particular objectives, the legal foundations necessary to provide adequate support for privatization, tax structure, and politics.

In some ways, the political issues are the most important. Experts agree that the most significant barriers to privatization that government decisionmakers in less developed countries must overcome are political rather than financial.[34] The government may be fully aware of the financial drain of subsidies to state-owned enterprises, but it may also refuse to reduce or eliminate them because of the political risks involved.

Whenever the government explores the steps necessary to privatize, it will probably face opposition from the following groups:

- Political parties and opposition groups with conflicting partisan or ideological goals;

- Segments of the private sector that share in any special concessions made to public sector firms through allocation of foreign exchange, tax rates, or preferred markets;

- Ministry officials who benefit from positions on the boards of state-owned enterprises and managers who run the companies and do not believe that a change in management will improve operations; and

- Labor unions that may foresee a loss of jobs, a reduction of union strength, and a possible weakening of government responsibility for pension and job security rights.

A successful privatization program must overcome strong resistance from people who perceive it as a direct threat to their livelihood. Because many sectors of the population in Third World countries are employed in state enterprises, the potential for widespread public opposition exists.

In less developed countries, state-owned enterprises are often used as a means to disguise unemployment problems. Although some developing countries deal with unemployment through a compensation system or through a military draft, many leaders seem to view state enterprises as a place to absorb unemployed workers.[35] As a result, many agency or department heads see their task as providing employment rather than developing and delivering goods and services.

Observers agree that by using state-owned enterprises as a welfare mechanism, many workers are underemployed, resulting in a misdirection of their talents and skills. Although state-owned enterprises do provide nominal jobs, in the long run, they divert people from full development of their talents and skills. Long-term employment prospects will be improved as more efficient private enterprises create new market opportunities.

Another critical concern associated with the sale of state-owned enterprises in the developing world involves the purchasers. Governments attempting to transfer state-owned enterprises to the private sector must, on occasion, create legal and financial mechanisms to do so. They must identify potential buyers, decide upon the form of transfer and develop public support, sometimes for an innovative program such as an employee stock ownership plan or a debt-equity swap.

In many countries, some investors are politically unacceptable, either to the government or to the general population. Not only are foreign investors suspect, but local ethnic minorities are sometimes excluded from the purchase of domestic firms. For example, Indians in certain African countries or the Chinese in various Southeast Asian nations are prohibited from ownership. In many nations, sale of state enterprises to close friends or relatives of the country's leadership is highly resented. In this case, privatization could mean the replacement of a government monopoly with a private one.

Divestiture of state-owned enterprises through broad equity ownership—as in the form of public stock offerings or employee ownership plans—is one means of creating popular support for the sale of state corporations to the private sector while minimizing public criticism and worker resistance. Moreover, such ownership offers unique opportunities to strengthen individual economic freedoms in developing nations.

In Jamaica, for instance, the government recently sold 51 percent of its holdings in the National Commercial Bank through the sale of over 30 million shares of bank stock. Apart from the nearly 2,000 bank employees who invested (98 percent of bank employees), 15,000 applications from the general public were for under 300 shares, and 7,000 applications were for 300 to 1,000 shares.[36] This broadly based ownership of privatized state-owned enterprises not only involved the "redistribution of wealth," it also served to create a constituency for future privatization activities.

Plans whereby corporate equity is transferred to employees via a trust established by the corporation have been viewed as a means to democratize privatization in less developed nations.[37] At the La Perla coffee and spice plantation project in Guatemala, for example, the owners transferred 40 percent of the plantation's stock to an employee association, to be paid from the future earnings of the plantation plus employee and employer contributions averaging 3 percent of pay.[38] Funds generated through this type of plan enable workers to purchase the state-owned enterprise and participate in management and policy decisions.

Conversion to employee ownership requires careful planning and promotion. In many cases, it is far from certain that the workers could be persuaded to trade current cash payments for shares in a company whose future is uncertain. In addition, unions might object if their position could be weakened under such an ownership plan. Moreover, if the firm fails and liquidation of the enterprise is necessary, the workers (who under an employee ownership plan assume most of the risk) will lose the employment and benefits that are now secured through the government.

The Commission recommends:

Recommendation (4)

Employee stock ownership plans should be promoted by the Agency for International Development as a method of transferring state-owned enterprises to the private sector in developing countries.

International Financial Issues

Financing the sale of state-owned enterprises is a key privatization issue in developing nations. Depending on the size of the enterprise being sold, possible sources of financing include local entrepreneurs, domestic lending institutions, multinational corporations, international lending agencies, and foreign governments.

The privatization of small state enterprises usually can be financed in less developed countries through local capital sources—especially if an organized market exists. Private sector buyers may be able to pay the full cost from their own resources or with assistance from domestic lending institutions.

Loans for the purchase of relatively large state-owned enterprises in less developed countries are likely to be more difficult to secure. Local commercial banks are frequently more interested in short-term loans with greater security than a recently privatized state enterprise usually provides. In the case of large business loans, commercial bankers will often require full collateral or government guarantee. Governments are reluctant to guarantee these loans because, if the firm defaults, the government may find itself the unwilling participant in a "reverse privatization."

Because of the potential difficulties in arranging finances to transfer state-owned enterprises to private entrepreneurs, many governments in developing countries have turned to international or regional lending organizations and agencies. International financial institutions such as the World Bank, however, have displayed ambivalent attitudes toward privatization in these countries. Multilateral lending agencies and organizations often have rules and regulations that can stifle private sector investment. In addition, they have hesitated to depart from the traditional practice of lending to the public sector, because of a continuing belief—or hope—that state-owned enterprises might be made more efficient with additional funds.

Bilateral donors and multilateral or regional banks have, on some occasions, worked at cross purposes, with one donor attempting to assist privatization of a state-owned enterprise, while another funds the enterprise to keep it in the public sector. Some international banks, however, are experimenting with private sector alternatives and directing their staffs to explore further opportunities to encourage the privatization of state-owned enterprises in less developed countries.

The Commission recommends:

Recommendation (5)

The Agency for International Development should continue to encourage multilateral financial institutions and regional banks to act more decisively in private sector lending, privatization, and divestiture in less developed countries.

Foreign investors could provide a majority of the capital needed for privatization. In return, they could retain a share in the ownership of the new firm or a percentage of its profits. A key issue for governments in less developed countries which wish to attract private foreign investors and companies is how to accomplish this task, especially when many of these governments are in the midst of a major debt crisis.

When a government is interested in transferring a state-owned enterprise to the private sector and is prepared to seek foreign investors, debt-equity swaps, in particular, may provide inducements to foreign businesses and corporations that might not otherwise be interested in financing new private sector enterprises.

In debt-equity swaps, foreign or local investors purchase international commercial bank debts at a discount, convert the debt to local currency, and buy all or part of the equity in the enterprise. When the transaction is completed, the country's external debt is reduced, the investor has acquired a company at a discounted price, and a government agency has successfully shifted one of its holdings to the private sector.

Debt swapping has been accomplished mainly in Latin America, especially in Chile. Since introduced in 1985, swaps have totaled almost 10 percent of Chile's debt to foreign commercial banks and have played an important role in financing the privatization of state-owned enterprises.[39]

Not all indebted developing countries may choose to participate in debt-equity swaps, however. Some of the countries see no great advantage in debt-equity swaps, as it is possible to reschedule debt as long as interest payments can be met. Furthermore, there is the hope that the debt may be cancelled altogether by the lending institutions, who have grown frustrated over the years in their attempt to collect these outstanding debts.

Even for those countries interested in pursuing debt-equity swaps, there can be difficulties. Debt-equity swaps may promote inflation within the country if the government prints new money to meet the local currency needs resulting from the swaps. If large multinational corporations, in particular, purchase the debt, the government might face charges of selling indigenous firms to foreign interests. Moreover, privatizing state-owned enterprises in the Third World can be difficult enough without the complications of debt-equity swaps.

Nevertheless, debt-equity swaps can be an important means of financing the privatization of state-owned enterprises in developing countries. At the same time, these swaps can help both to reduce the debt pressures on developing nations and to stimulate the flow of capital from developed nations to indebted countries.

The Commission recommends:

Recommendation (6)

The Agency for International Development should support debt-equity swaps as one means of financing privatization activities in less developed countries and solving the problem of Third World debt.

Summary

Privatization should be a well-integrated part of the U.S. foreign assistance program. Many developing countries are voluntarily taking steps to expand private ownership in their economies. The United States, through the Agency for International Development, can encourage these efforts and pave the way for an infusion of innovative ideas from the private sector to enhance these nations' progress. The effectiveness of the U.S. foreign assistance will improve as private sector initiatives become an integrated aspect of these programs.

URBAN MASS TRANSIT

At the turn of the century, urban mass transportation in the United States was largely a private and profitable enterprise. There was little competition, and private trolleys and buses generally operated as monopolies. Regulation of transit began with exclusive horsecar franchises in the 1860s, often placing tight limits on fares and preventing companies from dropping unprofitable routes. However, it was the advent of the electrified streetcar, with its apparent economies of scale,* that ushered in the era of urban transit as regulated monopoly.[40]

As the use of automobiles increased in the 1920s, many transit companies struggled to collect enough fares to meet expenses. To assure continued service, governments gradually began to take over failing companies or to subsidize their operations. Soon after the introduction of the federal transit grant program in 1964, both takeovers and subsidies increased dramatically.

Overview of UMTA

The Urban Mass Transportation Administration (UMTA), a separate agency within the U.S. Department of Transportation (DOT), was created in 1964 to provide federal subsidies to local governments to fund urban mass transit systems. Nationwide, there are approximately 300 transit authorities, and virtually all receive some form of assistance from UMTA. UMTA has an annual budget of about $3.2 billion, 88 percent of which is distributed to local governments in the form of matching grants to buy buses, build subways, and maintain facilities. Grants typically cover 75 to 80 percent of the cost of purchasing transit equipment. In addition, UMTA grants will cover up to 50 percent of a local transit authority's operating deficits; these expenditures account for the remaining 12 percent of total grant assistance.

Government Involvement in the Provision of Mass Transit

Government takeovers of mass transit companies were based on three premises. First, transit was viewed as having social benefits that exceeded private benefits, thus justifying public subsidies. Urban mass transit is a textbook example of a service providing "positive externalities," that is, benefits that are not fully reflected in the market price.[41] Equivalently, one can say that there are "negative externalities" associated with

---

*Economies of scale are said to exist when average costs per unit produced decline with an increased volume of production because fixed costs are high.

driving—such as traffic congestion, air and noise pollution, wear and tear on the infrastructure, and lost time (to others because of congestion)—that are not reflected in the cost to the individual traveler who is choosing whether to drive or to take mass transit. Thus, it is quite possible for driving to be the optimal choice from the individual's perspective of the relative costs (based on a comparison of transit fares with gasoline prices and some consideration of wear and tear on the car), at the same time that mass transit is the optimal choice from society's perspective. In effect, the cost of driving may be too low relative to the cost of using mass transit from a social standpoint. Because of the existence of externalities in these markets, governments have in many instances subsidized urban mass transit so as to make its price relative to the price of driving better reflect the relative cost to society of that choice.

Second, transit systems were deemed to be natural monopolies exhibiting economies of scale and scope.* Thus, having first committed to subsidizing urban mass transit, governments tended to impose monopoly restrictions on it in order to maintain volume and permit cross-subsidization of the most costly routes by the least costly routes. The rationale was the same as for imposing the postal monopoly: in this view, the competition would "skim the cream" by operating only the more profitable routes, leaving the government with only the least profitable routes and insufficient volume to keep average costs down.

Third, faced with a monopoly, albeit in some cases of its own making, the local government had to choose whether to run the transit system as a public service or to leave it private and regulate its operations. As with any publicly subsidized and regulated monopoly, there was concern that the profit motive, combined with difficulty in verifying costs, would make a privately run transit system more costly and perhaps less responsive to public needs than a nonprofit, government operated system.

By 1970 less than a quarter of transit service was provided by private transit companies. This figure dropped to 6 percent in 1980, despite subsidies covering more than half the cost of riding. There were also fewer passengers. Although the federal government spent $20 billion on mass transit between 1975 and 1984, compared with a total of $2.2 billion between 1965 and 1974, ridership decreased from 13 to 9 percent of all urban commuting over that period.[42] **

Between 1964, when the federal subsidy program began, and 1985, the combined operating subsidy (excluding the cost of equipment) from all

---

*Economies of scope are said to exist when average costs per unit produced decline with an increase in the number of product lines. This occurs when product lines are similar enough that some of the costs of producing them are "joint."

**The absolute number of riders increased from 7 billion in 1975 to 8.4 billion in 1985.

levels of government rose to more than $6 billion per year. Public transit employees' wages and the cost per mile traveled increased at nearly twice the rate of inflation through 1984.[43]* Critics of federal transit programs cite these statistics as evidence that federal subsidies have not increased ridership but have indulged inefficiency and inflated wages.

Increasing Private Sector Involvement

Growing concern about the escalating cost of providing public transit to a shrinking percentage of urban commuters has led to a rethinking of the form that government support should take in the transit industry. The lack of profit incentives in a publicly run firm leads to a lack of incentives to contain costs or to innovate. These dampened incentives are often viewed as the price that must be paid for preserving the market from "cream skimming" competition in order to realize scale economies and for ensuring that a natural monopolist does not extract monopoly profits and reduce service. But economists are increasingly questioning whether the economies-of-scale argument, arguably appropriate in the days when electric trolleys were the principal form of mass transit, holds today.[44] Fostering competition is increasingly seen as a viable method of injecting normal cost-minimizing incentives into the provision of mass transport.

Even when the transit system does appear to exhibit the characteristics of a natural monopoly, many people believe that the lack of appropriate incentives under public management outweigh the monitoring costs of turning management over to a private entity.[45] Similarly, there has been increased emphasis on contracting out work to private firms as well as encouraging the sale of assets to the private sector.

Under UMTA's administrative authority, private sector involvement in mass transit is currently taking four forms: contracting out of public transit services; private financing; development of independent, privately operated services; and privately owned assets.

Contracting out increases efficiency and lowers costs by introducing competitive forces to transit provision. To support the introduction of competition, some localities have separated policymaking and operations, to remove the conflict that can result when both are held within the same organization. Contracting also allows public oversight, planning, and subsidies to continue, but forces public transit operations to operate efficiently or lose their right to operate the tendered portion of their service.

The transit contracting business—whereby local governments pay private contractors a fixed fee instead of turning over the fare box receipts—

---

*Increases in energy costs over this period account for relatively little in the increased cost per mile because more than 70 percent of mass transit costs derive from labor.

is growing. The volume of competitive service contracts totaled $237 million in 1986.[46] Because they have lower labor and overhead costs, contractors can usually provide the same services as those provided by government but with a much smaller subsidy. According to a study by researchers at the University of California, competition has demonstrated savings averaging between 10 and 50 percent, and sometimes even more.[47] Successful contracting, however, requires policymakers to monitor closely the work of the winning bidder.

Using private financial resources to support transit operations is a second type of privatization initiative being implemented by mass transit authorities. For example, private funds are often raised by selling development rights near subway stations or by collecting fees from the businesses that benefit from a particular transit link. The latter method is rapidly gaining popularity around the country; it is under consideration for funding a major transit link on Manhattan's West Side.

Encouraging independent entrepreneurs to develop transit services to meet emerging demands in the suburbs and inner cities is a third form of private sector involvement. It is expected that entrepreneurs can develop new service strategies tailored to the needs of riders and client groups. A recent report estimated that transit authorities could save $70 million annually by turning over subsidized commuter express transit services to for-profit private operators.[48]

Shifting more responsibility to the private sector for owning and financing transit assets—buses, subways, maintenance garages, and the like—is a fourth form of transit privatization. Supporters of this initiative believe that the private sector is better at allocating and conserving capital than government, and will, for example, choose more durable buses and allocate and maintain them better. Moreover, private companies usually acquire their equipment and contract their facilities more quickly and with fewer cost overruns than government.

The success of the initiatives just discussed is generating interest in private financing and ownership of whole systems. In cities ranging from Minneapolis to Boston, private companies have offered to build and operate the rapid rail transit systems cities want, albeit with at least some form of subsidy.

Grant Programs

The enabling legislation, regulatory language, and administrative procedures for UMTA give it flexibility to support greater private sector involvement in transit. The enabling act requires local plans and programs to encourage private sector involvement "to the maximum extent feasible." (49 U.S.C. Sections 1602(e) and 1603.) This statutory provision is the fulcrum for UMTA's innovative private sector involvement program begun in 1983.

Directed by the Office of Private Sector Initiatives, which was established in 1985, the program has helped 84 percent of UMTA grant recipients develop a routine process for private sector involvement. Grant programs have been restructured to encourage public-private partnerships, and a network of experts in the field has been established to provide support to local mass transportation privatization efforts. UMTA has also funded a series of demonstrations of private transit finance, competition, and joint development.

In his testimony to the President's Commission on Privatization, Alfred DelliBovi, UMTA Administrator, stated, "Our privatization program was built on the foundation that competition is indispensable. We do not view privatization as an end in itself. Its purpose is public benefit, not private gain."[49]

In its review the Commission sought to assess the value and effectiveness of UMTA's current program and to consider ways to advance private sector involvement in transit. Based on its study, the Commission recommends:

Recommendation (7)

The proper stewardship of federal funds requires that the Urban Mass Transportation Administration administer its grant programs so as to foster public-private partnerships and healthy competition among public and private providers of mass transit service.

Privatization Incentives

Approximately two-thirds of UMTA's annual budget is allocated to states and localities by formula. Although most of the remaining funds are in an account to be spent at the agency's discretion (called the Section 3 account, for the part of the Urban Mass Transportation Act of 1964 that relates to it), Congress has traditionally earmarked much of this money for special projects of its choosing. Still, UMTA does have some discretion to fund worthwhile projects, but applications for Section 3 grants far exceed the available funds. Exercising its administrative discretion, UMTA decided, in 1984, that cities demonstrating significant private sector involvement in their transit system would be given higher priority for Section 3 discretionary grant awards.

In recent years UMTA has supported several legislative initiatives that would have strengthened provisions relating to competition and public-private partnership. Congress rejected these proposals but did not discourage UMTA's existing Section 3 Private Sector Incentive Program. The Commission recommends:

Recommendation (8)

The federal government should utilize UMTA grant funds as incentives to encourage grantees to use competition to improve mass transit efficiency.

Section 13(c)

Section 13(c) of the Urban Mass Transportation Act of 1964 was originally written to protect the private sector transit employees who were affected by federally assisted buyouts of transit companies by local governments (49 U.S.C. 1609[c]). As it is currently interpreted by the Department of Labor (DOL), Section 13(c) provides public transit employees with extensive protection against any federally supported (via transit grants) activity that threatens their jobs. The local transit union and the federal grantee must negotiate satisfactory protections—with a recourse to appeal to DOL in the event of an impasse—that the Secretary of Labor certifies as meeting the requirements of the section. This broad application of Section 13(c) often enables the union to block a transit agency from using federal funds to offer services for competition.

Critics argue that DOL's interpretation singles out public transit authorities for a degree of federal labor protection higher than that of any private sector employee and misconstrues the purpose of the section. The lack of strong guidelines from DOL has been criticized as enabling unions to hold up grants for indefinite periods of time.

Transit labor officials have stated they are not opposed to competition so long as wages are not targeted. In his testimony to the Commission, Arthur Luby of the Transport Workers Union of America said, "We [aren't] afraid of competition . . . but the question we've always had, is competition on what terms?" He called Section 13(c) a "crucial provision" for his union.[50]

The Commission believes that Section 13(c) is an effective barrier to private sector involvement in mass transit as long as federal assistance to transit authorities remains necessary. Thus, the Commission recommends:

Recommendation (9)

The Department of Labor, in consultation with the Department of Transportation, should issue substantive guidelines outlining the requirements and limits of Section 13(c). Transit authorities should have the ability to achieve economies through privatization. Limits on the power of local transit authorities to amend or revise existing section 13(c) agreements or to phase out or delete those decisions not required by section 13(c) can result in higher transit expenditures because innovative and economical actions cannot be taken.

Asset Sales Procedures

Current federal rules require local transit authorities to reimburse the federal government based on straight-line depreciation when any asset purchased wholly or partially with federal funds is sold. UMTA requires transit buses purchased with federal funds to remain in service for 12 years. If buses are sold before that time, the grantee must reimburse UMTA for the federal share (usually 80 percent) of the depreciated purchase price. Thus, if a transit agency sold a 6-year-old bus under straight-line depreciation, the grantee would owe UMTA 50 percent of the (80 percent) federal share of the purchase price. If a bus cost $100,000 new, in the event of a sale the grantee would owe UMTA 50 percent of $80,000, regardless of the amount the grantee obtained by selling it. Since selling equipment before it reaches the minimum age may often cost the grantee money, these requirements have strongly discouraged localities from selling even their unwanted assets. The fact that more than 30 percent of buses in the fleets of local transit authorities are spares illustrates the strength of this disincentive.

Private contractors who now provide only labor have shown an interest in owning and maintaining the equipment they operate. They believe the reimbursement rule discourages the establishment of private transit contractors by making used equipment unavailable for sale to entrepreneurs. Therefore the Commission recommends:

Recommendation (10)

UMTA should allow grantees to sell UMTA-funded equipment to private operators where service is being permanently contracted out or reduced, and UMTA should be reimbursed only for the federal share percentage of the proceeds.

In early 1988 a record 60 cities had applications before UMTA for funds to begin work on various subway, trolley, and train systems.[51] Because its budget cannot meet these financial demands, UMTA needs to help local public transportation authorities find alternative sources of funding. At the same time the private sector has demonstrated its willingness to become involved in the provision of mass transportation. UMTA's efforts to capitalize on this willingness are consistent with its enabling legislation and can be implemented without further congressional action. UMTA has demonstrated initiative by creating an environment in which local transit authorities are beginning to look to the private sector as well as the federal government for assistance. Continued emphasis on the cultivation of private sector provision of transportation services, combined with the recommended policy changes within the executive branch, should give local transit authorities the opportunity to make greater strides toward privatization.

SUMMARY

Private sector initiatives to strengthen Medicare, urban mass transit, and international development hold out the promise of improved quality and efficiency in the provision of services. The Commission supports the efforts of the Health Care Financing Administration, the Agency for International Development, and the Urban Mass Transportation Administration to increase private sector participation and urges continued efforts to realize the benefits that privatization can confer. In particular, AID's support for privatization in less developed countries provides a mutually beneficial link between U.S. privatization initiatives and the growing world privatization movement.

Where the private sector shows initiative with popular support, government's role is to avoid impeding its people's progress. This is being done with increasing frequency around the world, as more and more nations acknowledge the limits of governmental programs in meeting their peoples' needs. Greater private sector involvement could provide solutions to current problems.

NOTES FOR CHAPTER 10

1. *Consumer Price Index Detailed Report*, March 1987.

2. For a thorough discussion of the Private Health Plan Option, see Paul B. Ginsburg and Glenn M. Hackbarth, "A Private Health Plan Option Strategy for Medicare," The Rand Corporation, 1987, R–3540–HCFA.

3. Testimony submitted by the American Medical Association for the Hearings on Health Care Financing (hereinafter cited as Health Hearings), January 8, 1988.

4. See "Worker Health Plan Proliferation Hit," *Washington Post*, Sunday, November 29, 1987.

5. Testimony of John Rother, American Association of Retired Persons, Health Hearings, January 8, 1988.

6. The classic paper showing that a pooling equilibrium results when everyone's relative risk is the same, but that a separating, or sorting, equilibrium results when individuals' risks vary, is Michael Rothschild and Joseph Stiglitz, "Equilibrium in Competitive Markets: An Essay on the Economics of Imperfect Information," *Quarterly Journal of Economics*, vol. 90 (1976), pp. 629-50.

7. Rother testimony.

8. Testimony of Geza Kadar, Health Insurance Association of America, Health Hearings, January 8, 1988.

9. U.S. General Accounting Office, "Medicare Contracting: Existing Authority Can Provide for Effective Program Administration," HRD-86-00, 1986, Executive Summary, pp. II-III.

10. Testimony of James Doherty, Group Health Association of America, Health Hearings, January 8, 1988.

11. See ibid. and Harold S. Luft, "On the Use of Vouchers for Medicare," *Milbank Memorial Fund Quarterly/Health and Society*, vol. 62, no. 2, 1984.

12. For a discussion of the evidence, see Ginsburg and Hackbarth, "A Private Health Plan Option Strategy for Medicare," pp. 70-73.

13. Alain C. Enthoven, "Managed Competition in Health Care and the Unfinished Agenda," *Health Care Financing Review*, 1986 Annual Supplement, p. 106.

14. Paul B. Ginsburg, "Market Oriented Options in Medicare and Medicaid," chapter 6 in Jack A. Mayer, ed., *Market Reforms in Health Care* (Washington, DC: American Enterprise Institute, 1983), p. 106.

15. Alain C. Enthoven, "Managed Competition," p. 109.

16. Kadar testimony.

17. Doherty testimony.

18. Elliot Berg, "The Role of Divestiture in Economic Growth," in Steve Hanke, ed., *Privatization and Development* (San Francisco: Institute for Contemporary Studies, 1987), p. 24.

19. Berg, "The Role of Divestiture in Economic Growth."

20. L. Gray Cowan, "Privatization: A Technical Assessment," unpublished manuscript, Bureau for Program and Policy Coordination, U.S. Agency for International Development, September 1987.

21. George B.N. Ayittey, "A Blueprint for African Economic Reform," *Journal of Economic Growth*, vol. 2, no. 3, (1987), p. 9. See also John R. Nellis, *Public Enterprises in Sub-Saharan Africa* (World Bank Discussion Papers, November 1986).

22. From *The World Bank's World Development Report, 1983*, cited in Cowan, "Privatization," p. 3.

23. From *1986 Inter-American Development Bank Annual Report*, cited in *SWAPS: The Newsletter of New Financial Instruments* (Washington, DC: Intrados Group, January 1988), p. 3.

24. Cowan, pp. 70-73.

25. James Brooke, "In Africa, A Rush To Privatize," *New York Times*, July 30, 1987. See also Donald May, "Third World Warms Up to the Private Sector," *Washington Times*, February 28, 1987.

26. L. Gray Cowan, "A Global Overview of Privatization," in Hanke, ed., *Privatization and Development*, p. 12.

27. Testimony of Richard E. Bissell, Bureau for Program and Policy Coordination, U.S. Agency for International Development, submitted to the President's Commission on Privatization, Hearings on Agency for International Development (hereinafter cited as Hearings on AID), January 8, 1988.

28. Ibid. See also Elliot Berg and Mary Shirley, *Divestiture in Developing Countries* (World Bank Discussion Papers, June 1987).

29. Frances Moore Lappe, et al., eds., *Betraying the National Interest* (New York: Grove Press, 1987), pp. 119-23.

30. Bissell testimony. See also *Economic Growth and the Third World: A Report on the A.I.D. Private Enterprise Initiative* (Washington, DC: Bureau for Private Enterprise, U.S. Agency for International Development, April 1987); Neal Zank, "A.I.D.'s Private Enterprise Initiative," *The World and I* (January 1988), p. 42.

31. U.S. Agency for International Development, *A.I.D. Policy Determination-14, Implementing A.I.D. Privatization Objectives*, June 16, 1986, p. 2.

32. Ibid., pp. 10–11.

33. Bissell testimony.

34. Testimony of Gordon Johnson, Center for Privatization, Hearings on AID, January 8, 1988.

35. Ibid. See also Hay Group, Inc., *Privatization and Employment Policy: Issue Analysis* (Washington, DC: Bureau for Program and Policy Coordination, U.S. Agency for International Development, June 1987).

36. Bissell testimony. See also Roger Leeds,"Privatization of the National Commercial Bank of Jamaica: A Case Study" (Cambridge, MA: John F. Kennedy School of Government, Harvard University, September 1987).

37. *High Road to Economic Justice: U.S. Encouragement of Employee Stock Ownership Plans in Central America and the Caribbean* (Washington, DC: Presidential Task Force on Project Economic Justice, October 1986). See also testimony of Stuart Butler, Heritage Foundation, Hearings on AID, January 28, 1988.

38. *SWAPS: The Newsletter of New Financial Instruments*, p. 5.

39. Steve Hanke, "The Anatomy of a Successful Debt Swap," in Hanke, ed., *Privatization and Development*, p. 164.

40. George W. Hilton, "The Rise and Fall of Monopolized Transit," chapter 2 in Charles A. Lave, ed., *Urban Transit, The Private Challenge to Public Transportation* (San Francisco: Pacific Institute for Public Policy Research, 1985), pp. 31–46.

41. For example, see Edwin S. Mills, *Urban Economics* (Glenview, IL: Scott, Foreman and Co., 1972).

42. Testimony of Alfred DelliBovi, submitted to the President's Commission on Privatization, Hearings on Urban Mass Transportation (hereafter cited as Urban Mass Transportation Hearings), December 22, 1987.

43. Ibid.

44. See, for example, Stephen Glaister, "Bus Deregulation, Competition, and Vehicle Size," *Journal of Transportation Economics and Policy*, May 1986; Kofi Obeng, "Bus Transit Cost, Productivity and Factor Substitution, *Journal of Transportation Economics and Policy*, May 1985; and Edward K. Morlok and Philip A. Viton, "The Comparative Costs of Public and Private Providers of Mass Transit," chapter 10 in Lave, *Urban Transit, the Private Challenge to Public Transportation*.

45. U.S. Department of Transportation, Federal Highway Administration, "Private Sector Involvement in Urban Transportation," December 1986.

46. Urban Mass Transportation Administration, Office of Budget and Policy.

47. Roger F. Teal, G. Guiliano, and E.K. Morlok, "Public Transit Service Contracting," prepared for Urban Mass Transportation Administration, March 1986, p. 3.

48. Urban Mobility Corporation, "Unsubsidized Transit Services: Potential to Meet Public Needs and Reduce Subsidy Requirements," prepared for Urban Mass Transportation Administration, December 1985, p. 14.

49. DelliBovi testimony.

50. Testimony of Arthur Luby, Transport Workers Union of America, Urban Mass Transportation Hearings, December 22, 1987.

51. "Mass Transit to the Suburbs," *Wall Street Journal*, January 27, 1988.

Chapter 11

Economic Public Policy
and Privatization

After more than a century in which the worldwide trend has been toward the growth of governments, a strong movement has emerged in the past decade to reduce government. Outside the United States, this movement is best known as the privatization movement and has frequently involved the outright divestiture of government properties.[1] However, the two most important forms of privatization in the United States have been deregulation and tax reduction. Whereas other nations were most likely to nationalize an industry, the United States was more likely to subject the industry to systematic government regulation. The widespread deregulation movement in the United States has been a home-grown version of what in other nations has taken the form of outright divestiture of government properties.

The United States has also been a leader in the effort to reduce the intrusiveness of taxation in the private economy. By the 1980s tax rates in many nations had reached the point of inhibiting private initiative, and taxes were exerting a pervasive influence on the behavior of private corporations and individuals. The major reductions and simplifications in federal taxation that occurred in the 1980s were intended to diminish this form of government influence over private sector activity.[2]

In rethinking the proper relationship between government and the private sector, the worldwide privatization movement has once again raised fundamental political and economic questions. This chapter takes a broad view of privatization by showing how it has emerged from an evolution of political and economic thought. Government is facing a major challenge, because the political and economic concepts that have traditionally given legitimacy to government actions have come under growing criticism. The nature of this challenge and the types of public policy effects that have resulted are illustrated below for three policy areas: deregulation, asset sales, and contracting out. Finally, it is suggested that the potential influence of the privatization movement has only begun to be felt. Current political and economic trends will make privatization a policy direction of fundamental social significance for the future.

Intellectual Origins of the Privatization Movement

Worldwide, the privatization movement has developed mainly as a reaction against the socialist and Marxist visions that have exerted so much influence in the 20th century.[3] In the United States, however, the growth of government has been based on the political and economic design that emerged from the Progressive movement around the turn of this century.[4] The American privatization movement has represented in significant part a reaction against the themes and results of Progressive thought.

The Progressive Foundations for American Government

Progressivism was itself a reaction against the social Darwinism and laissez-faire theories that were prevalent schools of public philosophy in the late 19th century.[5] Although historians have characterized Progressivism as the "gospel of efficiency," it was not an efficiency to be achieved through the survival of the fittest.[6] Rather, the allocation of resources was to be achieved on a more modern and in fact more truly efficient basis through the pervasive application of science to all manner of social decisions. Dwight Waldo, one of the leading students of Progressive thought, has written on the great public faith of the time in the powers of scientific reasoning:

> Following the lead of many of the scientists and of most of the persons whose province of study was human affairs, they frequently concluded that the New Day would not dawn until science was applied to the realm of human affairs just as it had been to the physical world, until the "power-controlling sciences" were as well developed as the "power-producing sciences." An easy . . . optimism abounded that at last a technique for solving these problems themselves lay hidden within the mystery of science.[7]

In business, Frederick Taylor became the leading apostle for use of the scientific methods of management.[8] In government, Woodrow Wilson (especially in his early academic career), Frank Goodnow, and others performed a similar proselytizing role.[9] Progressivism sought the substitution of scientific decisions throughout American government for decisions previously based on habit, tradition, casual opinion, common sense, and other less rigorously scientific methods. The question of whether decisions should be made in government or in the private sector was not itself a prime concern, because in either case the decisions should be made on the same rational and scientific basis and be made by members of the same professional elites. Even in the business world, old assumptions of self-interested behavior to earn profits were often replaced by assumptions that future business decisions would be based on professionalism and the expertise of engineers and other technicians.[10]

Progressive theories of government were built on the concept that government could be divided into two domains, one of politics and the other of administration.[11] Politics would be the realm of democratic government, where value and other subjective questions not suitable for scientific resolution would be answered. The larger part of government, however, would consist of administration. Here, politics and interest groups would be strictly excluded in favor of professional expertise. Over time, it could be hoped that the expert domain of government would expand, following the march of human progress (hence "Progressive") under the banner of science.

Another key aspect of Progressivism was its promotion of a new sense of national community in the United States. The scale of business activity in the late 19th century had reached a level that commonly transcended state and local boundaries, seeming to demand the involvement of the federal government and encouraging the transfer of citizen loyalties to the entire nation. William Schambra has written that the Progressives offered a vision of a "genuine national community . . . Americans would be asked to transcend their traditional laissez-faire individualism in order to bind themselves as one to the 'national idea.' " [12] In seeking to advance this national community, Progressives also sought reforms of American democratic institutions to curb the corrupting role of special interests, which had dominated American government in the "Gilded Age" of the late 19th century. In those efforts, Progressivism took on a moral and crusading quality that went well beyond the boundaries of the scientific method itself.

In summary, the hallmarks of the Progressive theory of government were a deep faith in the powers of science in human affairs, a reliance on professional experts to apply these powers for the social good, the exaltation of efficiency to the degree that it became a virtual gospel, the strict separation of democratic politics from the basic administration of government, and the systematic use of scientific planning by professionals as a basis for the administration of government. In many ways Progressivism was a domestic version of the "scientific socialism" of Europe. In America, however, it was necessary to make greater concessions to democratic politics, reflecting a deeper and stronger attachment to the principles of democratic government and individual liberty, which were not as embedded in the more authoritarian European tradition.

The Political Theory of Interest-Group Liberalism

Progressive themes still dominate much of the official public discourse in America today. Whatever the actual facts of the matter, it is still obligatory to say a law is enacted to serve the public interest, which is itself determined by the appropriate technical experts. Yet, the utterance of such themes has become more rite and habit than conviction. Among intellectuals and opinion leaders, a disillusionment with Progressive ideas set in many years ago. The undermining of the Progressive vision—much like the undermining of the orthodox socialist vision that was occurring worldwide at much the same time—was a critical step in the intellectual evolution that has paved the way for the contemporary privatization movement.

Dwight Waldo, for instance, found that, contrary to Progressive assertions, the actual conduct of government involved a "seamless web" in which politics and administration were thoroughly interwoven.[13] Others argued that effective administration depended on the strong political skills of the leaders at least as much as on their level of technical expertise.[14] Students of Progressive thought also questioned the Progressive conviction that administrative and management questions could almost always be reduced to matters of science. Herbert Simon (later to win a Nobel Prize in economics in 1978) wrote in 1946 that the allegedly scientific "principles" in the field of public administration were actually little more than a set of practical "proverbs"—and some of them were mutually contradictory at that.[15]

In another much-noted commentary, Charles Lindblom in 1959 characterized the normal functioning of government as "the science of 'muddling through.' "[16] Decisionmaking was typically incremental, seldom based on clear goals, and seldom planned in advance in any comprehensive or systematic way.[17] As a result, the Progressive prescription—that democratic politics set the goals and expert administration followed—was bound to fail. Government could not work in this fashion because goals and objectives were only realized after the fact.

Perhaps the most influential of all the criticisms of Progressive views was offered by political scientist David Truman.[18] Truman saw a government process in which interest groups played a pervasive role, not only in the domain of democratic politics, but also in the supposedly expert aspects of government administration as well. The conviction that American government was a process of interest-group negotiation and bargaining became the conventional academic wisdom of the 1950s and 1960s. At first, it was presented merely as a matter of the scientific description of the reality of American governmental workings. However, a more positive view of the interest-group role gradually emerged. As Robert Dahl and other prominent political scientists argued, interest-group politics was the only satisfactory way of reaching decisions in an American society characterized by a great pluralism of interests and viewpoints.[19] Moreover, the results reached so far had seemed to serve the nation well.

Nevertheless, while political scientists such as Dahl defended American pluralist politics, others such as Theodore Lowi found cause for great concern. Lowi coined the term "interest-group liberalism" (which has since come into wide use) to highlight the shift among the opinion leaders of American liberalism away from the old technocratic vision of Progressivism to a new vision of pluralist politics with interest-group negotiation and compromise at the center.[20] Lowi, however, strongly criticized interest-group liberalism as depriving government of its legitimacy, turning government into a vehicle for the expression of private purposes. He suggested that theories of democratic government in which Congress made policies for all the people and disinterested administrators implemented these policies were perhaps best left in the high school civics classes.

Yet, in view of the large discrepancy between the realities of American government and the popular ideals, it was likely to be only a matter of time before a public protest would develop. Moreover, as long as the Progressive principles had been widely believed and accepted, they had acted as a brake on the assertion of interest-group power. However, if greater intellectual legitimacy was to be given to this exercise of power, such encouragement in itself was likely to exacerbate matters. The contemporary privatization movement is in significant part a reaction to the excesses of current interest-group politics.

The Public Choice School

Despite an occasional critic, most members of the political science profession—at least until recently—have held a generally favorable view of interest-group government. Initially, economists did not pay close attention. One exception was John Kenneth Galbraith with his 1950s pluralistic theory of a system of "countervailing power."[21] A more important exception developed among a group of economists who have since come to be known as the "public choice" school.[22] James Buchanan produced the seminal work in this field, frequently in collaboration with Gordon Tullock.[23] Buchanan's receipt of the Nobel Prize for economics in 1986 gave public recognition to the significant impact that the public choice school has had on American political and economic thought.

If economists had traditionally analyzed the social consequences of self-interested behavior in the private market, interest-group liberals and other proponents of pluralistic politics now made the same assumption with respect to the actual motive for behavior in the public sector. Although the context was different, many of the familiar tools and analytical methods of economics could readily be transferred to the circumstances of American politics.[24]

The literature of public choice is by now voluminous, but the basic conclusion is not complicated.[25] A political system of interest-group bargaining will almost certainly result in very large inefficiencies by society in the use of its available resources. For example, each interest group will face the following incentive: If government can be pressured to provide greater goods and services for that particular group, the full benefits will flow to the group. Yet, the costs are likely to be much smaller, because the burden of taxation to pay for the benefits will be spread over the full body of taxpayers. Each interest group will typically have a strong incentive to demand as much in goods and services from government as it can get.[26] It will also have little if any incentive to oppose individual demands of other interest groups. (Each of these individual demands would be too small to affect the overall budget and tax situation.)

A similar set of incentives will apply on the revenue side. Each interest group will have an incentive to resist paying taxes levied on it, and no interest group will have much individual incentive to support general taxes. With intense pressures to raise government delivery of goods and services and similar pressures to hold down taxes, interest-group interaction will act to create a large gap between the costs of government and the revenues collected. In addition, since future taxes are perceived as less painful than current taxes, there is a bias in favor of raising government revenue through borrowing rather than direct taxation. The public choice theory thus predicted that government would tend toward ever-growing budget deficits. The fulfillment of this prediction in the 1980s did much to move public choice ideas from the margins of American intellectual life to center stage. Buchanan himself has taken the view that a solution to these problems can be achieved only through a significant reworking of the constitutional arrangements for American democratic government.[27]

The public choice analysis of a system of interest-group government also concluded that both the absolute magnitude and the distribution of goods and services provided by government are likely to be economically irrational. Political exchanges accomplished through democratic institutions are in effect a special form of barter. Yet, like any other barter system, political trading lacks a common currency (other than political power) or prices to rationalize the system of exchange. Compared with exchanges accomplished in private markets, the allocation of resources achieved by interest-group trading is likely to be no more rational or efficient than a barter economy would be in relation to a market economy.

Much of the intellectual inspiration of the contemporary privatization movement in the United States has been derived from the writings of the public choice school. This school has, in turn, been significantly influenced by Friedrich Hayek, Milton Friedman, and the tradition of economic analysis long associated with the University of Chicago.[28] Before them were some of the great names in political and economic philosophy. The doubts about government intentions and capabilities raised by the public choice school are not so much a new discovery as a restatement for modern times and modern circumstances of some old and familiar themes. The privatization movement traces its intellectual history through a line of succession that runs back to Adam Smith.[29]

Economic Progressivism

Unlike the public choice school, the mainstream of the economics profession has served as the leading proponent of a new and updated version of the Progressive political vision.[30] If orthodox Progressivism was labeled the gospel of efficiency, economists in the years following World War II defined their mission with a similar focus on efficiency, although with less moralism and righteousness. Like the Progressives, they believed that the application of expert knowledge—economic knowledge, in many cases—should both guide government and be separated from the undermining influence of special-interest pressures. Economists generally shared the strong faith of the Progressives in the powers of science and rational analysis and in the ability of government to put these powers to use in the service of the public interest.

If leading economists subscribed to basic tenets of the Progressive vision in these respects (and others as well), there were also several critical differences. Aside from Galbraith and a few others, most mainstream economists were not prepared to assume that technocratic elites would assume control over the management of private industry, thereby substituting professional standards of expertise for private profit as the chief driving force in business behavior. Compared with the old Progressives, most economists were also much more sceptical about the feasibility and merits of comprehensive state planning. In short, any system that relied on centrally imposed commands and controls to run the economy was likely to be inferior to a decentralized system of decisionmaking.[31]

Instead, for the members of the economics profession, the market provided an instrument that was highly decentralized in its operation and based on the realistic assumption that the private sector would behave in a self-interested way. Moreover, a new element was introduced in the years following World War II. Economists now argued that markets did not necessarily operate freely. Rather, it would be possible to plan or control the direction of the market—creating a "planned market" rather than a "free market." By manipulating monetary policy, taxes, budget levels, or other levers, society could guide the market according to its needs. These attitudes were reflected in the new use by economists of the term "market mechanism."[32]

In this fashion economists arrived at what might be called "Economic Progressivism." Like the old orthodox Progressivism, there would be separate domains for politics and expertise. However, in the expert domain, instead of administrative bureaucracies and command and control methods, policy decisions would now be implemented much more efficiently through the mechanism of the market itself.

The great architect of Economic Progressivism was John Maynard Keynes. Keynes argued that a private market system produces goods and services very efficiently, but that it suffers from macroeconomic instability.[33] Rather than abolish the private market, as many socialists were proposing, the better answer was to achieve a scientific understanding of macroeconomic behavior, and to use this knowledge to control the market to curb its instabilities. As Lawrence Klein, one of Keynes's leading American disciples and the 1980 Nobel Laureate in economics, later put it, "The Keynesian economic system is essentially a machine which grinds out results according to where the several dials controlling the system are set." [34]

Besides macroeconomic instruments, economists have subsequently proposed to manipulate market behavior with negative income taxes, environmental pollution taxes, education vouchers and tax credits, among a wide variety of such proposals. In recent years, the leading statement of this political and economic vision has been made by Charles Schultze. In *The Public Use of Private Interests*, Schultze contended:

> There is a growing need for collective influence over individual and business behavior that was once the domain of purely private decisions. But as a society we are going about the job in a systematically bad way that will not be mended simply by electing and appointing more competent public officials or doing better analysis of public programs.   . . .
> We usually tend to see only one way of intervening—namely, removing a set of decisions from the decentralized and incentive-oriented private market and transferring them to the command-and-control techniques of government bureaucracy. With some exceptions, modifying the incentives of the private market is not considered a relevant alternative. For a society that traditionally has boasted about the economic and social advantages of Adam Smith's invisible hand, ours has been strangely loath to employ the same techniques for collective intervention. Instead of creating incentives so that public goals become private interests, private interests are left unchanged and obedience to the public goals is commanded.[35]

The public choice school made a major contribution to the development of the contemporary privatization movement by applying economic analysis to show the inefficiencies and other failings of a system of interest-group dominance in American government. The contribution of Economic Progressivism was to show that, even if interest-group politics were rejected in favor of the Progressive vision, the preferable Progressive answer should in the main be a private market answer.

To be sure, Economic Progressivism does allow for direct government intervention in the market. In fact, over the years economists have identified a number of reasons why private markets might fail to allocate resources efficiently.[36] These reasons include the existence of "public goods," the presence of "externalities," the existence of monopoly power, and the lack of necessary information on the part of consumers. Nevertheless, the trend among economists in recent years has been to find fewer and fewer occasions on which government intervention is warranted.[37] For example, economists formerly argued that the presence of externalities required government regulations to control the external impact. They often argue that a respecification of property rights could serve to eliminate the externality, thus also eliminating the cause of market failure and the need for government regulation.[38] Economists have similarly come to see the existence of monopoly power in less threatening terms. They now often find that monopoly is a matter of degree—that there are in fact some unique features to the products of the great majority of firms—and that sufficient competition can arise in many forms.[39] For instance, a railroad that possesses the only track between two cities possesses a form of monopoly, but there may still be plenty of competition from the trucking industry.

Such thinking has caused mainstream economists in recent years to narrow significantly the circumstances thought to require government intervention to correct market failings. Such a narrowing has also reflected a growing penetration of public choice concepts into mainstream economics. Even where significant market failings are identified, the mainstream of the economics profession has now begun to ask more and more frequently whether government intervention might not be more harmful than beneficial. Given that corrective measures taken by government must be implemented through the institutions of American politics, including the likelihood of heavy interest-group involvement and compromise, the actual form of government intervention is likely to deviate substantially from the theoretical ideal. Attempts to manipulate the market mechanism for more positive purposes face the same problem. Economists saw clearly that such concerns were more than academic according to the authors when President Lyndon Johnson ignored the advice of his own economic experts to raise taxes and thereby may have set off a new round of inflation that proved exceedingly difficult to bring under control.[40]

As mainstream economists have felt more and more doubts concerning the wisdom of government involvement in the market, the policy differences between the public choice school and the mainstream of the profession have been significantly diminished. In the field of microeconomic policy, there has been a blurring of the old lines between conservative and liberal economists, with the great majority of economists now taking a stance sceptical of government intervention and favorable to market allocation of resources. This promarket trend within the economics profession has been another important intellectual factor in advancing the contemporary privatization movement.

The Rise of Ideology in American Politics

Not long ago, many political scientists wrote almost as though interest groups were all that counted and ideas scarcely mattered in government. Yet, in the past decade a reaction has set in among political scientists themselves. Many have noted that ideas—indeed, political and economic ideology—seem to be playing a growing role in American government. Nathan Glazer recently described how even in the 1960s "new passions were rising, passions not attached to interests but to world view, moral outlook, deeply held values. These were to govern American politics and the possibilities of social policy increasingly in the 1970s and have become dominant in the 1980s." [41]

One key ideology is that associated with the mainstream of the economics profession, earlier labeled Economic Progressivism. More and more economists have been employed by government to evaluate programs, do cost-benefit studies, and perform other tasks. The growing role of economics in government reflects the public sense that some grounding in the public interest is necessary for governmental legitimacy and that economic ideas can contribute significantly to this process. [42]

As part of the revival of ideology, however, other groups have entered the policy debate who challenge the core assumptions both of the old orthodox Progressives and now the Economic Progressives. These groups see a dehumanizing and alienating influence in a pervasive application of scientific methods to human affairs. Although they are at the margins of the environmental movement, writers such as Bill Devall and George Sessions capture a widespread mood when they assert that "technological society not only alienates humans from the rest of nature but also alienates humans from themselves and from each other. It necessarily promotes destructive goals which often destroy the basis for stable viable human communities interacting with the natural world." [43]

A growing libertarian influence is another part of the spread of ideological debate. The libertarian outlook finds surprising agreement with the environmentalist rejection of the Progressive vision. In the effort to persuade the public of the great powers of professional expertise, Progressivism is seen as having encouraged a public willingness to engage in social engineering that has significantly advanced the growth of modern government and that now threatens the liberty of the citizenry. [44] Viewing the instances of genocide, mass murder, and other evils of 20th-century history around the world, social critic Paul Johnson was moved to write of "a growing disesteem for the social sciences, which have done so much to usher in the age of politics and to advance its illusory claims. Economics, sociology, psychology, and other inexact sciences—scarcely sciences at all in the light of modern experience—had constructed the juggernaut of social engineering which had crushed beneath it so much wealth and so many lives." [45]

Another important new influence in American politics represents a return to a state of affairs that has characterized most human history. In recent years, religious leaders have increasingly concluded that, if government and society are to reflect religious values, these leaders will have to participate more closely in the development and implementation of government policies. [46] The U.S. Catholic bishops in 1984, for example, published a major statement on the significance of church teachings for the conduct of economic affairs.[47]

In the old Progressive theory, it was possible to argue that ideology and religion were part of the political domain that would be distinct and separate from the expert administration of the government. Yet, political scientists convincingly argued that the Progressive separation of value decisions from administrative decisions is not workable in practice and is not commonly found in the operation of American government. Hence, in a world of political pluralism and incremental decisionmaking, religious, ideological, and other groups that see government as necessarily asserting values cannot avoid becoming involved themselves in the administrative and other details of government. At least in some measure, therefore, the greater efforts of religious groups to become involved in government are another of the consequences of the breakdown of the Progressive vision and the rise of interest-group pluralism.

The greater role in American politics of ideology and religion is another important factor acting to further the contemporary privatization movement. In a nation as large and diverse as the United States, there is little prospect of a social consensus on many questions of basic belief and value. Yet, if government actions must assert some values, the possessors of different values will inevitably be thrown into political conflict. The immense destruction caused in the past by religious and ideological wars warns us today against any political arrangement that would act to promote such conflicts in American society.

In some cases, there may be no alternative but to seek a national agreement that involves a compromise on value questions. However, whenever possible, the better solution may well be to decentralize government powers to levels where much greater social homogeneity and agreement on values can be found. Decentralization can be accomplished within government by transferring responsibility to lower levels.[48]

In summary, the privatization movement also represents an attempt to avoid the fostering of greater social divisions and conflicts in American life. As American politics becomes more ideologically and religiously pluralistic, it becomes more and more difficult to see government as the valid expression of any single national community of common values, such as the Progressives presumed to exist and sought to advance.

The Privatization Movement in Practice: Lessons from Three Cases

The privatization movement has drawn support from a wide range of critics of the current scope of government.[49] These diverse strains have come together in the past decade behind several important efforts to reduce the role of government. The deregulation movement and the movement to reduce and simplify federal taxation have had the broadest range of support within American society and the greatest effect on U.S. public policy. Since 1975, major industries including banking, transportation, communications, oil and gas, securities, and others have been deregulated. By contrast, efforts to divest government-owned properties outright have been few in number. In the case of the most publicized such effort, the plan to sell some of the public lands, the effort was a failure. A third important field of privatization has been the contracting out of government services, a rapidly growing practice whose ultimate policy impact has yet to be determined. Examination of these cases offers some important lessons and sheds light on the prospects for privatization in the development of U.S. public policy.

Privatization and the Deregulation Movement

Like many other institutions of American government, federal regulation of industry was a product of the Progressive Era.[50] The Progressive idea was that disinterested experts, operating from regulatory commissions independent of politics, would administer the regulated industry to maximize the efficiency of its operation. Regulation was designed in part to control monopoly power, but also to curb "wasteful" duplication that might result from excessive market competition, and in general to impose a rational plan on an industry in place of the less orderly trial-and-error methods of the marketplace.

Later students of regulation found that the Progressive regulatory concept typically was not being realized.[51] Rather than the achievement of a more efficient industry, the actual purpose of regulation had become the protection of the industry from competition, benefiting existing industry members and unions as well. Regulation also served as a vehicle for internal cross-subsidies whereby one set of consumers of the industry product paid more than their share of costs in order that other consumers might pay less. Congress found it attractive to distribute the benefits of these cross-subsidies as part of the normal process of distributing its favors among the various interests in American politics. Economic analysts undertook a number of studies that documented the major inefficiencies resulting from all these practices and the high costs that were thereby imposed on the consumers of industry products.[52]

The question still remained whether the political will could be summoned to challenge the beneficiaries of regulation. Many political scientists predicted otherwise, taking the view that interest-group opposition would always be too strong. However, arguments of proponents of deregulation proved to have a large political influence. One point of view was expressed by Martha Derthick and Paul Quirk who concluded in a study of deregulation for the Brookings Institution, "If economists had not made the case for pro competitive deregulation, it would not have occurred—at least not on the scale the Nation has witnessed."[53]

Around the world, privatization has not been particularly associated with the political right or left. Steps toward privatization in China and the Soviet Union (however tentative) have made perhaps the greatest impact on world opinion.[54] In the United States, the deregulation movement had broad bipartisan support; Democratic and Republican leaders both played important roles in advancing deregulation.[55]

Supporters of deregulation were influenced by the principled argument that markets represent a superior mechanism for allocating resources. Because industry members often opposed deregulation, some supporters of deregulation saw their efforts as an attempt to eliminate special interest favors now being obtained by the business world. In this way, combined with other promarket advocates, a broad coalition of political support for deregulation was assembled.

A similar set of forces combined to bring about the enactment of the Tax Reform Act of 1986, the most recent of the tax reduction measures designed to diminish the intrusiveness of government in private sector decisions.[56] The income tax itself was another product of Progressivism (approved by constitutional amendment in 1913) that over the years had succumbed to numerous interest-group pressures, leaving it riddled with special provisions for the benefit of particular groups. Many political scientists had predicted that a comprehensive tax reform would be politically impossible, because so many interests had such a large stake in its provisions.[57] However, economists and others over the years had made an intellectual case for tax reduction and for a more neutral tax system, which eventually proved to carry significant political weight.[58]

In summary, the deregulation of various industries (as well as the tax reduction movement) illustrated new forces at work in the formulation of American public policy, forces that resulted in significant shifts away from government control over the economy and toward greater reliance on private market forces. In the case of regulation, government institutions were founded on Progressive principles of disinterested expertise applied in the service of the public interest, but operated in practice in response to the imperatives of interest-group pressures, yielding highly inefficient results. Despite widespread doubts that it was possible, the campaign waged against a number of types of regulation in the end proved successful. To be sure, interest groups that benefited from deregulation also played an important part in its political success. But the deregulation movement (and the tax reduction movement) showed that the privatization movement had itself become a significant ideological force in an American political system.

A Failure to Privatize: Public Lands

The worldwide privatization movement has involved substantial divestiture of government-owned properties in other nations, but the sale of

Conrail was almost the only such example in the United States. At the federal level, there are few government-owned businesses or industries. There is one form of property, however, in which the federal government still has very large holdings. The public lands constitute about one-third of the land area of the United States, a huge federal domain of ownership that is hard to reconcile with the reputation of this country as a citadel of reliance on markets and the private sector.[59]

The public lands were one more product of the Progressive Era and Progressive political theory. The Forest Service was formed in 1905, the National Park Service in 1916, and Congress enacted a policy of the leasing rather than the sale of energy minerals in 1920. In practice, the administration of the public lands was never the rational exercise, governed by expert planning, that the Progressives had envisioned. Rather, as had happened to most institutions formed on the Progressive model, the subsequent results were driven by the pressures of interest-group negotiation and compromise—one more vindication of the realism of interest-group liberalism.

Furthermore, it had been demonstrated that the resulting government management of the public lands exhibited pervasive inefficiencies.[60] Managing a vast wealth of natural resources, the Forest Service spent almost $2 billion in 1980, while its lands generated fewer than $1 billion in mineral, timber, grazing, and other revenues. Marion Clawson, perhaps the best-known economist in the public lands field (and a former Director of the Bureau of Land Management), wrote in 1976 in *Science* magazine that the Forest Service management of the national forests had been economically "disastrous."[61] In his view, "the national forests emerge as a great feudal estate, land poor, managed extensively, relatively unproductive."[62]

The public lands thus offered a set of circumstances very similar to those surrounding deregulation and tax reduction. The Reagan Administration in 1982 announced a major initiative to privatize portions of the public lands, the most visible effort at outright divestiture of government property thus far attempted by the privatization movement in the United States. The actual proposal was fairly modest, to sell no more than 35 million acres, or 5 percent of public lands. Yet, the extensive press coverage and level of controversy generated reflected a sense that the debate concerned broader principles of public land ownership in the United States.

A year later, in July 1983, the entire effort was unceremoniously canceled.[63] It had foundered on the existence of de facto property rights.[64] Over 50 years or more of continued use, ranchers had acquired a de facto property right to graze on particular parcels of public lands—rights even bought and sold in the market on occasion.[65] As a practical matter and whatever the legalities, such informal rights cannot be taken from their holders without the government providing fair compensation. In such instances, the best strategy for achieving privatization may be to give (or to sell cheaply) to the holders of political property rights some portion—or conceivably even all—of the rights to the government property being divested. This strategy, however, had not been followed in the 1982 planned sales.

A related lesson is that sale revenues may be a subsidiary consideration. Indeed, in the case of public lands, management costs substantially exceed the revenues earned by the government for many of the lands, so even an outright grant of the land free of charge would be a revenue-enhancing device. More important than revenues is the goal to relieve the government of subsidy burdens, at the same time opening the way for a more efficient use of resources in the private sector.

Separating Politics and Administration Once Again: Contracting Out

As pointed out earlier, in the Progressive vision government administrators were to be a class of disinterested experts guided by professional knowledge and norms to serve the public interest. However, in practice, it turned out that government administrators frequently had less exalted motives. They were all too often concerned with expanding their area of responsibility, obtaining a larger number of subordinates, capturing greater privileges of office, and concentrating on other matters more related to the self-interest of the administrator than to the service of the public interest. Just as the public choice school formalized the analysis and developed the full implications of a system of interest-group politics, economists also formalized and developed the implications of assuming a set of government administrators motivated by self-interest. In one leading study, William Niskanen in 1971 argued that the best way to understand individual bureaucratic behavior was to view it as motivated by the desire to maximize the budget of the bureaucrat.[66]

Similarly, self-interested government workers will seek to maximize their pay and other benefits, while reducing their work load. Political leaders will have a private incentive to improve the compensation of public employees in ways that burden only their successors in office. The adverse effects of the incentives faced by public managers were confirmed by studies showing high costs, inefficient service delivery, large unfunded pensions, and other problems being experienced frequently in government management at all levels throughout the United States.[67]

One response to these problems—probably the most common—is to try to reform government management. However, another response found more and more frequently is the contracting out of government service delivery to the private sector.[68] Contracting out, for some, represents a revival in a new form of the old Progressive distinction between politics and administration, with the private contractor now taking the former place of the expert government administrator. Under contracting, political leadership sets the policy goals and directions in one domain, while the private contractor then implements these goals and directions in a second separate domain, one that is to be insulated from political interference. Just as the Progressives emphasized efficiency, the goal of contracting is to achieve maximum efficient service delivery for the price the government is willing to pay.

Contracting out can thus be distinguished from other forms of privatization in several respects. Unlike most forms of privatization, contracting out does not necessarily have as a direct goal the reduction of the ultimate scope of government responsibility. It is neutral in this regard. Contracting, nevertheless, can still be linked to the broader aims of the privatization movement in the following respect. Although the absolute scope of government service responsibility may not decline, the actual size of government—the number of government employees and the extent of government owned resources—will diminish. Reducing the size of government may be an important goal in itself, especially if there is a concern that big government might at some point in the future pose a threat to the political freedom and individual liberty of its citizens.

Contracting has demonstrated impressive results in a number of jurisdictions where it has been employed, reducing costs of service delivery and improving the quality of services.[69] Yet, given a long history in which the Progressive political vision has been undermined by interest-group pressures, there must always be a concern that the same factors could undermine the effectiveness of contracting out. If private contractors are assumed to behave in self-interested ways, the contractor will have an incentive to understate or obscure any deficiencies that arise in contractor delivery of services. Contractors and their employees will also represent important interest groups who may possess substantial political power and exert substantial political influence on government contracting practices. These problems and others have, in fact, been experienced at one time or another in the U.S. Defense Department, which has long contracted many of its activities.

Contracting is likely to be most successful where the terms and measurements of service delivery are clear and easily defined, where at least several firms have the capacity to perform the contract, where the contractor does not have to make large new capital expenditures, and where the contract can be subject to renewal and renegotiation regularly. When enough of these conditions are missing, the contractor may become an extension of the government, freed from many of the government personnel practices and other limitations that inhibit effective government management. In that case, contracting may offer significant benefits, but many of the problems of the American governing process identified by the public choice school and other critics will still be fully applicable.

Future Political Dynamics of Privatization Policy

Although deregulation and tax reduction have represented major developments in U.S. public policy, overall the privatization movement has had a limited effect in the United States.

The most important force favoring a prominent future for privatization is the rapid pace with which a single world economy is developing and the intense competitive pressures thereby being created on each nation to rationalize its economic system. A second force is the tendency of interest-group politics to weaken the legitimacy and the authority of large government. Interest-group liberalism itself may contain the seeds of privatization, as interest groups seek to ensure that their past gains from government programs are maintained, pressuring governments to convert these gains to privately held and salable property rights.

Privatization and Growing World Competitiveness

The Progressives believed that large government was needed in order to provide a balance to the great political and economic power being newly exercised by large companies in increasingly concentrated industries.[70] The need to check excessive corporate power has continued to be a rationale for large government—contained, for example, in Galbraith's theories of countervailing power in the 1950s.[71]

Current trends in the world economy, however, are creating a much different set of concerns. As symbolized for many Americans by developments in world oil markets of the past 15 years, the world is increasingly becoming a single large economic system. The growth of this system is a product of reduced transportation costs, immensely improved communications, and the rapid spread of Western science and culture throughout the world. The American automobile industry currently finds its products competing with automobiles assembled in Japan, Germany, France, Italy, Korea, Brazil, and Canada, among other nations. In the world economic environment of today, the old concern of excessive political and economic strength of large American corporations is hardly the most pressing one. Rather, government worries today whether American industry and its work force will be able to survive in the face of intense world competition.

Historically, the principal rationale for larger government has been the existence of market failures due to externalities or the "public goods problem." In addition, considerable concern in the early 20th century about the perceived power of big business led to the passing of the Clayton and Federal Trade Commission Acts in 1914, and hence, the implementation of a large body of anti-trust regulation.

As discussed above, economists have increasingly advocated addressing market failures by altering market incentives rather than dictating behavior by means of regulation. At the same time, anti-trust concerns have changed their focus in part because of increasing recognition that the United States is part of a growing world economy.

In this newly competitive world economy a corporation that may have a large share of the American market still has only a small share of the world market. Industries that are highly concentrated on the scale of a single national market become highly competitive when the scale becomes a world market, thus acting to restore the conditions of strong competition in which markets function best.

The growth of a highly competitive world economy has implications for the political practices of nations that are only beginning to be appreciated. All over the world, the instruments of government have been used to advance narrow social classes, special interests, and other parochial or private groups.[72] In the absence of the forces of world economic competition, political change required that the citizens of a nation collectively act to assert a broad national purpose against these privileged classes and other beneficiaries of existing government arrangements. Now, however, the forces of world economic competition may simply make the social burdens imposed by governments—a kind of "tax" on the rest of the citizenry—impossible to sustain. The nation may simply find that it cannot sell its products on world markets.

To be sure, government could maintain inefficient domestic industry by imposing tariffs, providing subsidies, and in other ways seeking to protect its industries.[73] Yet, the national cost of such protective measures would be much more visible to the citizenry than have been the internal inefficiencies resulting from weak government management, poorly conceived regulations, and other government actions. The pressures created in this way on national political systems are similar to the effect that has been seen in the United States when competition arrives in newly deregulated industries. The first introduction of competition creates great pressure on the management of existing companies to abandon superfluous layers of middle management, wasteful production methods, unsustainable wage rates, and other business practices that may have been tolerable before, but now leave the company uncompetitive and threaten its survival.

The growth of world economic competition is related to another important development that has contributed to the movement for privatization. As the pace of economic change has accelerated, events today occur too rapidly for the transmission, in large, rigid organizations, of adequate information from the field to central officials, whether they be corporate executives or government planners and regulators. In the government sector, resulting demands for greater decentralization can be met in part by privatizing functions, allowing market incentives a much greater leeway.

The trend of technological development also favors privatization. In the first half of this century the great new corporations of America were found in industries where huge size conveyed a great competitive advantage. Today, the most rapid areas of economic growth are in high technology, services, and other fields where such advantages of large scale do not exist. This characteristic of current technology is a key reason why even within individual nations, the competitive market of small firms is increasingly a reality—no longer merely the theoretical construction of economists.

Interest-Group Liberalism and the New Property

Although the privatization movement has emerged chiefly as a reaction against interest-group government, its future may depend on whether privatization objectives can be made compatible with the forces of interest-group politics. In fact, such an outcome is not unlikely. In many cases, interest groups have strong private incentives to support the shift of the government benefits that they currently receive as matters of publicly granted privileges to become matters of privately possessed property rights. For example, public housing residents have a strong personal interest in seeking the transfer to them of the ownership of their housing units, thereby seeking to convert their occupancy of the housing from a public privilege to a salable private right. The political dynamics created by interest-group politics could, in fact, create strong pressures for widespread privatizations of this sort in many areas of public policy.[74]

A limited number of examples can already be found. Ranchers who long ago received privileges from government to graze on particular parcels of public land in the West have by now acquired de facto rights that are transferable and salable with their private "base" property. Holders of what were formerly airport landing privileges have seen their privileges transformed to become private salable rights at several airports. The use of telecommunications frequencies, initially granted as a privilege for public service, gradually became a salable right.

The economist George Stigler once commented that government regulatory agencies took on the character of a personal possession of business, administered to maximize the profits of the regulated industry.[75] On the social welfare side, some argue that welfare payments and other entitlement benefits should be assured to recipients as a matter of right. The courts accepted such arguments in part, establishing new procedural and other protections against arbitrary loss of benefits. In an influential series of 1960s articles in the *Yale Law Journal*, former law professor Charles Reich sought to lay the groundwork for such a policy:

> Among the resources dispensed by government which it would seem desirable to treat as property are social security pensions, veterans' benefits, professional and occupational licenses, public assistance, unemployment compensation, public housing, benefits under the Economic Opportunity Act, Medicare, educational benefits and farm subsidies.

Planning with respect to such rights can be done on a general basis; the rights themselves should be distributed to all who qualify for a certain status. Governmental decisions concerning such rights should be and are increasingly subject to the requirements of due process of law; such rights should not be denied or revoked without a full adjudicatory hearing.[76]

The treatment of government program benefits as "property" is partly an outgrowth of the fading of the Progressive political vision and its supplanting by interest-group politics.[77] In the Progressive concept, government benefits were granted because there was a sound reason, identified by professional experts and spelled out through planning. In interest-group liberalism, changes in government program distributions represent merely realignments in political power and in the bargaining strength of interest groups. As a result, in the eyes of the courts and the public, the legitimacy of government actions and the authority of government officials to make programmatic changes in a discretionary fashion have been significantly weakened.

If government program benefits are to be treated as forms of "property," the question arises whether this property ought to be owned outright by the beneficiaries. On the surface, an outright transfer of rights to government-provided benefits might be seen as undesirable. Yet, if these property rights already exist as a practical matter, formal transfer would not alter the loss of government discretion and control, which already exists. Moreover, private ownership and the right to sell the property in many cases would serve the causes of social efficiency and equity. If program benefits are available only for direct personal receipt, the recipients lose their mobility. They may be locked into use of a benefit that takes up resources possessing a much higher social value in an alternative use. Yet, as long as there is no incentive for the recipients to move (such as a salable right), the inefficiency will be perpetuated. A failure to establish private rights in such circumstances may also have little to recommend it in terms of social equity.

Consider, for example, a small farmer to whom government has granted permission to use publicly provided and subsidized water for irrigation but who is not able under current law to sell the permission to use the water, even though this water might have a much higher value for use in a nearby municipality.[78] Recognizing a new salable property right to the water would allow its transfer and might thereby advance substantially the social efficiency of water use. It might also improve significantly the overall well-being of the small farmer; this may be a socially equitable policy in that the farmer may never have earned more than a modest income.

Future proposals to privatize government functions could be aligned with the interests of current program beneficiaries. For example, a proposal to divest a government business might suggest transferring it to the employees, who might be the group with the greatest interest in the continuation of this particular function. A proposal to divest government power-generating facilities might suggest giving the facilities (or selling them cheaply) to the current power customers, whose historic receipt of subsidized power rates may be seen as having created a de facto entitlement to continued low rates. A proposal to divest government conservation lands might suggest giving them to a current conservation organization, representing the main existing users of these particular lands.[79]

In summary, if privatization consists simply of eliminating government programs and cutting off benefits, change may come at a slow pace. If privatization consists, however, of forming and recognizing new private rights for the beneficiaries of existing programs, the pace of privatization could accelerate. In fact, privatization in this form might even be an inevitable long-run result of the dynamics of interest-group politics.

Summary

The growth of government in the 20th century has been based on a number of assumptions and predictions. It was assumed that the process of government would become steadily more objective and rational, as scientific methods were applied ever more widely to administrative and other governmental matters. It was assumed that, as science established an objective basis for government, the role of religion, ideology, and other such "subjective" forces would gradually diminish in government. It was also assumed that the introduction of rational and scientific methods into government would gradually decrease the scope of responsibility of democratic politics, a domain in which interest-group involvement inevitably exerted a major influence. Finally, as mass education produced a full citizenry enlightened by the discoveries and knowledge of modern science, there would be a growing homogeneity of American life and culture, yielding a single national community of Americans with common values and beliefs.

These earlier assumptions have, at times, seemed to be coming true, if perhaps more slowly than the greatest enthusiasts had expected. During the two world wars of this century (and especially the second), a set of professional and technocratic elites managed the nation with what seemed to many citizens to be extraordinary success. During World War II, for example, the role of democratic politics was significantly curtailed, and the United States acted to a great degree as a single community with common goals and values. These attitudes, outlooks, and political practices carried over in some measure into the later 1940s and then into the 1950s. Since the 1960s, however, it has gradually become apparent that new, and for many, unanticipated forces are at work in American society. Many of the assumptions and predictions on which the earlier growth of government was based have proved either to be false or at least to be subject to much greater doubt.

The scientific administration of government has seemed much less certain, as the professional elites central to this task have often failed to deliver. Doubts have arisen as to whether the social and administrative sciences are really sciences at all, or perhaps have instead dressed earlier philosophical and ideological convictions in a new technocratic garb.[80] The Vietnam War, a war initiated and managed by the "best and the brightest," was particularly damaging to public confidence in professional elites. But the trend is much broader, as virtually every profession has had its "crisis."

Contrary to earlier expectations, the role of democratic politics and of interest groups in American government can hardly be said to have diminished. As professional elites have found it increasingly difficult to sustain their claims to authority, the role of interest groups seems instead to have increased correspondingly since the 1960s. At present, many of the actions of government are widely perceived as benefiting narrow interests more than they serve as the expression of any clear public interest. A widespread sense of excessive interest-group influence has weakened the legitimacy and public acceptance of government actions and policies. The level of concern is such that public discussion of constitutional reform of a significant structural nature has taken on a more serious character than at any time since the Progressive Era.[81]

The ability of government to serve—even to define—the public interest itself depends on the actual existence of a national community that shares many common goals and values. Yet the trend since the 1960s has instead been toward a growing religious and ideological diversity and pluralism in American life. The number of government questions for which there is a single objective answer, the answer given by science and rational analysis, has seemed more limited than many had earlier expected. In an incremental system in which government policymaking involves a continuous interaction between legislative, administrative, and judicial decisionmaking, religious and other values may have to be asserted in each step of the process, if they are to be asserted at all. Yet, in a pluralistic American society where in some key areas there is little social agreement on values, who is to say what values are to be asserted throughout the process of governing? Indeed, does it make any sense to favor one set of values over another? If not, then a reduction in the scope of national government may be the only answer.

The ultimate consequences of the new forces at work today in American political and economic life, including whether these forces will be longer lasting or shorter lived, will not be seen for some time. What can be said is that the privatization movement is likely to be at the center of the response to these forces. In seeking to reduce the role of government and to rely more heavily on the private sector, the privatization movement is a reflection of the failure of many of the past assumptions on which large government has been based. It is a critical part of the continuing effort in American life to rethink the purpose and role of government, now that this rethinking seems to have become unavoidable. The outcome will depend not only on intellectual trends but also on changing economic circumstances as the world becomes much more competitive, and on the dynamics of interest-group politics, as it inevitably continues to play a major role in American governmental processes.

As analyzed here, all these factors suggest that the impact of the privatization movement, broadly understood, is only beginning to be felt. Privatization in this broad sense may well be seen by future historians as one of the most important developments in American political and economic life of the late 20th century.

NOTES FOR CHAPTER 11

1. Madsen Pirie, "Privatization Techniques and Results in Great Britain," and Eamonn Butler, "How the Thatcher Revolution Was Achieved," in John C. Goodman, ed., *Privatization* (Dallas: National Center for Policy Analysis, 1985).

2. Paul Craig Roberts, *The Supply-Side Revolution: An Insider's Account of Policy Making in Washington* (Cambridge, MA: Harvard University Press, 1984).

3. Paul Johnson, *Modern Times: The World from the Twenties to the Eighties* (New York: Harper and Row, 1983).

4. Stephen Skowronek, *Building a New American State: The Expansion of National Administrative Capacities, 1877–1920* (New York: Cambridge University Press, 1982), p. 288.

5. Robert Green McCloskey, *American Conservatism in the Age of Enterprise* (Cambridge, MA: Harvard University Press, 1951); Sidney Fine, *Laissez-Faire and the General Welfare State* (Ann Arbor: University of Michigan Press, 1964).

6. Samuel P. Hays, *Conservation and the Gospel of Efficiency: The Progressive Conservation Movement, 1890–1920* (Cambridge, MA: Harvard University Press, 1959).

7. Dwight Waldo, *The Administrative State: A Study of the Political Theory of American Public Administration* (New York: Holmes and Meier, 1984; 1st edition, 1948), p. 12.

8. Frederick W. Taylor, *The Principles of Scientific Management* (New York: Harper and Bros., 1911).

9. Woodrow Wilson, "The Study of Administration," *Political Science Quarterly*, June 1887, reprinted in *Political Science Quarterly*, December 1941. See also Robert H. Wiebe, *The Search for Order, 1877–1920* (New York: Hill and Wang, 1967).

10. Samuel Haber, *Efficiency and Uplift: Scientific Management in the Progressive Era, 1890–1920* (Chicago: University of Chicago Press, 1964).

11. Frank Goodnow, *Politics and Administration: A Study in Government* (New York: Russell and Russell, 1967; 1st edition, 1900).

12. William A. Schambra, "Progressive Liberalism and American 'Community,' " *The Public Interest* (Summer 1985), p. 36.

13. Waldo, *The Administrative State*, p. 121.

14. Norton Long, "Power and Administration," *Public Administration Review*, Autumn 1949.

15. Herbert A. Simon, "The Proverbs of Administration," *Public Administration Review*, Winter 1946.

16. Charles E. Lindblom, "The Science of 'Muddling Through,'" *Public Administration Review*, Spring 1959.

17. Aaron Wildavsky, *The Politics of the Budgetary Process* (Boston: Little, Brown, 1964).

18. David B. Truman, *The Governmental Process: Political Interests and Public Opinion* (New York: Alfred A. Knopf, 1951).

19. Robert A. Dahl, *Who Governs?* (New Haven: Yale University Press, 1961); and Robert A. Dahl, *Pluralist Democracy in the United States: Conflict and Consent* (Chicago: Rand McNally, 1967).

20. Theodore J. Lowi, *The End of Liberalism: Ideology, Policy and the Crisis of Public Authority* (New York: Norton, 1969).

21. John Kenneth Galbraith, *American Capitalism: The Concept of Countervailing Power* (Boston: Houghton Mifflin, 1956).

22. James M. Buchanan, *What Economists Should Do?* (Indianapolis: Liberty Press, 1979); James M. Buchanan and Robert Tollison, eds., *Theory of Public Choice* (Ann Arbor: University of Michigan Press, 1972).

23. James M. Buchanan and Gordon Tullock, *The Calculus of Consent: Logical Foundations of Constitutional Democracy* (Ann Arbor: University of Michigan Press, 1962).

24. Anthony Downs, *An Economic Theory of Democracy* (New York: Harper and Bros., 1957).

25. Mancur Olson, *The Logic of Collective Action: Public Goods and the Theory of Groups* (Cambridge, MA: Harvard University Press, 1965). Also, more recently Mancur Olson, *The Rise and Decline of Nations: Economic Growth, Stagflation, and Social Rigidities* (New Haven: Yale University Press, 1982).

26. James M. Buchanan, "Public Finance and Public Choice," *National Tax Journal*, December 1975.

27. James M. Buchanan, *The Limits of Liberty* (Chicago: University of Chicago Press, 1975); James M. Buchanan and R.E. Wagner, *Democracy in Deficit* (New York: Academic Press, 1977).

28. Friedrich Hayek, *The Road to Serfdom* (Chicago: University of Chicago Press, 1944); Milton Friedman, *Capitalism and Freedom* (Chicago: University of Chicago Press, 1962); see also Joseph A. Schumpeter, *Capitalism, Socialism and Democracy* (New York: Harper and Brothers, 1950; 1st edition, 1942).

29. Adam Smith, *An Inquiry into the Nature and Causes of the Wealth of Nations* (Indianapolis: Liberty Press, 1981; 1st edition, 1776).

30. Charles L. Schultze, *The Public Use of Private Interest* (Washington, D.C.: Brookings Institution, 1977).

31. Friedrich Hayek, "The Use of Knowledge in Society," *American Economic Review*, September 1945; also Friedrich Hayek, *Individualism and Economic Order*

(Chicago: University of Chicago Press, 1948); Thomas Sowell, *Knowledge and Decisions* (New York: Basic Books, 1980).

32. Paul Samuelson, *Economics* (New York: McGraw-Hill, 1961).

33. John Maynard Keynes, *The General Theory of Employment, Interest and Money* (London: Macmillan, 1964).

34. Lawrence R. Klein, *The Keynesian Revolution* (New York: Macmillan, 1961; 1st edition, 1947), p. 153.

35. Schultze, *The Public Use of Private Interest*, p. 2.

36. Richard A. Musgrave and Peggy B. Musgrave, *Public Finance in Theory and Practice* (New York: McGraw Hill, 1976); Francis M. Bator, "Anatomy of Market Failure," *Quarterly Journal of Economics*, August 1958.

37. James Buchanan and W. Craig Subblebine, "Externality," *Economica*, November 1962; Gordon Tullock, *Private Wants, Public Means: An Economic Analysis of the Desirable Scope of Government* (New York: Basic Books, 1970).

38. J.H. Dales, *Pollution, Property and Prices* (Toronto: University of Toronto Press, 1968); Ronald Coase, "The Problem of Social Cost," *Journal of Law and Economics*, 1960.

39. Richard Posner, "The Chicago School of Antitrust Analysis," *University of Pennsylvania Law Review*, 1979.

40. Erwin C. Hargrove and Samuel A. Morley, eds., *The President and the Council of Economic Advisors: Interviews with CEA Chairmen* (Boulder, CO: Westview Press, 1984).

41. Nathan Glazer, "Interests and Passions," *Public Interest*, Fall 1985, p. 19.

42. Stephen E. Rhoads, *The Economists' View of the World: Government, Markets, and Public Policy* (New York: Cambridge University Press, 1985).

43. Bill Devall and George Sessions, *Deep Ecology* (Salt Lake City: Peregrine Smith Books, 1985), p. 48.

44. Friedrich Hayek, *The Counter Revolution of Science: Studies on the Abuse of Reason* (Glencoe, IL: Free Press, 1952).

45. Johnson, *Modern Times*, p. 730.

46. A. James Reichley, *Religion in American Life* (Washington, DC: Brookings Institution, 1985).

47. U.S. Catholic Bishops, *First Draft—Bishops Pastoral: Catholic Social Thinking and the U.S. Economy*, printed in *Origins*, November 15, 1984. See also Michael Novak, *The Spirit of Democratic Capitalism* (New York: Simon and Schuster, 1982).

48. Advisory Commission on Intergovernmental Relations, *An Agenda for American Federalism: Restoring Confidence and Competence* (Washington, DC: 1981).

49. Ronald C. Moe, *Privatization: An Overview from the Perspective of Public Administration*, Congressional Research Service, Report No. 86–134 GOV (Washington, DC: June 30, 1986).

50. Marver Bernstein, *Regulating Business by Independent Commission* (Princeton, NJ: Princeton University Press, 1955).

51. Roger G. Noll, *Reforming Regulation: An Evaluation of the Ash Council Proposals* (Washington, DC: Brookings Institution, 1971); Paul W. MacAvoy, ed., *The Crisis of the Regulatory Commissions: An Introduction to a Current Issue of Public Policy* (New

York: Norton, 1970); Roger G. Noll and Bruce Owen, eds., *The Political Economy of Deregulation: Interest Groups and the Regulatory Process* (Washington, DC: American Enterprise Institute, 1983).

52. Richard Caves, *Air Transport and its Regulators* (Cambridge, MA: Harvard University Press, 1962); George Douglas and James Miller III, *Economic Regulation of Domestic Air Transport: Theory and Practice* (Washington, DC: Brookings Institution, 1974).

53. Martha Derthick and Paul J. Quirk, *The Politics of Deregulation* (Washington, DC: Brookings Institution, 1985), p. 246.

54. Harry Harding, *China's Second Revolution: Reform after Mao* (Washington, DC: Brookings Institution, 1987).

55. Stephen Breyer, *Regulation and its Reform* (Cambridge, MA: Harvard University Press, 1982).

56. Jeffrey Birnbaum and Allan Murray, *Showdown at Gucci Gulch* (New York: Random House, 1987).

57. John F. Witte, *The Politics and Development of the Federal Income Tax System* (Madison: University of Wisconsin Press, 1985).

58. Joseph A. Pechman, *Federal Tax Policy* (Washington, DC: Brookings Institution, 1983, 4th edition).

59. Sterling Brubaker, ed., *Rethinking the Federal Lands* (Washington, DC: Resources for the Future, 1984).

60. Thomas M. Lenard, "Wasting Our National Forests—How to Get Less Timber and Less Wilderness at the Same Time," *Regulation*, July/August 1981.

61. Marion Clawson, "The National Forests," *Science*, February 20, 1976, p. 766.

62. Marion Clawson, *The Economics of National Forest Management* (Washington, DC: Resources for the Future, June 1976), p. 84.

63. Phillip O. Foss, ed., *Public Lands Policy* (New York: Greenwood Press, 1987).

64. Stuart M. Butler, *Privatizing Federal Spending: A Strategy to Eliminate the Deficit* (New York: Universe Books, 1985), p. 88.

65. Delworth Gardner, "A Proposal to Reduce Misallocation of Livestock Grazing Permits," *Journal of Farm Economics* (1963).

66. William A. Niskanen, *Bureaucracy and Representative Government* (Chicago: Aldine and Atherton, 1971).

67. Thomas E. Borcherding, ed., *Budgets and Bureaucrats: The Sources of Government Growth* (Durham, NC: Duke University Press, 1977).

68. Philip E. Fixler, Jr., ed., *Privatization 1986: Annual Report on Privatization of Government Services* (Santa Monica, CA: Reason Foundation, 1986); Martha A. Shulman, *Alternative Approaches for Delivering Public Services*, Urban Data Service Reports, vol. 14, no. 10 (Washington, DC: International City Management Association, October 1982).

69. Stuart M. Butler, ed., *The Privatization Option: A Strategy to Shrink the Size of Government* (Washington, DC: Heritage Foundation, 1985); Harry Hatry, *A Review of Private Approaches for the Delivery of Public Services* (Washington, DC: Urban Institute, 1983).

70. Richard Hofstadter, *The Age of Reform: From Bryan to F.D.R.* (New York: Vintage Books, 1955).

71. Galbraith, *American Capitalism*.

72. P.T. Bauer, *Equality, the Third World and Economic Delusion* (Cambridge, MA: Harvard University Press, 1981).

73. Keith Marsden and Therese Belot, *Private Enterprise in Africa: Creating a Better Environment* (Washington, DC: World Bank Discussion Paper, 1987).

74. Bruce Yandle, "Resource Economics: A Property Rights Perspective," *Journal of Energy Law and Policy*, 1983.

75. George Stigler, "The Theory of Economic Regulation," *Bell Journal of Economics and Management Science*, Spring 1971.

76. Charles Reich, "The Law of the Planned Society," *Yale Law Journal*, July 1966, p. 1266.

77. Ibid.; also Charles Reich, "The New Property," *Yale Law Journal*, April 1964; and idem, "Individual Rights and Social Welfare: The Emerging Legal Issues," June 1965.

78. Terry L. Anderson, ed., *Water Rights: Scarce Resource Allocation, Bureaucracy, and the Environment* (San Francisco: Pacific Institute for Public Policy Research, 1983).

79. John Baden and Richard Stroup, "Saving the Wilderness," *Reason*, July 1981.

80. Donald N. McCloskey, "The Rhetoric of Economics," *Journal of Economic Literature*, June 1983.

81. James L. Sundquist, *Constitutional Reform and Effective Government* (Washington, DC: Brookings Institution, 1986).

Appendix A

Executive Order
12607

President's Commission on Privatization

By the authority vested in me as President by the Constitution and laws of the United States of America, and in order to establish, in accordance with the Federal Advisory Committee Act, as amended (5 U.S.C. App. I), a Commission to revise the appropriate division of responsibilities between the Federal government and the private sector, it is hereby ordered as follows:

Section 1. Establishment. (a) There is established the President's Commission on Privatization. The Commission shall be composed of not more than 13 members appointed or designated by the President. The members shall be drawn from among a bipartisan cross-section of distinguished leaders.

(b) The President shall designate a Chairman from among the members of the Commission

Sec. 2. Functions. (a) The Commission shall study and evaluate:

(1) Past and current privatization efforts by the Federal government, State and local governments, and foreign governments, including asset sales by the Federal government;

(2) Literature and writing on privatization; and

(3) The environment for additional privatization efforts by the Federal government.

(b) The Commission shall review the current activities of the Federal government, including asset holdings, and identify those functions that:

(1) Are not properly the responsibility of the Federal government and should be divested or transferred to the private sector, with no residual involvement by the Federal government; or

(2) Require continuing oversight by an Executive Branch agency but can be performed more efficiently by a private entity, including the use of vouchers as an alternative to direct service.

(c) The Commission shall develop the framework for a privatization program, identifying:

(1) Privatization opportunities, including those identified in (b) above, listed in order of priority;

(2) Legislative and administrative actions necessary to effect the privatization initiatives or remove existing privatization restrictions;

(3) Needed improvements to personnel and administrative policy to create an environment conducive to privatization;

(4) Organizational and resource requirements necessary to implement successfully the privatization program; and

(5) Actions necessary to create broad-based support for privatization efforts.

(d) The Commission shall submit its findings and recommendations to the President and the Director of the Office of Management and Budget by March 1, 1988. Interim recommendations shall be transmitted to the Director for consideration in the formulation of the President's FY 1989 budget.

Sec. 3. Administration. (a) The heads of Executive departments, agencies, and independent instrumentalities shall, to the extent permitted by law, provide the Commission, upon request, with such information as it may require for purposes of carrying out its functions.

(b) Members of the Commission shall serve without compensation for their work on the Commission. While engaged in the work of the Commission, members appointed from among private citizens of the United States may be allowed travel expenses, including per diem in lieu of subsistence, as authorized by law for persons serving intermittently in the government service (5 U.S.C. 5701–5707).

(c) To the extent provided by law and subject to the availability of appropriations, the Director of the Office of Management and Budget shall provide the Commission with such administrative services, funds, facilities, staff, and other support services as may be necessary for the performances of its functions.

Sec. 4. General Provision. (a) Notwithstanding the provisions of any other Executive Order, the functions of the President under the Federal Advisory Committee Act that are applicable to the Commission, except that of reporting annually to the Congress, shall be performed by the Director of the Office of Management and Budget, in accordance with guidelines and procedures established by the Administrator of General Services; and

(b) The Commission shall terminate 30 days after submitting its final report to the President.

RONALD REAGAN

THE WHITE HOUSE

September 2, 1987.

Appendix B

Business Meetings and Hearings

BUSINESS MEETINGS
- September 18, 1987
- September 30, 1987
- October 20, 1987
- November 9, 1987
- December 1, 1987
- December 21, 1987
- January 7, 1988
- January 28, 1988
- February 5, 1988
- February 22, 1988

HEARINGS

Witnesses at Commission Hearings

October 20, 1987 LOW-INCOME HOUSING
- The Honorable Dan Coats, U.S. Representative, Indiana
- Stuart M. Butler, Director, Domestic Policy Studies, Heritage Foundation
- Carl D. Covitz, Under Secretary, U.S. Department of Housing and Urban Development
- Carol T. Crawford, Associate Director, Economics and Government, Office of Management and Budget
- Dale P. Riordan, Executive Vice President, Administration and Corporate Relations, Federal National Mortgage Association

October 21, 1987 LOW-INCOME HOUSING AND HOUSING FINANCE
- Paul L. Pryde, Jr., Chairman, Pryde, Roberts and Company, Inc.
- Rosalind R. Inge, Vice President, National Center for Neighborhood Enterprise
- John C. Weicher, American Enterprise Institute

- Richard F. Muth, Chairman, Department of Economics, Emory University, Atlanta, Georgia
- Rene A. Henry, Jr., President and Chief Executive Officer, National Institute of Building Sciences
- Gregory T. Barmore, President, General Electric Mortgage Insurance Company, Raleigh, North Carolina, on behalf of Mortgage Insurance Companies of America
- Warren Lasko, Executive Vice President, Mortgage Bankers Association
- Lee Holmes, Executive Vice President, Internal and External Affairs, Federal Home Loan Mortgage Corporation
- John D. Luke, Associate Director; Dennis Fricke, Group Director, both on behalf of the Resources, Community and Economic Development Division, General Accounting Office
- Richard B. Geltman, General Counsel, National Governors' Association
- Dennis J. Jacobe, Senior Vice President, U.S. League of Savings Institutions, Chicago, Illinois

November 9, 1987 FEDERAL LOAN PROGRAMS

- The Honorable Richard K. Armey, U.S. Representative, Texas
- Joseph R. Wright, Jr., Deputy Director, Office of Management and Budget
- Donald A. Clarey, Deputy Administrator, Small Business Administration
- John Sloan, President, National Federation of Independent Business
- Mary M. Rose, Deputy Under Secretary, Office of Management; Mike Korbey, Comptroller; Tom Stack, Director, Credit Management Improvement Staff; Ann Hewitt, Vice President, Chemical Bank, New York, New York; all on behalf of the U.S. Department of Education
- William A. Inglehart, President; William I. Davis, Executive Vice President; both on behalf of GC Services Corporation, Houston, Texas

November 10, 1987 FEDERAL LOAN PROGRAMS

- The Honorable Charles E. Grassley, U.S. Senator, Iowa
- Carol D. Olson, Legislative Assistant, Senator Grassley, Iowa
- John R. Price, Jr., Managing Director of Public Finance, Manufacturers Hanover Trust Corporation, New York, New York
- Miner Warner, Former Vice President, Salomon Brothers, Inc., New York, New York
- Marvin Markus, Vice President, Asset Finance Department, Kidder, Peabody and Company, New York, New York

- La Verne Ausman, Acting Under Secretary, Small Community and Rural Development; Vance L. Clark, Administrator, Farmers Home Administration; Jack Van Mark, Deputy Administrator, Rural Electrification Administration; all on behalf of the U.S. Department of Agriculture
- Harold O. Wilson, Executive Director, Housing Assistance Council, Inc.
- R.J. Vogel, Chief Benefits Director; Keith Pedigou, Director, Loan Guarantee Service; both on behalf of the Veterans Administration
- Dennis Cullinan, Assistant Director, National Legislative Services, Veterans of Foreign Wars of the United States
- Lisa Miller, Acting Director; Paula Schnepp, Program Analyst; both on behalf of the Operations and Liquidations Division, Federal Savings and Loan Insurance Corporation
- Frederick D. Wolf, Director; John F. Simonette, Associate Director; Ernst F. Stockel, Group Director; all on behalf of the Accounting and Financial Management Division, General Accounting Office
- William A. Niskanen, Chairman, Cato Institute
- Carol G. Cox, President, Committee for a Responsible Federal Budget

December 1, 1987 AIR TRAFFIC CONTROL AND OTHER FAA FUNCTIONS

- Vice Admiral Donald D. Engen, Former Administrator; J. Lynn Helms, Connecticut, Former Administrator; based on experiences with the Federal Aviation Administration
- Carol T. Crawford, Associate Director, Economics and Government, Office of Management and Budget
- Lloyd K. Mosemann, II, Deputy Assistant Secretary for Logistics, U.S. Air Force; representing the Department of Defense's Committee on Federal Aviation
- Kenneth M. Mead, Associate Director; Dave Balderstadt, Evaluator; both on behalf of the Resources, Community, and Economic Development Division, General Accounting Office
- Robert W. Poole, Jr., President, Reason Foundation, Santa Monica, California
- Fred L. Smith, Jr., President, Competitive Enterprise Institute
- James L. Gattuso, Senior Policy Analyst in Regulatory Affairs, Heritage Foundation

December 2, 1987 AIR TRAFFIC CONTROL AND OTHER FAA FUNCTIONS

- The Honorable James L. Oberstar, U.S. Representative, Minnesota
- The Honorable Guy V. Molinari, U.S. Representative, New York
- Rudolph A. Oswald, Director, Economic Research, American Federation of Labor and Congress of Industrial Organizations
- William F. Bolger, President, Air Transport Association
- W. Dan Todd, Senior Vice President, Government and Technical Affairs and Aviation Policy, Aircraft Owners and Pilots Association
- John F. Thornton, National Coordinator, National Air Traffic Controllers Association
- J. Donald Reilly, Executive Director, Airport Operators Council International
- Spencer Dickerson, Senior Vice President, American Association of Airport Executives
- Jonathan Howe, President, National Business Aircraft Association, Inc.
- Ward J. Baker, Senior Staff Engineer, Engineering and Air Safety Department, Airline Pilots Association
- Jim Burnett, Chairman, National Transportation Safety Board
- Clifford Winston, Senior Fellow, Brookings Institution
- Robert W. Lynch, Jr., President, Barton Air Traffic Control, Inc., Murfreesboro, Tennessee
- Robert J. Butler, Partner, Wiley, Rein and Fielding; on behalf of George F. Mansur, Chairman of the Board, Aeronautical Radio, Inc.
- William A. Kutzke, President, Air Transport Holdings, Inc.

December 21, 1987 EDUCATIONAL CHOICE

- John E. Chubb, Senior Fellow, Brookings Institution
- Keith Geiger, Vice President, National Education Association
- Albert Shanker, President, American Federation of Teachers, New York, New York
- Douglas L. Alexander, Executive Director, Citizens for Educational Freedom
- Michael P. Farris, President, Home School Legal Defense Association

December 22, 1987 EDUCATIONAL CHOICE, MILITARY
COMMISSARIES, PRISONS, AND URBAN MASS TRANSIT
- Chester E. Finn, Jr., Assistant Secretary of Education for Educational Research and Improvement; Patricia M. Lines, Research Analyst; both on behalf of the U.S. Department of Education
- William J. Gainer, Associate Director; Ellen B. Sehgal, Senior Evaluator; David D. Bellis, Social Science Analyst; all on behalf of the Human Resources Division, General Accounting Office
- John E. Coons, Professor of Law, University of California, Berkeley, California
- Joan Davis Ratteray, President, Institute of Independent Education, Inc.
- Lieutenant General Anthony Lukeman, U.S. Marine Corps, Deputy Assistant Secretary of Defense, Military Manpower and Personnel Policy, Office of the Secretary of Defense
- Michael C. Bourgoine, President, Andover Division of Wetterau Inc.; representing the Food Marketing Institute, Andover, Massachusetts
- L. Wayne Arny, III, Associate Director, National Security and International Affairs, Office of Management and Budget
- Thomas W. Beasley, Chairman, Corrections Corporation of America, Nashville, Tennessee
- James K. Stewart, Director, National Institute of Justice
- Ira P. Robbins, Professor of Law, American University, representing the American Bar Association
- Arthur Luby, General Counsel, Transport Workers Union of America, AFL-CIO, New York, New York
- Arlee T. Reno, Jr., Director, Transportation Studies, The Urban Institute
- Alfred A. DelliBovi, Administrator, Urban Mass Transportation Administration, U.S. Department of Transportation

January 7, 1988 CONTRACTING OUT
- Robert P. Bedell, Administrator; Allan V. Burman, Deputy Administrator; David Muzio, Deputy Associate Administrator; all on behalf of the Office of Federal Procurement Policy, Office of Management and Budget
- Constance Horner, Director; Thomas J. Simon, Senior Administrator for Intra Government Affairs; both on behalf of the Office of Personnel Management
- Gene L. Dodaro, Associate Director; Edward Fritts, Group Director; both on behalf of the National Productivity Group, General Government Division, General Accounting Office
- Robert A. Stone, Deputy Assistant Secretary of Defense for Installations

- Major General M. Bunker, Director of Management, U.S. Army
- Major General Peter T. Kempf, U.S. Air Force, Commander, U.S. Air Force Tactical Fighter Weapons Center at Nellis Air Force Base, Nevada
- Captain Philip Jacobs, U.S. Navy, Commander, Naval Air Stations, Cecil Field, Florida
- Linda M. Lampkin, Director, Department of Research, American Federation of State, County, and Municipal Employees
- Robert E. Edgell, Government Procurement Specialist, American Federation of Government Employees, AFL-CIO

January 8, 1988 CONTRACTING OUT, MEDICARE, AND INTERNATIONAL DEVELOPMENT PROGRAMS

- Frank S. Swain, Chief Counsel for Advocacy, U.S. Small Business Administration
- William D. Russell, President; Gary D. Engebretson, Executive Director; both on behalf of Contract Services Association
- Anton S. Gardner, County Manager, Arlington County, Virginia
- Geoff Bogart, International City Management Association
- William L. Roper, M.D., Administrator, Health Care Financing Administration, Department of Health and Human Services
- Geza Kadar, Jr., Assistant Washington Counsel, Health Insurance Association of America
- James F. Doherty, President and Chief Executive Officer, Group Health Association of America, Inc.
- Richard E. Bissell, Assistant Administrator, Bureau for Program and Policy Coordination, United States Agency for International Development
- Gordon O.F. Johnson, Deputy Director, Center for Privatization in Washington, D.C.

January 28, 1988 POSTAL SERVICE

- John W. Crutcher, Commissioner, Postal Rate Commission
- Louis A. Cox, General Counsel, United States Postal Service
- Earl W. Ogle, National President, National Association of Postmasters of the United States
- William Burrus, Executive Vice President, American Postal Workers Union, AFL-CIO
- Vincent R. Sombrotto, President, National Association of Letter Carriers, AFL-CIO
- Gene A. Del Polito, Executive Director, Third Class Mail Association
- Thomas Gale Moore, Member, Council of Economic Advisers
- Douglas K. Adie, Professor of Economics, Ohio University, Athens, Ohio

January 29, 1988 FEDERAL ASSET SALES, NAVAL PETROLEUM
RESERVES, AND AMTRAK

- James C. Miller, III, Director, Office of Management and Budget
- Stuart M. Butler, Director, Domestic Policy Studies, Heritage Foundation
- Jeffrey A. Jones, Director, Energy Policy, Office of the Assistant Secretary of Defense, Production and Logistics, Department of Defense
- Richard D. Furiga, Deputy Assistant Secretary, Petroleum Reserves; Howard Borgstrom, Office of Planning and Financial Management; both on behalf of the Department of Energy
- Flora H. Milans, Associate Director, Fossil Energy and Renewable Resources; Clifford L. Gardner, Group Director, Emergency Preparedness; Jay Cherlow, Group Director, Economic Analysis Group; all on behalf of the Resources, Community, and Economic Development Division, General Accounting Office
- John T. Cameron, Vice President, Producing, Exploration and Land Functions, Western Region, Chevron, U.S.A., Inc., San Ramon, California
- W. Scott Lovejoy, III, Executive Director, American Independent Refiners Association, West Coast Division, Los Angeles, California
- Thomas R. Hunt, II, Executive Vice President, California Independent Producers Association, Fountain Valley, California
- W. Graham Claytor, Jr., President and Chairman of the Board, National Passenger Corporation (Amtrak)
- John Riley, Administrator; Jim McQueen, Associate Administrator, Passenger and Freight Services; both on behalf of the Federal Railroad Administration
- Ross B. Capon, Executive Director, National Association of Railroad Passengers
- Byron A. Nordberg, Vice President, Government Relations, United Rail Passengers Alliance, Inc., Oceanside, California
- Lawrence A. Hunter, Deputy Chief Economist, U.S. Chamber of Commerce

PRESIDENT'S COMMISSION ON PRIVATIZATION

1825 K Street, N.W., Suite 310
Washington, D.C. 20006   (202) 634-6501

David F. Linowes, Chairman

Annelise Graebner Anderson
Michael D. Antonovich
Walter F. Bish
Sandra Mitchell Brock
Garrey E. Carruthers
Richard H. Fink
Melvin R. Laird
James T. McIntyre, Jr.
George L. Priest
Ralph L. Stanley
Walter B. Wriston

March 18, 1988

President Ronald W. Reagan
The White House
Washington, D. C.   20500

Dear Mr. President:

I am pleased to transmit to you the report of the President's Commission on Privatization, <u>PRIVATIZATION: Toward More Effective Government</u>.   Created by your Executive Order No. 12607 on September 2, 1987, the Commission has devoted the past several months to examining the appropriate division of responsibilities between the federal government and the private sector.

During the conduct of our examination, we reviewed extensive literature on privatization, considered the testimony of 140 witnesses, and analyzed information and data provided by the pertinent federal agencies in each of the subject areas addressed in this report.

In our deliberations, we considered first and most critically the needs of the American consumer and how those needs can best be satisfied.   In this report we recommend alternative approaches for administering many government programs and services, when we determined that they could be better managed at less cost by involving the private sector and/or providing for individual consumer's choice.

It is our belief and hope that this report of findings and recommendations, if adopted, would serve as the linchpin in the identification and transfer of federal activities that can be performed more effectively by the private sector.

For all of us, participation in the work of the Commission has been a challenging and stimulating opportunity to serve our nation.   We appreciate having had this privilege.

Sincerely,

David F. Linowes
Chairman

PRESIDENT'S COMMISSION ON PRIVATIZATION

1825 K Street, N.W., Suite 310
Washington, D.C. 20006   (202) 634-6501

March 18, 1988

The Honorable James C. Miller, III
Director, Office of Management and Budget
Washington, D. C.   20503

Dear Mr. Miller:

I am pleased to transmit to you the report of the President's Commission on Privatization, PRIVATIZATION: Toward More Effective Government. Created by Executive Order No. 12607 on September 2, 1987, the Commission has devoted the past several months to examining the appropriate division of responsibilities between the federal government and the private sector.

During the conduct of our examination, we reviewed extensive literature on privatization, considered the testimony of 140 witnesses, and analyzed information and data provided by the pertinent federal agencies in each of the subject areas addressed in this report.

In our deliberations, we considered first and most critically the needs of the American consumer and how those needs can best be satisfied. In this report we recommend alternative approaches for administering many government programs and services, when we determined that they could be better managed at less cost by involving the private sector and/or providing for individual consumer's choice.

It is our belief and hope that this report of findings and recommendations, if adopted, will serve as the linchpin in the identification and transfer of federal activities that can be performed more effectively by the private sector.

For all of us, participation in the work of the Commission has been a challenging and stimulating opportunity to serve our nation. We appreciate having had this privilege.

Sincerely,

David F. Linowes
Chairman

COMMISSIONERS

David F. Linowes is Chairman of the Commission. He is Professor of Political Economy and Public Policy, and Boeschenstein Professor Emeritus at the University of Illinois. Prior to 1976 he was the national partner of a worldwide management consulting and auditing firm. He also served as Chairman of the U.S. Privacy Protection Commission from 1975 to 1977.

Annelise Graebner Anderson is Senior Fellow at the Hoover Institution at Stanford University in California and former Associate Director of the Office of Management and Budget.

Michael D. Antonovich is a member and former Chairman of the Board of Supervisors for Los Angeles County, the largest local government in the country.

Walter F. Bish is President of the Independent Steelworkers Union at Weirton Steel Corporation, the largest industrial employee-owned company in America.

Sandra Mitchell Brock is an independent government relations advisor, specializing in the areas of transportation and financial services.

Garrey E. Carruthers is Governor of New Mexico since January of 1987.

Richard H. Fink is Founder, President, and Chief Executive Officer of Citizens for a Sound Economy.

Melvin R. Laird has served as a member of Congress for 16 years, Secretary of Defense from 1969 to 1973 and Counsellor to the President from 1973 to 1974. Currently he is Senior Counsellor for Reader's Digest Association, Inc.

James T. McIntyre, Jr., is a partner in the Washington, D.C., office of the law firm of Hansell & Post, and served as Director of the Office of Management and Budget from 1978 to 1981.

George L. Priest is the John M. Olin Professor of Law and Economics, Director of the Program in Civil Liability, and Director of the Center for Studies in Law, Economics, and Public Policy at Yale Law School.

Ralph L. Stanley is Vice Chairman of Municipal Development Corporation, and former Administrator of the Urban Mass Transportation Administration.

Walter B. Wriston is former Chairman of the Board and Chief Executive Officer of Citicorp.

PRESIDENT'S COMMISSION ON PRIVATIZATION
COMMISSION STAFF

Frank Sellers
Executive Director

Joan Simmons
Research Director

Wiley W. Horsley, Jr.[1]
Staff Manager

Susan R. Solomon [2]
Director of Public Affairs

Norma J. Campbell [1]
Report Coordinator

Office of General Counsel
John P. Giraudo,[3]
General Counsel
Ralph J. Benko,[4]
Deputy General Counsel
(10/15/87–12/1/87)
Michael J. Wootten,[3]
Deputy General Counsel
(1/4/88–3/15/88)

Project Management
Lisa Marie Daniel [8]
Stephen S. Greene [6]
Devin T. Hagerty
Thomas Hugh Upton [7]
(10/15/87–1/15/88)

Advisor
Stuart M. Butler

Consultants
Peter Hannaford
E. Steven Savas

Senior Research Staff
Edward J. Lynch,[5]
Senior Research Associate
Stephen K. Moore,
Senior Research Coordinator
Robert H. Nelson,[1]
Senior Research Manager
(12/1/87–3/1/88)

Professional Staff
Elizabeth B. Burke [2]
(1/4/88–3/18/88)
Richard H. Feen [9]
Charles Logan [3]
Andrew Strasfogel [1]
Ralph Sullivan [6]

Project Consultants
Jerome R. Ellig
Charles B. Oliver
William J. Silvey
Steven A. Steckler
Daniel A. Witt

Administrative Secretary to the Chairman
Betty L. Hildebeidel

Administrative Staff

Jillian T. Detweiler,
Editorial Assistant
Hilda H. Maness [8]
(10/19/87–12/18/87)

Jacqueline Mayberry [1]
Dennis R. Rhinow
(2/11/88–4/15/88)

On detail from:
[1] Department of the Interior
[2] Department of Commerce
[3] Department of Justice
[4] Department of Energy
[5] Department of Transportation

[6] Environmental Protection Agency
[7] Department of Defense
[8] Federal Trade Commission
[9] Agency for International Development

INDEX